THE **COMPLETE IDIOT'S GUIDE** TO

WITHDRAWN

Publishing Children's Books

Third Edition

by Harold D. Underdown

A

A member of Penguin Group (USA) Inc.

To Ann, of course. —H. U.

ALPHA BOOKS

Published by the Penguin Group

Penguin Group (USA) Inc., 375 Hudson Street, New York, New York 10014, USA

Penguin Group (Canada), 90 Eglinton Avenue East, Suite 700, Toronto, Ontario M4P 2Y3, Canada (a division of Pearson Penguin Canada Inc.)

Penguin Books Ltd., 80 Strand, London WC2R 0RL, England

Penguin Ireland, 25 St. Stephen's Green, Dublin 2, Ireland (a division of Penguin Books Ltd.)

Penguin Group (Australia), 250 Camberwell Road, Camberwell, Victoria 3124, Australia (a division of Pearson Australia Group Pty. Ltd.)

Penguin Books India Pvt. Ltd., 11 Community Centre, Panchsheel Park, New Delhi—110 017, India

Penguin Group (NZ), 67 Apollo Drive, Rosedale, North Shore, Auckland 1311, New Zealand (a division of Pearson New Zealand Ltd.)

Penguin Books (South Africa) (Pty.) Ltd., 24 Sturdee Avenue, Rosebank, Johannesburg 2196, South Africa

Penguin Books Ltd., Registered Offices: 80 Strand, London WC2R 0RL, England

Copyright © 2008 by Harold D. Underdown

International Standard Book Number: 978-1-59257-750-7
Library of Congress Catalog Card Number: 2007941477

10 09 08   8 7 6 5 4 3 2 1

Interpretation of the printing code: The rightmost number of the first series of numbers is the year of the book's printing; the rightmost number of the second series of numbers is the number of the book's printing. For example, a printing code of 08-1 shows that the first printing occurred in 2008.

Printed in the United States of America

Note: This publication contains the opinions and ideas of its author. It is intended to provide helpful and informative material on the subject matter covered. It is sold with the understanding that the author and publisher are not engaged in rendering professional services in the book. If the reader requires personal assistance or advice, a competent professional should be consulted.

The author and publisher specifically disclaim any responsibility for any liability, loss, or risk, personal or otherwise, which is incurred as a consequence, directly or indirectly, of the use and application of any of the contents of this book.

Most Alpha books are available at special quantity discounts for bulk purchases for sales promotions, premiums, fundraising, or educational use. Special books, or book excerpts, can also be created to fit specific needs.

For details, write: Special Markets, Alpha Books, 375 Hudson Street, New York, NY 10014.

Publisher: *Marie Butler-Knight*
Editorial Director: *Mike Sanders*
Senior Managing Editor: *Billy Fields*
Acquisitions Editor: *Michele Wells*
Senior Development Editor: *Christy Wagner*
Production Editor: *Megan Douglass*
Copy Editor: *Cate Schwenk*

Cartoonist: *Steve Barr*
Cover Designer: *Becky Harmon*
Book Designer: *Trina Wurst*
Indexer: *Joan Green*
Layout: *Ayanna Lacey*
Proofreader: *John Etchison*

Contents at a Glance

Appendixes

Contents

Appendixes

Foreword

In this honest and precise book on writing for children, Harold has managed to cram in almost everything about writing and illustrating books for children and getting them published there is to know.

With so much to cover, it's surprising that there were only three things about which I wish he'd said a little more: joy, gathering, and ducks.

I know this is an odd list. But read on a bit and see what I mean.

Joy. Too many writers talk about the difficulties of writing. How it takes blood and bile. How it's enormously difficult and lonely. How no one in his or her right mind would plan to make a living at it.

But I always want to come down on the side of joy.

Think of it: you'll be writing down stories, poems, anecdotes, and information that might change lives.

I always told my children that they should leave the world a little better than they found it. Some might say it's an easy task, given in what awful shape the world is now. But I believe they have taken that mother line to heart. They are good, moral adults, and in their work do make a difference to the world.

Well, I'm not modest about it. I get enough letters from children whose lives I have changed with my fictions and my poetry to know that it happens. On a small scale—certainly. One reader at a time—absolutely.

Art can work miracles.

Story can.

Now about *gathering*, here is what I mean.

My son Adam, his wife Betsy, and their little children Alison and David live in Minneapolis. When I travel there, I know I'll visit with family. Have good meals. See friends. Indulge in amusing conversations. Lots of fun music. (Adam is in two bands.)

What it doesn't mean is writing.

I can still accomplish daily things like keeping up with e-mail and phone calls.

But I do no writing.

Still, I consider these kinds of trips "gathering days." Good writing is made up of details. So on these hours away from the computer, away from actual writing, I become a collector of details. Some I collect actively, most passively.

The sweet talcum smell of the baby's neck, under the chin. How John, who plays backup guitar in Adam's Irish band, sweats in large discontinuous swatches on his T-shirt. The silhouette of my daughter-in-law holding Alison and how they pat one another on the back simultaneously. The damp Minnesota heat that leaves moist patches, like tears, under my eyes. The exact arch of a Catalpa tree leaning over the street.

It may look as if a writer uses such stuff to keep her away from the actual hard work of writing. And in fact many authors will tell outsiders just that. But do not be fooled. It is actually all grist to the mill.

For example, while I'm speeding through the latest Dick Francis novel, I'm also noting how he keeps his story moving, how the arc of his telling forces the reader to keep going. Reading the latest issue of *Cricket* or Richard Peck's Newbery Award novel I'm taking in what's considered the best writing today. Working crossword puzzles, I'm discovering new words. Watching TV, I'm practicing dialogue. Listening to local gossip, I invest in character.

As I say in *Take Joy: A Book for Writers*:

> I never turn off my writer's head. Conversations are stuffed in there, the chalky sweet smell of paper-white roses, the sharp fishiness of herring fillets, the rough crumble of unharled stone, the way a rose bush points its wayward fingers upward in its search for some new purchase, how the ruined towers of a castle take on extra life against a gray sky, the feel of my granddaughter's small wriggly hand in mind.

> All this and more will be returned to me when I need it in a scene or a poem or as a central metaphor for a story.

> I didn't know that when I began writing. I thought any time away from the typewriter was wasted time. Then my husband and I spent nine months camping in Europe and the Middle East and I started throwing images of what I had seen into my stories. That's when I understood how important gathering days are for writers.

Finally, there are those *ducks*.

Often I feel as if my writing time is slowly being nibbled away by ducks. Other writers have made similar complaints. Life, we all say, simply gets in the way.

But then on reading a biography about Emily Dickinson, where she's shown making tea cakes and writing letters, helping in the house and playing with her nephew, etc., I realize that we writers still must live in the real world. That means cakes, letters, bills, clogged toilets, etc. That means reading other people's books, watching TV, doing crossword puzzles, chatting on the phone. That means taking children to school, to the orthodontist, to choir practice, to basketball games. That means working till 3, till 5, till 8, till midnight. That means vacuuming the living room of cat hairs, dog hairs, husband's hairs. That means running to the grocery store, the paint store, the shoe store. That means going to the doctor, the dentist, the hair salon.

What that means is life.

Besides, without life, what's there to write about?

Jane Yolen

Jane Yolen is the award-winning author of more than 200 books for children, young adults, and adults. Ms. Yolen's best-known title, the critically acclaimed *Owl Moon* (Putnam/Philomel), illustrated by John Schoenherr, won the prestigious Caldecott Medal for 1988. Among Jane Yolen's many other awards are the Catholic Library Association's 1992 Regina Medal for her work in children's literature and the University of Minnesota's Kerlan Award for the body of her work. She has also received numerous state awards, including New York's Charlotte, Nebraska's Golden Sower, and New Jersey's Garden State Children's Book Award.

Introduction

I speak at children's book conferences and I run a personal website on the world of children's publishing, and over and over again people ask me about how to get started, where the publishers are, how to get feedback on a manuscript, what you should have in a portfolio, and about other problems with which writers and illustrators struggle as they try to establish themselves. It's hard to find all the basic information about this cozy but mystifying world. And that, quite simply, is why I wrote this book—to bring together all that information. What you have in your hands is, I hope, a resource that lays out all the basics, takes you some steps beyond the basics, and points you in the correct direction when you are ready to learn still more.

Different people, of course, may have different ideas about what the basics are or need different kinds of information at different times. So I've written dozens of definitions of publishing terms and taken a philosophical look at how your motives can affect your work. I've dissected the parts of a book and sketched a mini-history of children's publishing. I provide help in understanding contracts and sample letters to accompany manuscripts. And I've included many places to turn to for more information.

I love being involved in children's books, but I know from personal experience that there's a lot to keep up with. I hope this book helps you to do that, to spend more time writing or illustrating, and to need to take less time trying to figure it all out.

How to Use This Book

The world of children's book publishing can be confusing and complicated to those unfamiliar with its traditions and procedures. I've organized this book into six parts to unravel the complexities for you, guiding you through the maze to your ultimate goal—publication—and beyond.

Part 1, "Where to Begin?" provides suggestions and information about moving your ideas from your imagination onto paper—the first steps of their journey to publication.

Part 2, "Get Ready, Get Set …," introduces some background about children's publishing, kinds of books, the parts of a book, and even books for writers.

Part 3, "Reaching Out," gives you guidance in assessing if your work is ready and then getting it from your desk or drawing table to the right company, and to the right editor or art director at that company, or to the right agent.

Part 4, "Understanding Publishers," explores the world of publishing, from types of publishers, to guidance in finding one, to other kinds of publishers and self-publishers.

Part 5, "Working With a Publisher," explains what happens after you sign on the dotted line. If you think the hard part is over when the publisher sends you a contract, these chapters are especially for you!

Part 6, "My Book Is Published! Now What?" discusses the many events that move your book up the sales chain. From publicity appearances to reading for school children, many opportunities are available for you to increase your book's presence in the marketplace. And I take a look further ahead, to building a career and dealing with such disappointments as out-of-print books.

I've also developed a glossary of terms used in children's publishing; a resource list of books, magazines, organizations, and websites; and sample letters and guidelines. You'll find all these in the appendixes.

Extras

Throughout the book, sidebars and margin notes highlight interesting information and important details. Here's what to look for:

Class Rules

Check these boxes for warnings and cautions.

def•i•ni•tion

These boxes explain terms and lingo common in the children's publishing industry.

Playground Stories

These anecdotes from, and profiles of, children's authors and publishers give you an inside view of the children's publishing world.

Can You Keep a Secret?

In these boxes, you'll find suggestions, tips, and resources to help you present yourself as a pro.

Acknowledgments

I'm always telling artists and writers that a book is a team effort. This one was no different, both in creating the original edition and the later revised editions. None of them would have happened without the help of dozens of people. Michele Wells and Christy Wagner put together a great team for the third edition.

Many others contributed their expertise and experience in e-mails and phone conversations, some of which I've quoted directly, others of which contributed to the thinking that shaped the book. They include Jennifer Armstrong, Bruce Balan, Susan Campbell Bartoletti, Miriam Bat-Ami, Carmen Bernier-Grand, Larry Dane Brimner, Toni Buzzeo, Evelyn Coleman, Sneed Collard, Bev Cooke, Elizabeth Devereaux, Muriel L. Dubois, Jennie Dunham, Lisa Rowe Fraustino, Sandy Ferguson Fuller, Charles Ghigna, James Cross Giblin, Lois Grambling, Megan Halsey, Tony Johnston, Jane Kurtz, Elaine Landau, Grace Lin, Diane Mayr, Lucas Miller, Stephen Mooser, Josephine Nobisso, Jules Older, Larry Pringle, Dana Rau, Deborah Kogan Ray, Pam Muñoz Ryan, Mary Ann Sabia, Aaron Shepard, Tema Siegel, Alexandra Siy, Donna Spurlock, Whitney Stewart, Ann Tobias, Chris Tugeau, Ginger Wadsworth, Jan Wahl, Rozanne Lanczak Williams, Carolyn Yoder, Jane Yolen, and Karen Romano Young. If I talked with you and you're not on this list, blame my record-keeping, not my lack of gratitude.

I interviewed a number of people by phone or e-mail and appreciate the time they took to deal with my sometimes lengthy lists of questions. So my special thanks to Mary Cash, Emma Dryden, Cindy Eagan, Beth Feldman, Bernette Ford, Jennifer Greene, Kate Jackson, Margaret K. McElderry, George Nicholson, Paula Quint, Mary Ann Sabia, Susan Sherman, and Christine Tugeau—and also to my work colleagues, for putting up with my sometimes distracted air while working on the book.

Alison James was a content reviewer beyond peer for the first edition; the work of her guiding hand is still apparent in this third edition.

My family and friends have been remarkably tolerant of my absence from their lives during the work on the first edition and during the revisions, and of my aura of preoccupation on the rare occasions when I came to the surface.

My thanks above all to my wife, Ann Rubin, who not only encouraged me to take on this project when it first was offered, but never once expressed regret at having done so, and even continued to encourage me. As an artist, not a publishing insider, she also brought perspective into what was truly important on the many occasions when I got lost in the details. Most of all, her confidence that what I might want to say was worthwhile kept me going. This book would not have happened without her.

And for the third edition, I again offer thanks to our daughter. When I was working on the second edition, though not yet 2, she was very accepting of the sad reality that sometimes Daddy had to work during our usual weekend time together. Now, not yet 6, she understands my work as an editor and is developing into an avid reader. I hope she'll be proud of this book when she's old enough to read it.

Special Thanks to the Technical Reviewer

The Complete Idiot's Guide to Publishing Children's Books, Third Edition, was reviewed by an expert who double-checked the accuracy of what you'll learn here, to help us ensure that this book gives you everything you need to know about writing your story, getting your children's story into the hands of a publisher, working with a publisher, and building a career. Special thanks are extended to Tere Stouffer.

Tere received her M.A. in children's literature from Hollins University and is now pursuing an M.F.A. in writing for children there as well. She is the author of *The Complete Idiot's Guide to the World of Harry Potter* and 14 other nonfiction books.

Trademarks

All terms mentioned in this book that are known to be or are suspected of being trademarks or service marks have been appropriately capitalized. Alpha Books and Penguin Group (USA) Inc. cannot attest to the accuracy of this information. Use of a term in this book should not be regarded as affecting the validity of any trademark or service mark.

Part 1

Where to Begin?

If you're not a part of it, children's publishing can be a confusing world. Part 1 gives you the basics so you can get started with what you want to do: write or illustrate books for children and get them published.

In the following chapters, you find ways to get started writing; learn about the best, most popular, and most recent children's books; and see how your motives can affect the work you do. Then it's time to set up your immediate world—your office space or studio—and get organized. Don't worry, I give you guidance for these tasks, too.

Adults Rule the World

In This Chapter

- ◆ What this book is all about
- ◆ Some basics about children's books
- ◆ The importance of taking yourself seriously
- ◆ An introduction to the challenges of writing and illustrating for children

Welcome to the wonderful and challenging world of writing, illustrating, and publishing children's books. You might think the title of this chapter, "Adults Rule the World," is odd considering the subject of the book, but I intentionally chose that title to remind us all of a strange paradox at the heart of children's publishing: we create books for *children*, but everyone involved in producing and buying them, with rare exceptions, is an *adult*. Even if, in your mind, you're creating for a child you know well, be it your own child or the child you once were, for your work to become a book for children, it must go through the hands of many adults.

Getting Started

So you want to write or illustrate a children's book (or both!). Maybe you already have. Maybe you've sent your work out to a few publishers and it's come back to you. Or maybe you've been working for a few years, with some success, but you want to push on ahead. Getting started is hard, and so is continuing. To make both easier, I've filled this book with information, advice, resources, and stories of success and failure.

Piercing the Static

Picture the thousands of manuscripts and art samples children's book publishers receive every year as static. You've got to pierce that static and get yourself and your manuscript or illustrations noticed. To do that, you need four things:

- You need to work hard on your writing or illustrating and keep striving to improve it.

- You need to learn as much as you can about the publishing world.

- You need to be persistent—over years if necessary.

- You need some luck.

That's a tall order, and many people never do get published. I aim to help you get through the static so you can have a chance of being among those who do.

No One Best Way

You may be looking for the best way to get published. If so, let me tell you up front that there isn't one. There are as many ways to get published as there are people, and that can be both frightening—because you'll have to figure out some things for yourself—and freeing—because it allows you to be yourself.

There's good news, though: in this book you learn about options you might not have considered—types of writing or illustrating to try, ways to approach publishers, kinds of publishers to investigate—and you learn how to chart your own path. Keep going down that path! If you don't, you won't reach the end of it.

It Takes Time

I hope you come to understand the value of patience along the way. As you'll see in some of the stories, writing or illustrating for children is not the simple task some outsiders assume. It's far more like becoming a brain surgeon than just starting a hobby, in fact. It takes years and years before you become a real practitioner, and during that time you learn many things, refine your technique, and gradually get better.

So don't be too hard on yourself, and don't compare yourself to other writers or illustrators. Deal with the challenges in front of you, whatever they may be, and after that you can worry about the next ones. As you learn and grow—and improve—you might not even notice your progress, but a day may come when you look up and find that you're on the top of that hill that only a short while earlier had looked like it was unclimbable.

> **Playground Stories**
>
> It can take longer than you might expect to feel that you've arrived, noted Simms Taback, illustrator, in his acceptance speech for the Caldecott Medal, the most prestigious award for illustrators. "What's really wonderful about getting this award is that I feel like a relative newcomer to the world of illustration, as if I have only just arrived as a practitioner of this craft. But actually, I have been illustrating for 40 years." He goes on to cite missteps and bad luck that kept him from feeling that he had ever "made it."

Lots to Learn—Start Here

Children's book publishing is a big business, with many kinds of publishers, many kinds of books, and right ways and wrong ways to do even such a simple thing as write a cover letter. This is a world unto itself, and you need to know the jargon and the shared assumptions of the people in it if you are going to have a better chance of succeeding.

Getting to Know Books and Publishers

Writing or illustrating is hard enough. But if you are to go from a few sketches or a neatly typed manuscript to an actual book, you need to make sense of the children's publishing industry. You need to figure out what kind of work you're doing and which publishers might be a good match for you.

Picture Books and Books with Chapters

There are many kinds of children's books, and I'll go into them in Part 2, but to start, you need to understand a basic distinction. *Picture books* are books in which the pictures and words tell the story together. Often they have pictures on every page and are read to children by the adults in their lives. *Books with chapters*, on the other hand, have chapters. They may also have pictures, but the pictures aren't as important; the words tell the story. These books are usually meant to be read by children or teenagers themselves.

Both of these basic types are divided into smaller categories. Do you have to know exactly what you've written, or the age group of the children for whom you want to illustrate? No, and sometimes a publisher will have a different idea about your work than you do. But it helps to know the basics because some publishers only publish one type or the other.

So Many Publishers!

At first glance, it might seem like there are hundreds of publishers all over the country. Or it can seem like there are only five—all in New York. It's tricky to sort them all out, especially because in the last decade publishers have bought out other publishers in what seems like a never-ending dance of mergers and acquisitions. Actually, although five or six very large publishers may seem to dominate the market, many other publishers around the United States and Canada are putting out books. I'll help you find them.

Types of Publishers

Different publishers, and sometimes different divisions of the same company, create very different types of books. A company selling books to libraries takes a different approach from one that sells its books in bookstores or one that puts its books in racks in drugstores. Depending on what you want to write, you've got to find the right match.

For the most part, *trade* publishers aim for bookstores, although some also sell to schools and libraries. *Mass-market* publishers target a wider audience and find it in supermarkets and other general retail stores. Beyond books, magazines and electronic publishing beckon, too. (You'll read a lot more about these different markets later in the book.)

def•i•ni•tion

Trade publishers sell mostly to bookstores, but also the "institutional" market—schools and libraries. **Mass-market** publishers aim for the masses, and their books are found in warehouse stores, newsstands, supermarkets, and similar outlets. Trade books are usually the more expensive of the two.

Putting Away Childish Things

As you read this book, and as you start to have contact with publishers, writers, and librarians, you'll find that children's publishing isn't all fluffy kittens and sad-eyed puppies. It may not be quite so cutthroat as some businesses, but it is a business—a "bunny-eat-bunny-world" according to some. Be prepared for this.

Take It Seriously

Begin by taking what you are about to do seriously. This isn't a hobby or a pastime, or something you can succeed in by working on it only during your summer vacations. On the other hand, you don't have to define success by making money from your writing. As many will tell you, you might never be able to quit your day job. Creating books for children is not easy and takes time, space, and dedication. As I detail in later chapters, it's important to set aside a space and time and remember that you need and deserve this.

Can You Keep a Secret?
How big is children's publishing? Estimates suggest about $2 billion in sales annually, with five publishers—Random House, Penguin, HarperCollins, Scholastic, and Simon & Schuster—accounting for about half. Each year, 4,000 to 5,000 new books for children are published, half by the big guys. But hundreds (maybe thousands) of smaller companies publish books, too, as well as individuals who self-publish.

Art and Commerce

Remember, too, that at the end of the process is a book or magazine or something similar that someone (actually thousands of someones) will have to decide to buy. You're an artist, but you're not creating one idiosyncratic work that needs to find only one buyer, or that you might even be keeping for yourself. Book publishing lies in an interesting middle area between art and commerce, between pure self-expression and the manufacture of millions of such useful but generic items as pencils and bars of soap. There's room for creativity, but you need to find an audience (your market), and a publisher will help you do that.

"When You Grow Up, Will You Write for Adults?"

Once you reach the point of identifying yourself as a writer or illustrator for children, it won't be long before you run into the condescension of those who assume that they, too, could write or illustrate wonderful children's books, if they could just find the time. Or those who exclaim that it's just wonderful that you've taken up such a charming hobby: "Painting pretty pictures for the little ones! How sweet ...."

Sadly, many people don't understand that creating books for children is as significant, challenging, and absorbing as any other form of creative endeavor, from investigative journalism to spoken-word poetics, from advertising design to land-form sculpture. Some people think that because children aren't as mature or intelligent as adults, it must be easier to write or illustrate for them.

You are doing serious work—work that's actually harder than similar work for adults. After all, you aren't creating for someone just like you, even if you are keeping in mind the child you used to be. It can be tricky to write or illustrate (or edit, for that matter) for this "other": adults publishing for other adults can use their own reactions as guides to how their audiences will react. You can't do that. Be proud of what you are doing. It's something special.

What This Book Can Do for You

Just how am I going to help you deal with the issues I've been discussing, as well as teach you what you need to learn? The following sections explain what I and this book realistically can and cannot do for you.

The Whole Picture

In these pages, I give you a comprehensive overview of this field. I don't just give you information about children's book publishers—I look at magazines and educational publishing, too. I get you started with tips on getting your manuscript or art samples to the right publishing companies, follow up with guidance on revision and contract negotiation, and help you complete the process through marketing and self-promotion. In short, I've tried to cover everything that someone just getting started would need to know—and then go beyond that and provide useful information for those already published.

Of course, I'll be happy to hear from you if there's something you think I've left out and you want to suggest for the next edition—I provide contact information in Appendix B.

There's No Magic Formula

Looking for guidance on writing? I give you help on getting started writing, examining your motives for writing, and getting feedback. But I don't tell you *how* to write. I'd have to write a whole other book to do that! But you can find many great how-to books for writers, and for this edition I've even added a chapter to help you choose the right one for you (Chapter 11).

X Marks the Spot

The many books, websites, and other sources for more help I identify throughout the book and in the appendixes make the book you hold in your hands a treasure map to the many places you can go for more detailed and advanced information. You could find those places yourself, of course, but you can also get some help with one of the hundreds of books on publishing and on children's books—or the as-many websites. I've checked them out and organized them and made some judgments on which ones are worthwhile so you don't have to take the time out from your writing to do a lot of digging.

How Others Did It

A book full of advice and information would be pretty dry without real-life stories. I don't include these just for the human interest; I include them because there's no better way to learn how to move forward in children's publishing than to see how others have done it—or failed to do it, as the case may be.

In the following pages, you'll read stories and tips from extremely successful people, from others just getting started, from people who've succeeded in many areas, and from others who've specialized. And when it's called for, you'll read stories from publishing insiders, too, so you can begin to get to know the people with whom you might be working.

Know the Forest, Not the Trees

Although I've packed it full of specific information—the trees—I hope most of all that this book will help you begin to get to know the forest of children's book publishing. The strange ecosystem that is children's publishing changes slowly, even though individual trees may come and go. From the trees in this book—individual publishers, editors, types of books—you'll begin to put together an understanding of how the forest works so that when you venture into new and uncharted parts of it you'll be less likely to get lost. You'll know how to survive, even if you don't recognize all the trees.

Above all, be inspired by the example of a J. K. Rowling, but don't be disappointed if a career like hers doesn't evolve for you. With the amazing worldwide sales of millions of copies of the *Harry Potter* books, Rowling did what no other author, whether for adults or for children, has ever done. *Ever!* Don't measure your success, or lack of it, against hers—or any other author or illustrator. Your personal best is what matters.

The Least You Need to Know

- You're starting out on a long and interesting road. Don't try to rush it.
- Getting a children's book published takes persistence.
- Understand the difference between picture books and books with chapters and between trade and mass market.
- Take yourself seriously, and take illustrating or writing for children seriously.
- Use this book as a reference manual and a starting point. I can't fit in all the answers, but I'll help you find them.

Chapter 2

I Don't Know What to Write!

In This Chapter

- ◆ Finding a direction
- ◆ Explore your interests with a journal
- ◆ Why writing must be practiced and how to do it
- ◆ What you need to do to write and tips on creating the time and space
- ◆ You think you're finished? Think again …

Few things are as terrifying as a piece of blank paper staring back at you. How can you overcome that? Writers, even established writers—maybe even *especially* established writers—don't just sit down and write.

In this chapter, I suggest ways to fill that page: how to discover what you want to write if you're unsure and how to practice your writing and imagining skills, in much the same way you might practice skiing or hitting a golf ball. These are getting-started exercises. When you're writing, you might need to be sure your work fits into the specific formats and types of children's books. (To do that, turn to Chapters 8 and 9. For more advanced help with writing, turn to Chapter 11.)

You Are What You Read

Do you have the writing bug but just don't know *what* to write? That happens to the best of writers, and you can get past it. Start by asking yourself what you like to read. Go over to your bookshelves and take a careful look at what it holds. Which books sit there, never opened? Which ones have cracked bindings, well-thumbed pages, and notes in the margins? Can you see certain kinds of books you usually read, or are your favorites fiction, nonfiction, light, heavy, or all over the map? Most importantly, do you read children's books? If you don't but think you want to write them, start reading them. Find out what you like to read; that's probably the kind of book you will write.

If you really like to read books that present science to a general audience, such as Lewis Thomas does for adults, try reading science books for children to see if such books interest you. Almost any kind of book you like as an adult points to a similar kind for children. Do you like vampire novels? They're popular with teenagers, too. Do biographies grab you? Libraries grab them. You get the point. And keep in mind that you don't *have* to write a classic. Write what you like to write, not what you think you should.

Later, you'll learn about particular kinds of children's books, but you don't need to begin by trying to write a specific type of book for a specific audience. Give yourself some time to explore ways of generating raw material, get in some practice, and set up the habits and schedule that will keep you going.

> **Class Rules**
>
> In your reading, as in your writing, rule one is to write what you *want* to write, not what you think you *should* write. *Should*s tend to clog your mind and get in the way of the clear thinking you need to do your best writing, so run away from them.

Dear Diary ...

Just about everybody has kept a diary at some time or another. Most diaries cover everyday events or feelings that are very important to the diarist but possibly to no one else. Now that you're writing, you should seriously consider keeping a diary that goes by a grander name—a *journal*, and specifically a *writer's journal*.

A journal can be many things. You can use it to write about whatever's on your mind at the time. You can use it to record observations that interest you, from the changing of the cloud patterns in the sky to the changing of emotions in the faces of passengers sitting near you on the bus. You can use it to note ideas,

> **def•i•ni•tion**
>
> The word *journal* is related to the French word for "day," *jour*. As that implies, a journal is a blank book to write in daily. Your journal should be as much a part of your life as your morning cup of coffee or your evening news time.

remember sentences that come to you, transcribe snippets of dialogue, or sketch portraits of interesting characters. You can use it to explore your feelings about writing or your reactions to books you've read. More practically, you can keep track of when you write, for how long, and how effectively, so you can figure out your best writing times.

To get the most out of your journal, you need to use it regularly. It's good to keep it with you so you can jot down something whenever you want to, but don't stop there. Make an appointment with yourself to write in your journal every day, preferably at the same time. If you can't, be sure you find times when you won't be interrupted.

Writing every day can be difficult to maintain, especially without a structure. Don't feel bad if you aren't inspired; give yourself a break and give yourself a structure. Take a month to explore your feelings about your parents and your siblings, or to note down some key memories from a particular year of your childhood. Or give yourself a theme of the day, such as Monday for family, Tuesday for friends, and Wednesday for writing.

These are just suggestions; choose whatever topics are most important to you. Make your journal your own, and in it, be as honest with yourself as you can be. Make a point of reading back through it from time to time. Gradually, ideas and areas of interest will start to emerge and become clearer. And with the added practice of writing in a journal, your writing will benefit.

You don't like to write in a journal, or just can't? You don't need a journal to write down what you observe. Write in e-mails, on backs of envelopes, etc. Some "journals" are actually shoeboxes or large envelopes that contain printouts of e-mails, copies of letters, notes made on napkins, etc.

Practice Makes Perfect

A journal isn't the only way you can practice your writing. There are many ways in which you can work on improving not only the quality of your writing but also your fluency. Getting words down on paper so you can go back and revise them later is a challenge to every writer, so the more easily and rapidly you can write, the better.

Writing exercises will also help you get started on a particular project. No writer starts a manuscript without a considerable amount of *prewriting*, which includes brainstorming, outlining, and the like. Jennifer Armstrong, a published author of fiction and nonfiction, observes: "I spend a lot of time on preparation. Lots of notes, lots of outlining, lots of character sketching. (This of course all depends on what I'm writing.) Not until I really know where the book is going do I begin writing prose."

Playground Stories

You can learn from general-purpose writing books. Natalie Goldberg's *Writing Down the Bones* and *Wild Mind: Living the Writer's Life* are great sources of inspiration and practical exercises. Or check out Jessica Wilbur's *Totally Private and Personal: Journaling Ideas for Girls and Young Women.* It's great for people of any age and either gender.

Don't give yourself writer's block by thinking that good writers are able to sit down and write, producing something that's very close to its final form—that doesn't happen very often. To write well, you have to do a lot of work first, and as you'll see a little later in this chapter, you have even more to do when you've come up with a first draft.

As you'll discover when you spend a little time exploring books about writing, there are many ways you can develop your writing without sitting down to write an actual story. The following sections offer a few suggestions.

Don't Stop

Writing without stopping to edit yourself or rethink what you just wrote is difficult to do, but you can learn to do it. Give yourself five minutes to write, without stopping and without going back and correcting a word or a spelling. If you can't think of anything to write, just write *I can't think of anything to write*, and keep going. Use a pen, a pencil, a typewriter, or a computer—the tool doesn't matter, as long as you feel comfortable with it. Do this every day, in your journal or not, as you choose.

After you've had some practice with this technique, try varying it. Give yourself a topic to start off with or a writing prompt (a sentence to complete), and see where it leads you. Write *I love to write children's books because …* or maybe *I'm scared to write children's books because ….* After some use of this technique, you might find that your conscious mind lets go a little, and you start writing things that surprise you. (My thanks to Natalie Goldberg, whose books on creativity inspired these ideas.)

Visualize

Clear, concise description is a joy—and difficult to achieve—whether you're writing about a dark and stormy night or a new scientific discovery. Practicing visualization can help you improve your description skills.

Settle on a scene you'd like to visualize, perhaps from your childhood, perhaps more recent, but not one that's right in front of you. Close your eyes and conjure it. Take some time to bring as much of it to your mind's eye as possible. If it's a room, imagine yourself walking around in it, looking under things, behind things, maybe even out the window. If you imagine yourself outside, walk around there, too. Settle on the limits of your scene. After you've looked your fill, listen. What sounds belong in your scene? What do you smell? What do you feel: the temperature of the air, the textures of the objects around you? If there's something edible, what do you taste?

After you feel you've fully placed yourself in your chosen scene, open your eyes and write. Describe what you just savored as fully and evocatively as you can. Don't edit! Just keep writing. After you've finished—and you may go on for pages and pages—you can go back and edit.

You might use this to help you imagine a setting for a story, or you might just use it for practice. But try it again, with a different place. With practice, your ability to picture places familiar and unfamiliar will improve, and so will your ability to describe them.

Memories

Many writers for children draw on childhood experiences and memories as the raw material of their writing. Even if that's not your intention, even if you plan to write only about American history or biology or sports, being in touch with your childhood and the feelings you had then can only improve your ability to connect with your audience.

Think about an important milestone in your childhood, maybe the moment when you first succeeded in tying your own shoelaces, or the moment when you walked up to the chalkboard and wrote the right answer to a difficult math problem, or the moment when you said something clever at lunch and you noticed that cute boy (or girl) smiling. Visualize it. Write about it. Or remember the time you got lost in the big department store, or the time you had a fight with the playground bully, or the time you saw the girl (or the boy) you had a crush on dancing with someone else at the school dance and obviously enjoying herself. Visualize that and write about it.

You might then develop something from your memory explorations. One or more of them could become the basis for a scene in a novel, or for an entire picture-book story. Or these explorations might help you understand what interests you in the world around you and find ways to present information to excite the child, you, and—we hope—your audience.

This Is Your Life

You have a life beyond writing, and your family and your day job can make it difficult to find time to write. But your day-to-day life can be an opportunity, too.

In the time you must spend in the rest of your life, do what children's novelist Jane Yolen calls *gathering*. Observe your family or your co-workers. Take in the scene outside your window. Watch for details that could bring a character or scene to life—how someone tugs at the top button of his shirt when explaining; the oil that leaks from the old car, making rainbow patterns when it rains. Make notes, mentally or physically. And of course, notice how other writers tell a story, describe a setting, or reveal a character.

Get a Feel for It

Do you think you're ready to write that story? Maybe you already have. Whether you have or not, here's a different kind of exercise that will help you get a feel for the form of a children's book.

> **Playground Stories** _____
>
> For some guidance on writing specific kinds of children's books, check out Katherine Paterson's *The Invisible Child: On Reading and Writing Books for Children* and Anastasia Suen's *Picture Writing: A New Approach to Writing for Kids and Teens*. But choose a how-to book *you* love (see Chapter 11).

Choose a favorite children's book and head to your keyboard. Type the book's text, breaking the paragraphs where they break in the book. If it's a picture book, do the whole thing. If it's a novel, do a chapter or part of it. This will help you to get a feel for some ground-level aspects of children's book writing: sentence length, word choice, paragraph length and structure, and how these things can vary with the age of your intended audience. You may find that your "natural" writing style needs to change.

Spontaneity or Results?

You're ready to be creative … now do you wait for inspiration to strike and then get to work? You may be waiting a long time, if so. Writers—*accomplished* writers, that is—learn early on that writing sometimes has to go ahead without inspiration. Writing is work: flashes of insight followed by the labor of translating that insight into words and then revision. Just like any other job, if you plan to succeed, you need to put your nose to the grindstone.

But unlike those lucky people in 9-to-5 jobs, writers don't have supervisors breathing down their necks to get the job done—especially unpublished writers without deadlines.

Your own willpower is what makes you finish your first book. And even after you've got a book contract or established yourself as a full-time children's book author, no one will be hovering over you with a whip each morning, yelling, "Write!" or telling you that your break ran too long. In one word, the profession you've chosen takes *dedication.* You need to look at your writing as you would any other job, set up a schedule, and stick to it.

Class Rules

Although I'm emphasizing the importance of setting aside time to write, don't leave out time to goof off, as Barbara Seuling notes in *How to Write a Children's Book and Get It Published.* If you feel guilty about doing things other than writing, sooner or later writing will become a drag. Give yourself writing time, yes, but give yourself nonwriting time, too.

Sitting behind a computer day-in and day-out in your bathrobe, barely showered, slaving away on a manuscript that might sell to a publisher or might not isn't exactly glamorous. Writing is hard work, and it's easy to procrastinate. Even established writers have times when washing the dog seems more urgent than writing. To succeed in the solitude of writing, consider these tips:

Set a schedule and stick to it. Tell yourself *I'm going to write every day from this time to that time* and then do it. If you can only manage 15 minutes, that's okay. Just make it every day. Post your schedule on the refrigerator, and ask your family to respect it.

Take breaks if you need them, whether the break is 2 minutes to let your eyes recover from the computer screen, or a brisk 30 minutes walk to keep you energized. But plan your breaks, and limit them.

Remove distractions, including children. Many, many parents hope to juggle the needs of their writing and of their children. But writing is a job. You'll soon learn that you can't concentrate on children and writing at the same time.

After you establish a schedule, every so often give yourself a change of scenery. When you write full-time from home, you'll find yourself turning into Howard Hughes if you don't get out of the house sometimes. So take a notepad and pen to your local coffeehouse or library and write there. Stick to your schedule, but just write somewhere other than home.

Let your neighbors and friends know you're working, not watching old movies. If you don't, you may find yourself the block baby-sitter or errand runner. Be firm and practice saying, "I'm sorry, but I'm working; I can't pick up your dry cleaning for you or baby-sit your son."

Can You Keep a Secret?

Jennifer Basye Sander, an author of more than 20 books and the mother of two small boys, hires a baby-sitter for several hours a day while she writes. If that's beyond your budget, call on grandparent day care, use parents day out at your local church, trade baby care with friends and neighbors, or talk your spouse into taking the kids for a day every weekend. And squeeze in writing whenever the kids are asleep. Be creative about making time for your writing.

Let the answering machine pick up the phone, and don't answer the door. You aren't home; you're writing.

You just need to do it—write! If you want it (the finished book) badly enough, you'll do it.

Do It Again!

Remember when you were in school you'd sit down and write an essay straight through from start to finish and hand it in? Professional writers don't work like that. You will write more and write better if you spend a good amount of time first getting ready to write—researching, brainstorming, outlining—and then write and revise. And it's no exaggeration to say that most writing is revision. But as you get started, be aware that you should be going back and revising everything you write.

Read it over, maybe out loud. Ask if the story does what you want it to do. If it doesn't, dig in and change it. Remember, it's always easier to revise than to write. Put it aside for a week and then read it again. When the story works, revise again to polish it, sentence by sentence.

Of course, you can go too far with revision. There's a point where more revision is just avoiding the dreaded time when you show your work to someone else. How do you know when you've reached that point? You'll have to learn your own work habits, but watch out for revisions that don't change much. Are you changing a word here and there on each round, just tinkering? Or are you switching back and forth between two approaches? Both of these are clues that you're done with the piece for now, and that it's time to see what someone else thinks of it. Before you send it to a publisher, get some good feedback on it, as you learn to do in Chapter 12.

The Least You Need to Know

- ◆ Knowing what you like to read helps guide you in discovering what you might like to write.

- ◆ Regular use of a journal can help you grow as a writer.

- ◆ Creativity exercises help you explore your interests and improve your writing.

- ◆ Set a schedule for yourself—and stick to it!

- ◆ Revise, revise, revise … but know when to stop.

The World of Children's Literature

In This Chapter

- ◆ The importance of your audience
- ◆ Discovering the different areas of children's literature
- ◆ Finding the most respected children's books
- ◆ What do children like to read?

Crucial to writing or illustrating for children is acquiring an understanding and knowledge of what children want to read, have read, and continue to read. You need to immerse yourself in the world of children's literature. Just as it's not enough to think you have a good idea for a business and immediately pour your life's savings into it, it's not enough to assume children's books are the right thing for you. What would you do if you were starting a business? You'd research your prospects. Check out the competition. Look at how a similar business might have thrived in the past. The same goes for children's books.

This chapter navigates you through your possibilities, giving you an overview of children's literature and touching on why understanding your audience is crucial.

The Children's Books Buffet Table

Remember how Mom used to nudge you into exploring new foods? "Just try it," she'd say, as she served avocados or a new casserole. And as you grew up, you encountered many new favorites.

Children's literature is like that. You have your favorites now, but there are many dishes you don't know. As you try new ones, you'll find many reading levels, age groups, styles of writing and illustration, and *audiences* you also like. You'll see there's no one right way to write or illustrate or one group who will be your audience. And you'll notice that the tone you use in a book for a witty and worldly sixth-grade boy isn't the same tone you'd employ in a toddler's picture book. For example, *Island of the Blue Dolphins* (a historical novel by Scott O'Dell) and *Goodnight Moon* (a picture book by Margaret Wise Brown, illustrated by Clement Hurd) are both considered classics of children's literature, but the audience for each is vastly different.

def•i•ni•tion

Your **audience** is your target reader. Your audience ultimately determines your style and tone.

To really get a feeling for what works for a toddler, 10-year-old, or early teen, you must get to know the various books out there for those age groups and learn how publishers differentiate genres. Don't rely on vague memories of the books you read as a child. Children's books are different today and are changing all the time.

Find out what children, as well as critics and librarians, think are the best. Now, don't overreact. You don't need to go out and get a Ph.D. in children's literature. I'm just suggesting some selections from the buffet table.

The Classics

Who can forget his favorite bedtime story? I loved Virginia Lee Burton's *Mike Mulligan and His Steam Shovel*. My daughter loved Molly Bang's *Ten, Nine, Eight*. Many titles endure the test of time and generations of readings: *Make Way for Ducklings*, *Curious George*, and *Charlotte's Web*. Even books published in the 1970s, 1980s, or 1990s, from picture books like Dr. Seuss's *Oh, the Places You'll Go*; Vera B. Williams's *A Chair for My Mother*; and Chris Van Allsburg's *The Polar Express*, to novels by Judy Blume, Virginia Hamilton, or Lloyd Alexander may now rank as classics.

Although you might rattle off the titles of adult classics such as *The Great Gatsby*, *Bleak House*, or *The Odyssey*, getting to know titles throughout the many age levels and genres of children's literature might prove more difficult. Here's an introduction (I go into more depth in Chapters 8 and 9).

Ask a Librarian

If you haven't read a children's book in 20 years and don't know where to look for a good starting place, ask your local children's librarian to show you around the world of classic children's literature. Children's librarians are experts on the classics and the very latest new books, and chances are they'll enjoy sharing their expertise with you.

Follow these steps to ensure you receive some good take-home reading material:

Be sure you hold an active library card. You'll want to check out titles to read and study.

Call the library and ask whether a children's resource specialist or children's librarian works there. If so, ask to speak to that person. If not, find out who handles the children's books. If your local branch doesn't have a children's area, find a branch or a main library that does. Call them.

> **Class Rules**
>
> Don't assume that books you loved as a child are actual classics or would be loved by children today. New classics come along and old ones retire.

When calling the librarian, explain that you're researching children's literature and, when convenient, would like the librarian to give you an overview of the classics as well as pull several examples within different categories and age levels for you to check out and read.

Finally, and most importantly, make an appointment and keep it.

Finding the Very Best

Newspapers, magazines, and even television shows often put together "best of" lists that you can consult for guidance. Some come out at the end of the year, while others are more occasional. For example, *School Library Journal*, one of the nation's most respected reviewers of children's books, got together a panel of experts as the millennium approached to determine the "100 Significant Books" of the twentieth century. The list was published in their January 2000 issue. Here are some examples from the list you might not know:

- *Tuck Everlasting* by Natalie Babbitt

- *Freight Train* by Donald Crews

- *And Then What Happened, Paul Revere?* by Jean Fritz

- ◆ *Shapes and Things* by Tana Hoban
- ◆ *Chicka Chicka Boom Boom* by Bill Martin Jr. and John Archimbault
- ◆ *The Alfred Summer* by Jan Slepian

If you want to learn more, consult a guidebook. Consider Anita Silvey's *The Essential Guide to Children's Books and Their Creators*. She's the former editor of the *Horn Book Magazine*, a highly respected children's book journal. Her guide compiles hundreds of entries on noted authors and illustrators, plus essays on specific genres. It's a great book to keep with you throughout your career. For now, you might want to start with the Basic Reading List at the beginning of Silvey's book, neatly broken down into different genres and age levels.

Playground Stories

In this chapter I advise you to consult experts, children, best-seller lists, and "best of" lists, but all this should lead in one direction: developing your own taste. When I was getting started in children's publishing, I read Alison Lurie's *Don't Tell the Grown-Ups: The Subversive Power of Children's Literature*. This had a big influence on my developing tastes because the book provided support for ideas I already had.

Hot! *Do* Touch That!

Beyond immersing yourself in the classics, you also need to know what's hot now—what kids are reading and parents are buying for their kids today—besides *Harry Potter!* After all, thousands of new children's books are published every year in the United States and Canada. The old standbys do retain steady sales year after year, but it's worthwhile to keep a finger on the pulse of kids' immediate reading preferences.

It might seem like an overwhelming endeavor as you explore all the new titles bursting forth from the publishers ("Just how am I going to read everything?" Answer: "Don't try to"), but you can streamline your mission. Follow the leader as we return to the library ….

Go Back to the Library

When you return all those children's classics you checked out, ask the librarian to show you today's hot titles. If the books are really hot, you might have to get on a waiting list for specific titles. Join the list and get an idea of what kids are enjoying nowadays. Or ask if the library has another list—one of the annual lists of recommended titles put out by different organizations.

What's Selling?

Get a different perspective on the latest books for children by visiting your local bookstore's children's department. From stocking the shelves and talking to customers, employees in this department know what's selling. They see what children and young adults choose, and they may have noticed that those self-selected titles are quite different from what parents and grandparents buy.

If you ask for books to give an elementary school student, they may suggest classics like *The Secret Garden* or *The Wind in the Willows*—books you'll also find on the *School Library Journal*'s list of 100! But the staff is just as likely to say "We see a lot of kids choosing titles from *The Magic Tree House* books and from Lemony Snicket's *A Series of Unfortunate Events*," two popular recent series. If you ask about picture books, you may be handed a classic such as Kay Thompson and Hilary Knight's *Eloise* or a recent book, Laura Vaccaro Seeger's *Dog and Bear: Two Friends, Three Stories*.

Can You Keep a Secret?
For recent books children like, check out the annual IRA/CBC "Children's Choices" list available at www.reading.org. For librarians' "best of" lists, find the "Notable Children's Books" list on the American Library Association's website at www.ala.org. To find out about what's hot in bookstores, check the American Bookseller's Association's "Book Sense" lists.

Booksellers also meet with sales representatives from book publishers, who provide overviews of all the new titles coming out each season. Pick a bookseller's brain sometime, and you'll probably hear about stacks of both really wonderful new literature and classic stuff.

Talk to Children

Most children tend to be honest and direct, so talk to them about what books they like. Ask your cousins', neighbors', and friends' kids what they like to read. Of course, if you have kids, ask them, too. If they feel comfortable with you, they'll tell you what they like and what they don't. Children like to make adults happy (well, most of the time), so don't telegraph the answers you want to hear when discussing books with them. Don't suggest possible titles, and don't settle for what they read in school. Ask them what they read when they get to pick their own books.

If you have time, go back to your library or bookstore. Sit quietly in a strategic spot and watch what children pull from the shelves and read. As you do, remember that children's tastes can outweigh any marketing plans. The initial popularity of the *Harry Potter* series came from word-of-mouth through kids in the United Kingdom, not what the publisher did. That's kid power!

Class Rules

If you're reading a picture book to a toddler and he starts to squirm, either he has to go potty or he's not interested. Now you need to find out why. Try different books and see which he prefers.

If you're able to gather a group and talk about certain books, do it. Perhaps a teacher you know will welcome you as a guest storyteller, or you might even become a regular volunteer. Bring a stack of various picture books and read for half an hour to first graders. Read the books beforehand, so you can keep your eyes on the children and not on the page. Gauge their interest and reaction to the material. Be careful of your delivery—you don't want to bore the kids with a monotone reading, but you also don't want to slant their reaction by giving an animated show. See if the story and the illustrations deliver the goods. This experience not only helps you continue to learn about what children respond to in books, it also helps you gauge reactions if you ever try out your writing on children—a tricky but potentially enlightening thing to do (see Chapter 12).

It all comes down to this: you want to write or illustrate for children, so get to know what they find amusing, interesting, or fascinating.

The Least You Need to Know

◆ Children's literature comes in various styles of writing and illustrating. There's a difference between what a toddler enjoys and what a teen enjoys, but they're both categorized as children's literature.

◆ Study myriad works—from classic picture books to contemporary young adult novels—to learn what kids read.

◆ Get help on your quest for kids' literature by asking a librarian, bookseller, or child to lead you toward what's out there and what's selling.

◆ Start to develop a sense of what children like, and how it's different from what adults *want* them to like.

4

Why Children's Books— and Why Not?

In This Chapter

◆ Why a desire for money and fame can let you down

◆ Predicting the likeliness of your success

◆ How your wishes for children can affect the way you work

◆ Why (and why not) self-expression and a love of the craft can be a good way to go

◆ How others have succeeded

We all have reasons for doing what we do, whether that's becoming a parent or having another slice of cake. That's good, because if we didn't have reasons, we wouldn't do it. But when we don't understand our own motives, they can affect what we do in unexpected and possibly damaging ways, and that's bad.

This happens with children's books, too. The motives and reasons that lead us to work on children's books are as varied and different as people are. But those who have been in the business for a while will tell you that they all boil down to one or a combination of a few things: some want fame or money, others want to teach children something or to make them feel good about themselves, and still others write or illustrate as a means of self-expression.

I'm Going to Be a Rich and Famous Children's Book Author!

From what you see in the news, authors of books for adults can expect million-dollar advances and national book tours, not to mention appearance on *Oprah* and other television shows. Children's books don't get quite so much attention, or at least they didn't until J. K. Rowling's *Harry Potter* books. Reading about these success stories, it's tempting to see an opportunity. Some think that because children aren't as discerning as adults, and their books are shorter, it must be easier to write or illustrate for them. This must be a path to fame and fortune!

Reality Check

Wake up and smell the hot chocolate. Like circumstances that led to the 100-foot waves in the *Perfect Storm*, several factors came together to create the once-in-a-century *Harry Potter* phenomenon. No other book has ever sold as well, and I believe that in the next 50 years, no other children's book will.

What's the harm of trying to emulate this kind of success, if it gets you motivated? If a desire for fame and fortune is what drives you, you can end up chasing the trends and the "hot" areas of the market. A few years ago, for example, you might have tried to write a scary/funny series à la the *Goosebumps* series—but by the time you finished it, the market had moved on. Or it might lead you into developing a "commercial" illustration style, to the detriment of the quality of your work. Ask any published authors or illustrators, and they'll tell you that it's better to do what you like to do, or you won't be able to stick to it.

It's a Living

In a more modest way, money *can* motivate you, if only to keep you at your work. Writing or illustrating can be a full-time job. This takes dedication, the ability to juggle multiple projects, and not least the will to face down the fear that sometime soon—tomorrow, next week, or next year—you will run out of inspiration and out of income.

Jennifer Armstrong, a successful full-time fiction and nonfiction writer, comments: "I don't know that I believe in inspiration, frankly. Either you want to write or you don't, but there won't be a beam of light coming through the window and into your ear. I always have multiple projects underway, so there's always something that has to be done. Deadlines are powerful motivators, as are mortgage payments and other bills. I've seldom known that whip not to work. I may be among a small group of writers for children and young adults who actually do make a living at this. I have to get my work done. That's all there is to it."

Jennifer has arrived at this point after several years of hard work, of course. And although many successful writers and illustrators never do make their work a full-time job, it is possible, with persistence and discipline. So appearing on *Oprah* may be out of reach, but if you want to write or illustrate, you may eventually earn a living at it.

What kind of a living can you earn, you ask? There's no simple answer to that question. Other than J. K. Rowling, only a few authors and illustrators earn hundreds of thousands if not millions of dollars annually, largely because their books have been turned into TV series or movies; Marc Brown, creator of the popular *Arthur* books, is one such person. More people, like Jennifer Armstrong, make a full-time job out of writing or illustrating, perhaps combining it with school appearances or a similarly related sideline. They have a solid middle-class income, but no more.

But for the vast majority, working in children's books is what they do on the side. They heeded some common advice: "Don't quit your day job." Children's books provide some additional income for them, but not even steady income; some writers may go years between contracts and, thus, between the advances received when signing a contract. Other writers never make any money from their passion. There's no telling which group you'll end up in, so I advise not using your income to measure your success.

The Chances of Getting There

If not money, what about recognition? What chance do you have of getting published? The odds don't look good when you consider that thousands of manuscripts usually pass through the doors of a typical publisher in a year, only a few of which are accepted for publication; publishers are similarly flooded with samples from illustrators. But consider that maybe 90 percent of those submissions and samples are just not very good, or are completely wrong for that publisher.

Those who keep working at their craft, and who find the right publishers, have a chance of getting there. They'll still have to compete with the others who have what it takes, but with the help of this book, you can get into that group.

> **Playground Stories** _____
>
> Sneed Collard, a well-known writer of nonfiction for children, says: "Writing is a _long_ road. I've been writing for 18 years now and only in the last 5 have I begun to understand what I'm doing. If you're not willing to put in the years and continue to grow, this field isn't for you. If you are willing to keep learning and growing, however, children's book writing can be an enormously satisfying ride."

Stephen Mooser, president of the Society of Children's Book Writers and Illustrators (SCBWI), says this about the path to success: "In my years with the SCBWI I have seen hundreds of people sell their first book. None of these books, however, came easy. They studied the market, studied published children's books, wrote and rewrote and wrote again. They were persistent and they succeeded, even if it took 10 years. There is a lot of competition and you have to give it your best. I've published 60 books, but probably had that many rejected."

I Want to Be the Teacher

You love the way children ask questions. Or maybe you're disturbed by the way children are raised today, or by the media's influence on them. Maybe you feel that you have something to teach children. This is a worthy motive, but how will it affect your writing? Your desire to teach can powerfully affect your writing (or your illustrations, for that matter), whether it's fiction or nonfiction.

def•i•ni•tion _____

Editors label a story in which the moral or message the author wants to convey overwhelms the plot **pedantic**. It's a story that teaches, but in a narrow way.

Writing fiction, in picture book or novel form, is one way to teach. If something bad happens to a child who acts in a certain way, the author hopes that this will teach the reader a lesson. This can be done effectively … and not so effectively. When a story is overwhelmed by its message, editors dismiss it as _pedantic_ and reject it immediately.

Here's an excerpt from a pedantic story I created:

Mary Who Doesn't Listen

by Mo Ralizer

Once upon a time there was a little girl named Mary. She was like most little girls her age, which was six. She liked ice cream, she liked to

---

play, and she liked to take care of her kitty. But in one way, Mary was not like other little girls. She never listened to her parents.

One day, Mary was playing *Treasure Chase* on the Zinblendo console for the TV. A fire truck went past, blowing its siren and making a big racket. Mary's kitty was scared and hid under the sofa. But Mary didn't hear the siren, she was so caught up in getting the next Gold Treasure. Mary played for hours. She was a very inattentive little girl. When her mother called her to supper, she didn't hear her. Her mother called her again, and still Mary didn't hear. Mary's supper was getting cold, and her father had to come upstairs and unplug the TV to get Mary to pay attention. Her mother and father were angry and said to her, "You are becoming Mary Who Doesn't Listen!"

I won't subject you to the entire story, but you probably can imagine how it develops. Mary continued to not listen and then something happened that made her decide to listen and become Mary Who *Does* Listen.

What's wrong with this story? We know nothing about Mary beyond her problem, which is that she doesn't listen, and nothing happens to her but an experience that teaches a lesson. Even worse, the author keeps hitting us over the head with the *bad* behavior. There's no humor and little dialogue. Imagine the illustrations that would carry the same message—literal and unimaginative, they would focus narrowly on Mary's bad behavior and its consequences. Put the text and illustrations together, and you'd get a book few children would want to read again, or even to finish.

If you want to teach good behavior, don't despair. There are ways you can do it and be effective. In fiction, use humor and exaggeration, as in the classic *Struwwelpeter* stories. These classic stories, originally published in Germany in 1848, each feature a child whose outrageously bad behavior leads to a rather gruesome end—one is eaten by a lion, one starves to death, and so on. Children old enough to recognize them as fantasies find them extremely funny and take them no more seriously than the violence they see all the time in cartoons. At the same time, they get the point.

Today, we take a gentler approach, but the humor of bad examples and the lesson they teach is exactly what Nancy Carlson plays on in *How to Lose All Your Friends*. David Wisniewski pokes fun at grown-ups while finding new reasons for the *rules* they enforce in *The Secret Knowledge of Grown-Ups*. You get the idea: a story in which a child who doesn't clean up his bedroom ends up being trapped inside could have a similar effect.

For older children, dramatizing a situation instead of talking about rules, even humorously, can work. Do you want to teach children about the dangers of drugs? Consider a novel in which one of the characters has a bad experience with drugs—but the author must let the experience develop naturally and refrain from commenting on it even through the mouth of another character.

Can You Keep a Secret?

Trust your ability as a storyteller. If the story tells itself, and the consequences of a particular action are clear, the reader will get the point with no need to underline it during the story or repeat it at the end. Vicarious experience puts your message across.

Playground Stories

Does nonfiction have to be presented in a fictional form to be effective? No, but don't forget to make an effective presentation and to use narrative form if it works, as Patricia Lauber does in *Volcano!* and Susan Campbell Bartoletti does in *Growing Up in Coal Country*.

On the other hand, you could teach through nonfiction. But again, your mission could overwhelm your writing. Even nonfiction—particularly nonfiction!—must be interesting. A list of facts or an essay that reads like an entry from an encyclopedia is a good solid piece of factual material. But it's also writing that's been overwhelmed by the author focusing too much on what she wanted to say and not enough on how to say it.

Instead, present your material simply and clearly, with a narrative if possible. Consider a book like Eve Bunting's *Ducky*, about a load of plastic toys washed off a freighter that ultimately became an opportunity for scientists to learn about the currents of the Pacific Ocean. The story and illustrations bring this event to life through the "eyes" of one plastic duck; compare this to newspaper stories from the 1990s to gain some insight into one way in which events or information can be transformed. For older children, Laurence Pringle's *An Extraordinary Life* follows the life and migration of a monarch butterfly in story format. Again, plenty of information is presented, but it's woven skillfully into the story.

If you want to teach, you can, but don't lose track of the fact that you are a storyteller first of all.

I Get to Be the Mommy

You like taking care of children; maybe you're a parent yourself. You want to write stories that will help children feel happy, and especially happy with themselves. This, too, is a worthy motive, but if it leads to you removing all conflict and difficulty from a story, it's gone too far.

In my work at Charlesbridge and other publishers, I saw many manuscripts submitted in which the author had worked very hard to remove anything painful or dangerous from the story. This invented excerpt shows this impulse in action:

The Happy Child

by Honey Syrup

Billy was a happy child. He lived in a big house with his mommy, his daddy, his dog Spot, and his sisters and brothers. Every day when he woke up he smiled, because he knew he was going to have fun! He didn't care if it was a school day or a weekend day. He knew he would enjoy it.

One day, he woke up and smiled even wider than usual because he was going fishing with his Grandpop. He got dressed and washed up. Then he went downstairs singing "I'm going fishing!"

When he got downstairs he said, like he always did, "Good morning, Mom!" and "Good morning, Dad!" He felt it truly was a good morning.

The story continues with everyone smiling at one another, Billy going fishing, sure he's going to have a good time, and Billy having a good time when he goes fishing.

What's the problem with this story? To start with, it isn't a story. Nothing happens. Billy accomplishes nothing because there's no tension or problem. The author has worked so hard to make the writing safe and reassuring that it's lost the feel of real life. Saccharine-sweet illustrations, perhaps featuring a child with unnaturally large eyes, would accompany this one-dimensional narrative.

What to do? It's more truly and deeply reassuring to a child to see a character realistically overcome a difficulty than to read a story about a world in which there are no difficulties because, much as we would like to believe otherwise, children know quite well that life is about difficulties and overcoming them.

Published authors know this, and you can find many wonderful examples of books that give true comfort to a child by showing a child dealing realistically with a real problem. For a child confronting death, for example, you can find picture books such as Judith Viorst's *The Tenth Good Thing About Barney*, nonfiction titles such as Janet Bode's *Death Is Hard to Live With*, or novels such as Ann Brashares's *The Sisterhood of the Traveling Pants*. Parents are there to take care of children, but for you as a writer, the challenge is to tell the story.

Class Rules

Children are in the middle of the process of growing from being helpless infants to resourceful, self-confident adults (or so we hope), and as they do, they experience many triumphs and failures. You do them no favors if you sugarcoat the world for them, and your writing suffers, too.

Having an Impact

One of the joys of writing and illustrating for children is that books *do* have a real impact on children's lives. Published authors and illustrators hear all the time from children who have been affected by their work. Children will learn from and be comforted, challenged, moved, and amused by your work—often in ways you hadn't anticipated.

Ironically, this is most likely to happen when you've successfully curbed an impulse to lecture or muted a desire to give a reader a verbal hug. Words and pictures that speak directly to children help them make sense of their world and their feelings and, therefore, have the biggest impact.

Look What I Did!

An enduring motive for writers and illustrators is self-expression, finding satisfaction through the use of words or pictures to get across their feelings and experiences. This approach is the one most likely to keep you going if you aren't published yet or you are published but can't land a new contract. Your own satisfaction with the way you put images or words together needs no outside validation. Self-expression can mean different things to different writers. What does it mean to you?

Personal Interests

Do you care deeply about some area of knowledge? In your passion for the subject, you'll find the motivation to get it across clearly, complete with the dramatic and exciting aspects of it that grab you right there, to grab your reader, too.

Writing or illustrating can lead you to learn even more about a subject that intrigues you, and from there, to other things about which you want to learn. For example, illustrator Michael Rothman did wonderful work for Sneed Collard's *The Forest in the Clouds*, showing the world of the Costa Rican "cloud forest." He already had considerable experience with rain forests, but this book gave him the opportunity to learn more, and he put what he learned into his illustrations.

Another example: I talked with noted nonfiction writer James Cross Giblin about his biography of Adolf Hitler. Jim told me that he got interested in this grimly fascinating subject while writing an earlier biography of Charles Lindbergh, the flawed American hero—his flaws most apparent in his open sympathy for the Nazis. So let your interests take you places, and pass on what you learn on the journey.

Open to Inspiration

When asked what inspires him, published poet and picture book author Charles Ghigna replied: "Nature, kids, animals, sports, travel, the weather, daily celebrations of life, and my own childhood memories. My son, Chip, and my wife, Debra, also inspire many of my poems, as do my editors, neighbors, and friends. I often receive inspiration from reading newspapers, magazines, and books. I guess one might say that everything inspires me!"

A writer or illustrator with this attitude—one that you can cultivate—will always be motivated and always have fresh ideas. Give yourself time to notice what's around you and time to think about where it could lead you.

> **Can You Keep a Secret?**
>
> No motive will carry you farther than your own desire to express yourself. Your own innate drive to learn, to be moved, and to find fresh language to express your passions will keep you going when hopes of fame or fortune wither.

The Inner Child

Jan Wahl, an experienced picture-book author with more than 100 books to his credit, has this to say about writing for children: "I don't try to write for editors or for librarians or for teachers—and, especially, I don't write for reviewers. I don't try to write for any specific child. I feel that's a big mistake."

Jan is not concerned with how people are going to react, and he doesn't even feel that a child he knows, or a classroom of children, can give him a clue as to whether or not he is succeeding. To him, writing for children means something else: "It means enjoying afresh, each day, those insights and glimpses of the universe I had as a child."

The Dark Side

Can you just sit down at your desk and start to express yourself? On a good day, yes, you might be able to do that. But even with the outside distractions removed, everyone wrestles at one time or another with feelings they would like to ignore: anxiety, fear, writer's block, or lack of motivation.

When you do get hit by one of these feelings, first be reassured that you are not alone. Then do something to counter it, such as talking to a friend, going for a walk, or reading a favorite book. And if you need it, an entire book has been written on this subject: *Art and Fear: Observations on the Perils and Rewards of Artmaking* by David Bayles and Ted Orland. Karen Romano Young, a novelist and nonfiction writer, recommended it to me, and this is what she said about it: "It's not just about art, it's about what we go through when we make things, the stories we tell ourselves and how we get in our own way. It puts a name on the different fears we have that stop us from pushing ourselves, starting, finishing, and succeeding, and offers ways out of this maze."

So there's a dark side to the creative life, but there are also ways to deal with it. You can make self-expression a lifelong and deeply satisfying quest. However you do it—by following your own interests, keeping yourself open, or listening to your inner child—express yourself. No one else has exactly your point of view or your way of saying things. Expressing yourself and getting better and better at doing so is a powerful motive. Hold on to it, develop it, and you'll find satisfaction, even if you never get published.

I Got a Star!

Real success is possible, although it can take many years. What does *success* mean? What *success* is varies from one person to another, but you may be surprised to hear that for most, it's not fame or money (although a steady income is a good thing) that matters.

An author I know, Miriam Bat-Ami, won a prestigious award for *Two Suns*, a historical fiction book about a detention camp for European refugees in upstate New York during World War II. Her success did not come out of nowhere: in the early 1990s, I had published a picture book and a short novel of hers. A few years later, she published a novel with another publisher. *Two Suns* came from a third publisher, six years after her first book. She says she needed that time, not only to work on the book but also to find the right publisher and the right editor for it. What does she most appreciate about her success? You might be surprised to hear what she told me, after acknowledging that good reviews and positive balances in a royalty statement are nice: "I like seeing a teenager at a table next to mine reading my book and seeming so concentrated on it …. But real success has to do with self-respect, and successfully working with an editor to tell the story I want to tell, and those are connected to my sense of myself as a writer."

There aren't any guarantees. You'll need persistence (possibly years of it), some talent, and a little luck—luck that you might be able to create—to have a chance of getting there. Do you have those prerequisites? You won't know until you try, so get to it!

The Least You Need to Know

◆ You probably won't become rich or famous writing children's books, but you might be able to make a full-time job out of it.

◆ If you want to teach, find ways to dramatize your lessons or present information in a narrative or other engaging form.

◆ To help children feel better about themselves, show children living in the real world and triumphing, not cocooned in a safe fantasy.

◆ One of the joys of working on children's books is the impact you can have on children's lives.

◆ Self-expression as a motive can lead to self-indulgence, but it's also an ever-expanding reason to keep working.

◆ Success is not assured, but the journey is worth it if you find the craft itself satisfying.

Chapter 5

Setting Up Shop

In This Chapter

- Gathering your supplies and getting organized
- What you need before you sit down to write
- Great reference books to have handy
- What files you may need
- Time-management tips

Now comes the nitty-gritty of being a writer. (If you're an illustrator, much of what's covered here is relevant to you, too. Turn to Chapter 6 for more details.) The desire to express yourself may get you started, but you need hard work and organizational skills to keep going.

This chapter covers the tools—both technological and traditional—you need to succeed in writing (especially after you earn a book contract) and also offers some organizational and time-management tips.

School Supplies

Remember when teachers sent home a list of required school supplies? Today, as you embark upon a career as a children's book author, you also need certain tools and supplies. You probably already have many of the following, in fact:

Telephone   This is a business, after all. You'll find that you use the telephone often and for long periods as a writer—even as a writer of children's books. You'll make calls to colleagues, editors, contacts, and sources for research. A separate line, which could be a cell phone, is ideal.

Computer with word processing capabilities and printer   An editor won't accept your manuscript scribbled out in pencil. If you can afford a computer, buy one. Otherwise, you can type your final drafts at a friend's house or rent time on a computer at stores such as Kinko's or perhaps your local library.

Backup capabilities   If you have a computer, be sure you also have a way to back up your files—by saving them to a flash drive or external hard drive, burning them to a CD-ROM, or sending them to online storage sites—so if something goes wrong with your computer you won't have to retype all your work.

Can You Keep a Secret?

Aaron Shepard's personal site, www.aaronshep.com, to see what one author has done with his website. The Society of Children's Book Writers and Illustrators site at www.scbwi.org is worth browsing, too.

Internet access   You need Internet access. You might be thinking, *I'm going to write a children's book. I just need my imagination! Why do I need the Internet?* First, you can do a lot of research online. Second, you'll find fabulous and helpful information for writers there.

E-mail   Nowadays, e-mail is *the* way to communicate with an editor. It's also a great way to stay in touch with writing and illustrating buddies.

Standard desk supplies   Think paper (for the printer, notes, outlines, etc.), sticky notes, pens, pencils, files, a stapler, paper clips, and anything else you use to keep organized.

Filing cabinet   You learn about organizing it and what types of files you find yourself making a little later in this chapter.

Access to a fax   You probably don't need to own a fax machine, but do need to know where you can send and receive faxes from in your neighborhood, or to set up a fax-to-e-mail service.

Class Rules

Don't foist your business cards on every editor you meet. Wait for them to ask.

Business cards   Identify yourself as a professional. Don't invest in anything fancy, but do print cards (perhaps on your own computer) with your name, phone, fax, home or office address, and e-mail address. You'll be glad you have them when you can hand one to another writer or illustrator.

That's it! Given these items, you can compete and do business in the world of publishing.

A Place for Everything

When it comes to organizing, you need to find a system that works best for you, but don't delude yourself into thinking that *disorganization* is your system. Putting everything neatly away in filing cabinets and desk drawers isn't necessary if you can find what you want in the umpteen stacks scattered around your workspace. (I said *stacks*, not strewn-about papers here and there.)

And when you're writing, you don't need to have an empty desk, but to thrive as a writer, you do need to set up your supplies *before* you begin writing. Have reference books, computer supplies, sharpened pencils, your notes, your files, extra paper, candy, or anything else you might need at hand so you don't have to break the flow.

> **Can You Keep a Secret?**
>
> Many writers can't break the momentum after they begin writing. If they stop, for example, to find a sharpened pencil, they can't get back to it for hours, days, or even months. So consider several organizational ideas before you sit down to write.

Here a Book, There a Book ...

You can't avoid it. You'll need to fill a shelf in your writing area with reference books. Following are some reference books every writer should have on his or her bookshelf:

Dictionary   Get a comprehensive one. Don't pick up the 200-pager at the 99¢ clearance center or even a pocket paperback edition. You need a quality, sturdy, hardbound, heavy dictionary: *Webster's Third New International* (the reference book copyeditors and proofreaders turn to) or the more portable *Webster's Collegiate*.

Chicago Manual of Style   This is the bible of editors and publishers everywhere. There's (almost) too much information, but you never know when you'll need to know when to capitalize something or how a book is laid out, right?

Roget's Thesaurus   Invest in a good, hardbound *Roget's* today and never fumble for a synonym, antonym, or perfect word choice again.

You should have a copy of this book on your shelf, too, of course!

Paper and Ink

Even in this technological age, where paper seems obsolete when we move documents via e-mail, you might want to proof your work the old-fashioned way—on paper, so be sure you have paper and printer ink on hand.

Back It Up!

And do be sure you own—and more importantly *use*—something to back up your writing files. I've heard horror stories from writers who lost years of manuscripts when their computer crashed. Save your work not only on the computer's hard drive but also on something you can take out of your work area as a backup, and save it regularly.

> **Class Rules**
>
> Do you need everything listed here to succeed? No. You'll know what you need and what you don't. But there is a minimum: you need writing tools, a quiet, distraction-free (and that means child-free) space in which to work, a work surface you don't have to clear off every time you want to use it, and a schedule your family and friends respect.

Research Within Reach

Are your research, notes, and any other documents necessary for your writing present and within reach? Be sure that when you sit down to write you can find important facts pertinent to your story line.

The Secret Files Garden

Part of maintaining your research is, of course, your file system, both for papers and on your computer. But how do you know what topics need their own folder? Short answer: you don't. You'll probably determine how to file things as you go along, but start with some obvious (and not so obvious) choices.

Keep separate folders for the following:

Book ideas   As one idea develops after another, it's easy to forget new ones. Note your ideas so you can come back to them. Use a notebook if that's easier.

Research of topics   Make a folder for every book that's gone beyond the idea stage. Whenever you come across related information or find yourself musing about a character, put the results in that folder. Then, when you're ready to work on that piece, just pull the file.

Contacts   You might choose to use experts in your writing or need to call upon experts for a project. Many writers keep files on people involved in a particular topic.

Contracts   After you sign them for a book deal, keep them.

Submission letters and proposals   Keep track of the submissions and proposals you've sent out. Maintain a separate file, perhaps even organized by months, with printed copies of your correspondence.

Business expenses   Writing is a form of self-employment, so keep a file for expenses such as telephone calls, printer cartridges, and any other item you may be able to write off if you have proof you used it in the course of your business.

> **Can You Keep a Secret?**
>
> When a folder gets too full, subdivide. Do the same thing on the computer. Don't save everything to the default "Documents" folder, or you'll end up with hundreds of documents—manuscript drafts, letters, notes, and pages saved from websites—all in one hard-to-navigate place. And you'll lose things, just as you can with a poorly organized filing cabinet.

A Time and a Space for Everything

Many years ago, Virginia Woolf wrote about the importance of having a room of one's own. She pointed out that in Britain, women had problems finding a space to call their own in which to write and the time to do it. Women weren't perceived as potential writers. Times change, but the situation for writers of children's books in North America today is not much different from what Woolf described.

Most of you are women, and if you're not, hey, you're a guy in a profession that's devalued partly because it's mostly an occupation of women. You probably have a hard time getting people to take you seriously—possibly even the people in your own family. And as a result, you have a hard time getting the space and time to write.

But you know what? You need that space. You need a desk, and good light, and room for the books you may need to refer to, and hours of time during which you don't need to worry about being interrupted or needed.

After you have that time and space—and if you don't insist on it you won't get it!—you need to cultivate the discipline you must have if you're going to stick with writing for the long haul. You've got to have that "butt-in-chair" time if you're going to write in your journal, try some writing exercises, plan out a project, and actually write it.

Give yourself a schedule, too. Maybe you can't get up every morning at 4 A.M. to write. How about two hours three nights a week while the rest of the family watches television? Throw in Saturday afternoon, and you've got 10 hours a week of solid writing time. You can get a lot done. Just do your best to resist the temptation to do laundry, or wash the dishes, or do any of those mundane things that suddenly seem *so* tempting when a blank page is staring up at you.

Playground Stories _____

Don't have time to write? Make time. Susan Campbell Bartoletti wrote and published several books while teaching full-time: "In order to make time to write, I woke at 4 A.M. to write before school. (My dog wouldn't even get up with me!) With my sixth book contract, I left teaching to write full-time. The morning hours still work best for me, and I have my best writing days when I'm at the computer by 4 A.M. I enjoy the early morning hours, while it's still dark outside. Ideas grow in the dark. It's the perfect time for creating, for taking that which is without form and void and separating darkness and light. I always feel as though I'm working toward the light."

The Least You Need to Know

- ◆ A writer today needs certain tools to compete in the publishing world and write: computer, phone, fax access, and online capabilities, including e-mail.

- ◆ Organize your writing area and have necessary supplies, reference materials, and research readily available to you before you sit down to write.

- ◆ Set up a filing system now to keep all the tidbits of information and ideas easily accessible to you.

- ◆ No writer should be without a good dictionary and thesaurus.

- ◆ Self-starters succeed as writers; schedule time to write and stick to it.

I Like to Draw

In This Chapter

- ◆ Illustration versus fine art
- ◆ Go to school? To draw? Yep!
- ◆ Setting up your work space
- ◆ Are you ready to contact publishers?

So far, I've introduced you to the world of children's literature and to getting started *as a writer*. In this chapter, we look at the first steps you need to take if your focus is on illustration.

Why Illustrate?

Let's start by drawing a couple basic distinctions. If your calling is fine art, you create works from out of your imagination, with no limitation in subject or approach. To make a living as a fine artist, you need to please only one other person, the person who purchases what you've created.

To *illustrate*, in contrast, you must start with someone else's text. Depending on the kind of illustration, your interpretation may have to be literal, or you may be able to bring considerable creative license to your work. But

def•i•ni•tion

To **illustrate**, if you look at the Latin roots of the word, means *to make bright,* implying that the illustrator interacts with and adds to a text. At its best, illustration is not merely decorative. It does not create its own artistic world, ignoring the mood and setting of a text—it develops from and meshes with a text to create a new, coherent whole.

in either case, you must start from the text. Your audience is also very different; to succeed, you must ultimately please thousands of book purchasers—customers in bookstores, librarians in charge of ordering books, teachers finding books to use in their classrooms, and so on.

If the challenges of illustration engage your interest, why illustrate for children? Not, I hope, because you've tried other fields and think you might make some money here, because you won't get rich as a children's book illustrator. And not, I hope, because you *love* children. As I tried to demonstrate in Chapter 4, your feelings about children can have some unfortunate side effects on writing and illustrating for them. Instead, as any practicing illustrator will tell you, it's a love of this craft that will keep you going: the challenge of developing your own unique style, rather than imitating what seems to be successful; the challenge of putting a picture book together so it functions as one single piece of art, not a series of disconnected illustrations; the challenge of showing character, interaction, and setting in a single piece for a jacket or textbook.

Does that sound good to you? Then let's get started.

Getting Started

Much of what you need to do now as an illustrator overlaps with what a writer needs to do: you need to have an understanding of what kinds of books are published for children, how to find the best ones, what the different parts of a book are called and what they do, and so on. So go ahead and read the rest of Parts 1 and 2 and then come back here.

Going to School (Again)

Although a lot of what writers and illustrators need to know and do is similar, there's one big difference: it's very hard, if not impossible, to succeed as a self-taught illustrator. Many writers pick up writing well after they leave college, perhaps when they have children, are able to hone their craft through writing and rewriting, and eventually get published. They don't need to go into a specialized writing program (although some do) because much of their education was built around reading and writing. Anyone who's graduated from a liberal arts college has spent years getting general training in dealing with words.

Unfortunately, an illustrator can't do what a writer does. A typical college graduate does not have an equivalent amount of what you could call *visual literacy*. Let's face it: our schools today don't spend much time teach-ing us how to draw and paint, how to interpret images, or how to present ideas visually. Just as someone who left school after the third grade is going to have a hard time writing novels, even the most dedicated self-taught illustrator might lack the specific skills needed to illustrate effectively. Drawing human beings, for example, can be a big challenge, because our figures and faces are so complex—and because people are so intuitively familiar with them.

> **Can You Keep a Secret?**
>
> While most authors pick up their pens some years after they leave college, most illustrators go to art school at some point. Publishers probably won't ask to see your diploma, but realistically, it's dif-ficult to reach professional stan-dards without some schooling.

Does that mean you need to go back to school for two years and get a degree in illus-tration? Not necessarily—some coursework may be all you need. Art schools like the Rhode Island School of Design, which has a well-known illustration program, have set up continuing education programs for people needing some specific training. Check an art school near you to see what's available.

Book Learning

What if you do have training as a fine artist or in illustration, but not children's book illustration, specifically? If you're a fine artist, you already know how to deal with the human face and body and perhaps animals as well; you know how to compose a scene, how to handle perspective, and how to choose a palette. You do need to learn how to illustrate. If you're already an illustrator, you need *only* to learn to work with the for-mats peculiar to children's books, and particularly how to compose a picture book—unless you want to limit yourself to book jackets and stand-alone illustrations.

For the fine artist, I recommend at least one course to introduce you to children's book illustration, and more if you can manage it. If you can't find a suitable course, two books will help you work your way into your new world. The first is Martin Salisbury's *Illustrating Children's Books: Creating Pictures for Publication*. This is a general introduc-tion to the field, written by a teacher of children's book illustration at an art college. Although not set up as a how-to, you can learn some basic principles and try them out.

When you're ready to go into more depth, or for the illustrator moving into children's books, check out Uri Shulevitz's *Writing with Pictures*. Shulevitz is a Caldecott Medal–winning illustrator who teaches a master class, concentrating on creating a picture book. Although written when preseparated art was still the norm, the basic principles—composition, page design, laying out a picture book as a whole—he teaches are still very relevant. Most of the children's book illustrators I know have this book.

Get Set Up!

To do anything well, you need a work area to practice your craft. In a pinch, a writer can work on a table in a corner, with a shelf or two set aside for supplies and reference books, but an illustrator needs more space. You don't need a huge studio, but you do need a room apart from family hubbub, where you can work in quiet and leave pieces to dry, or pin up a sequence of illustrations, and not worry that they'll be disturbed. This could be the guest bedroom or a nook up in the attic, so long as it's *your* space. Get a drawing table that you can adjust the angle and height of as soon as you can afford it.

Here are some other things you might want in your workspace:

- Supplies! Have *ample* quantities of your favorite paper, brushes, pencils, or whatever you use. You don't want to have to go get more while you're in the middle of a picture.

- A big piece of corkboard or something similar, so you can pin up sketches or a sequence of drawings.

- Visual reference materials: art books, files of pictures you've clipped, photo books, etc.

- No distractions! Unless you work on a computer, don't have one in the room. No TV, of course, although a radio is okay if you like to listen to music while you work.

Make your own list, based on what you want in your space, and make your space what you want it to be.

Get Some Books

Illustrators need a reference shelf. Start with Uri Shulevitz's *Writing with Pictures* if you don't already have it, and consider getting *Picture This! How Pictures Work* by Molly Bang, *Words into Type*, *Encyclopedia of Illustration Techniques*, *The Graphic Artists Guild Handbook: Pricing and Ethical Guidelines*, or *Words About Pictures: The Narrative Art of Children's Picture Books* by Perry Nodelman. These provide guidance in technique, book design, type, and other basics. (For brief descriptions of most of these books, see Appendix B.)

Are You Ready?

So you've gone to art school or taken some classes, and started building a stack of samples. Is your work good enough for you to put together a portfolio (see Chapter 14)? Are you ready to start contacting publishers? How can you know? Well, sometimes you can show your art to a published illustrator or an art director at a conference for children's book writers and illustrators and get feedback.

If you can't get a professional's feedback, try self-assessment. Choose a publisher that you feel could be a good match for your book. Research the company's most recently published books, following the procedures outlined in Chapter 19. Choose three that have illustrations similar in style and medium (such as paint or pastels) to yours, and get your hands on the illustrations through your local library system or bookstore. Look through all of them carefully. Check how the artists show characters in different situations, how they choose to use or not use different perspectives. See if you can get a sense of their pacing and how they create excitement. Look closely at how the illustrators depict movement and facial expressions. Whether or not they show animals or people, and regardless of whether the style is realistic or cartoonlike, evaluate how lively and real the characters seem.

Then turn to your own work. Are your characters as lively as those you see in the published books, or do they seem stiff or clumsy? Are your illustrations as varied and interesting? Does your book have pacing like theirs? Does it build to a climax? In short, can you confidently say that your work is at least as accomplished as what you see in these published books? If you can't, then don't start marketing yourself yet. You won't get hired, and you'll just waste time and money that would be better spent on classes or self-directed illustration exercises.

Class Rules

Sending out mailings and doing all the other things you need to do to make connections to a publisher are costly. Don't even think about doing them if you aren't ready. Take some more classes, set yourself projects such as creating a picture-book version of a folktale, and keep striving to improve.

The Least You Need to Know

◆ Illustration requires the illustrator to work with the text, not just create a nice picture.

◆ Unlike writing, illustrating requires formal training.

◆ As an illustrator, you need a work space and some reference books on your shelf.

◆ Assess your work carefully before jumping into marketing yourself to publishers.

Part 2

Get Ready, Get Set ...

Now you know the basics, but you have lots to learn if you want to reach your destination. Part 2 introduces the big world of publishing and explains what's happening there right now. I clue you in on the different formats and age levels books are slotted into and show you some of the genres within which you might be writing, from pure fantasy to the most straightforward nonfiction.

I also guide you on a detailed tour of a book, so you can call each book element by the correct name. And I help you figure out how to pick a good "how-to" to help you get beyond the writing basics. You're almost ready to go!

Chapter 7

It's a BIG World

In This Chapter

- ◆ A brief history of the children's publishing industry
- ◆ Why there are more and more paperbacks
- ◆ Buyouts and mergers
- ◆ How children's books are selling and to whom
- ◆ Internet, meet children's publishing

Once upon a time, children's book publishing was a genteel industry run by white-gloved ladies with backgrounds as librarians. Today, everything is different. Or so the story is usually told.

That the business was ever genteel may be something of a myth, but there's no denying that the business *has* changed. In this chapter, you find out how. You learn about the decline of the library market and the rise of the consumer market, the growth of paperbacks, and the buyouts that have hit publishing just as much as other industries. You also get an assessment of just how much the Internet has affected the business so far.

Why do you need to know this? Because you need to know who's buying the books. The business is not what it once was.

The Golden Age

Publishers have been making books for children for about as long as printing presses have been printing. Right through the nineteenth century, however, these were sidelines to their main business of publishing books for adults. In the United States, the first companies to create separate children's book divisions, with a dedicated staff, did so after World War I. In the 1920s and 1930s, other publishers followed suit, hiring librarians to run their children's divisions.

> **Playground Stories** _____
>
> Why librarians? Because at the time, children's books were mostly sold to libraries, so if a company wanted to be sure a book would appeal to the library market, it made sense to let someone with library training decide what books to publish. Librarians knew what they wanted. Solid informational books like Hendrik Willem Van Loon's *The History of the World,* which won the first Newbery Medal, and folktale collections with Arthur Rackham–style illustrations were in demand.

This was a fairly cozy little business, but a profitable one. More than one company had its literary but money-losing adult division sustained by its steady children's book sales. In the 1940s, following pioneering research into what appealed to children, books got livelier. The bright colors in *Goodnight Moon* don't look exceptional today, but it was a groundbreaking book when it was first published in 1947—and not much of a success at first, either. Influential librarians didn't like it.

Looking back, these times can seem like a golden age. "Commercial" considerations didn't rule the business. Publishers tried to put out quality books that conformed to a librarian's judgment of what was right for children. This started to change as early as the 1950s, when *Sputnik* spurred investment in science education in the schools and in funding for nonfiction books for libraries.

Paperbacks: Fun and Cheap

The publishing business really changed in the 1960s. Federal money from Lyndon Johnson's Great Society programs sparked a minor boom in children's publishing, and suddenly federal funds were available for schools and libraries to use to purchase books. Many more picture books, with more and more creative art, could be published. And publishers realized that Americans were not all white, and books that reflected our multiracial, multiethnic, and multicultural society started to come out in increasing numbers.

The rise of the paperback, which began in the 1960s and continues to this day, was possibly a more significant but less noticed change. Until that time, quality publishers, the ones focusing on the library market, published only in hardcover. Hardcover books were expensive, and few families could buy them. But when books like E. B. White's *Charlotte's Web* and *Stuart Little* came out in an attractive, large paperback format, more people could buy them.

Playground Stories

Ezra Jack Keats's *The Snowy Day*, a prize-winning book in 1963, was an early sign of the changes. This attractive and still popular book was one of the very first to matter-of-factly feature an African American child, a boy named Peter, as he enjoyed a snowy day in his urban neighborhood.

The bookstore market wasn't immune to change at this time. Back then, there were no children's-only bookstores and few large bookstores. Cheap, popular books such as those published by Golden Books were sold in department stores and the like, but no inexpensive editions of the quality books were sold to libraries. Those children's books took up a small section in most bookstores, and the booksellers expected to sell most of their children's books as gifts. When the "good" books started to be available in paperback, larger children's sections and children's-only bookstores started to appear, and gradually, bookstore sales became a larger part of the children's market.

Playground Stories

Until 1967, if a parent or a teacher wanted to buy a children's book, it had to be a hardcover or a low-quality paperback. But in that year, George Nicholson launched Dell Yearling, a trade paperback program. The first two titles, *Charlotte's Web* and *Stuart Little*, for which Dell paid Harper & Row $35,000—an enormous advance for the time—were not only huge successes, they also didn't hurt Harper's hardcover sales. Harper was willing to say so in writing, other publishers made deals with Dell, and the rest is history. Paperbacks, including books published as originals, not reprints of books first published in hardcover, have become a large part of the children's book market.

Starting in 1975, Random House published its new, inexpensive "pictureback" line of original picture-book paperbacks—serious competition to Golden Books's inexpensive hardcover books. They sold well in bookstores. Improving technology also made paperback versions of hardcover picture books possible. At the same size, and on the same quality paper, but half to a third of the price of a hardcover book, paperback picture books became more and more available. Today, almost every publisher publishes hardcovers and paperbacks, the paperback editions coming out a year or two after the hardcover, or less often at the same time. No longer do children's book publishers publish solely for the library market.

The Big Get Even Bigger

Other changes were taking place, too. In the 1970s, the federal funding that had supported the growth of children's publishing a decade earlier ended. Publishers laid off staff and hunkered down for hard times. Noted nonfiction writer and editor Jim Giblin points out that the photo-essay, a nonfiction picture book illustrated with photographs, began during this time. With library-oriented nonfiction not selling as well, publishers found that the photo-essay, which was more attractive, did sell in bookstores.

Better times came in the 1980s, but the industry was already beginning to change. Although shortsighted tax revolts had further cut funding that libraries could use to buy books, the economy was good and many parents had money to spend at the bookstores—and if they wanted to have books for their children, they had to spend money on them, because they could no longer count on finding them in the library. The business boomed—until the early 1990s, when sales went down and a round of buyouts, closures, and mergers began.

> **Class Rules**
>
> It's hard to keep track of the constant changes in publishing, but you need to try. Don't rely on out-of-date information. Use a guide such as *Children's Writer's and Illustrator's Market*, and buy a new one every year. Check publisher websites to confirm addresses. And don't send submissions to "Harper & Row" or "Macmillan Children's Books." Those names no longer exist.

To tell the story of children's book publishing since then is to tell a story of big fish swallowing big fish, big fish swallowing medium-size fish, and even a few cases of smaller fish somehow swallowing larger fish. Some of the biggest deals were the merger of Penguin and Putnam; the purchase of Macmillan by Simon & Schuster; the merger of Random House and Bertelsmann's Bantam Doubleday Dell; the purchase of the bankrupt Golden Books by Random House; HarperCollins's purchase of William Morrow; Scholastic's acquisition of Grolier (Franklin Watts, Children's Press, and Orchard); and the buyout of Harcourt by Houghton Mifflin. The largest children's publishers today are part of media conglomerates, many of them owned by multinational corporations. We've come a long way from white-gloved library publishing.

After all these mergers, five big companies make over half of the approximately $2 billion in annual sales in children's publishing—Random House, Penguin, Scholastic, HarperCollins, and Simon & Schuster. Not counting Scholastic, which only publishes for children, these companies are also the ones publishing most of the best-selling books for adults. These companies are *very* big fish, with thousands of employees, and are often part of even larger companies also owning cable channels, television stations, newspapers, and the like.

Who's Buying?

Children's books just aren't what they used to be because libraries no longer are the primary market for children's books. Publishers must reach individual consumers, and large companies dominate the landscape—but the effects aren't all bad! Many books are available reflecting the experiences of all Americans, although not as many as there might be. Books are available in a dazzling array of art styles and techniques. And many more affordable, but high-quality books are available. It's a different and bigger world. Children's publishing, in a way, has grown up. It's more like publishing for adults, for better or worse. What does that mean?

Eye-Catching Books

A few decades ago, thoughtful reviews in respected journals helped libraries choose which books to buy. They still do, but consumers are also buying more of the books now. And partly in an effort to get their attention, the art in children's picture books, and on the cover of children's novels and nonfiction, has become ever more eye-catching. Go to a bookstore and browse through the racks of paperback fiction in a children's department and an adult department, and you'll see what I mean.

Can You Keep a Secret?
Publishers actively market their children's books, even picture books, to adults. I've seen ads in the *New Yorker* for picture books every holiday season, free postcards showing children's book covers in coffee bar racks, and blurbs on the back cover of Ian Falconer's *Olivia* by David Hockney and Mikhail Baryshnikov. None of those are aimed at children.

TV, Movies, and Candy

If a consumer knows the name of an author, illustrator, or movie, he or she is more likely to buy a book with that name on it. So one strategy for publishers is to look for a *brand*—a name that's known and respected and therefore likely to help sell a book and its associated merchandise. Brand names may be those of a book or author or be brought into a book from the outside.

Don't be quick to exclaim in horror at this phenomenon! Licensing of this kind is not an entirely new phenomenon. Lewis Carroll of *Alice in Wonderland* fame licensed such products as a *Through the Looking Glass* biscuit tin.

Some publishers have been able to create children's book brand names:

◆ *Dr. Seuss* became a brand name because his books were so consistently good *and* easily recognizable.

◆ *Arthur* has become a brand name after the success of the TV series based on the book.

◆ HarperCollins has developed *The Little House on the Prairie* into a brand. You can buy Little House picture books and paper dolls.

◆ Houghton Mifflin has created new *Curious George* books, to extend another "classic" brand name.

◆ Celebrities from Shaquille O'Neal to Madonna have written or lent their name to children's books.

Publishers may also *license* a brand from another company. Licensing characters and the right to create books tied in to a movie or TV series (such as *Star Wars* or *Dora the Explorer*) has long been a way to associate a book with an already familiar brand name.

def·i·ni·tion

A **license** gives you the right to do something. In publishing, it gives you the right to publish a book or books, or to use a character or name or story created by someone else in a book (or some other product—a lunch box manufacturer might license the right to make a Dora the Explorer lunch box).

Licensing is just one part of the wider strategy publishers have developed to move into the consumer market to replace lost library sales. At the same time that publishers have cut back on books intended for libraries, they have opened or expanded divisions that do brand-name publishing. As one example, look at Simon & Schuster, a large children's publisher owned by Viacom. Viacom also owns Nickelodeon, and Simon & Schuster has successfully published a large number of Nickelodeon-derived books. Other publishers are doing the same.

Our Friend Harry Potter

Good old Harry! He's shown the world something we already knew—that a good children's book is a good book for children *and* adults. He's reminded us of the power of the imagination—the first four books came out before any movie or licensed product, leaving his millions of fans free to imagine him as they liked. He's reminded us of the power of word of mouth—the first book became a hit in England because children told their friends about it, they told their friends, and so on.

But will Harry have a lasting impact? Publishers do seem more open to publishing fantasy—and publishing books more than 200 pages in length—than used to be the case. Children's books seem a little more in the minds of the media than they used to be, meaning that it's not just the annual Newbery and Caldecott winners that get coverage. We can hope that older children will keep reading. (Until Harry, only a small minority of older children read books other than school books.) And we can hope that after swallowing the heftier price tag on a *Harry Potter* book, adults will be more willing to pay more than $16.95 for a children's book, allowing publishers to make longer, larger, or otherwise more expensive books. Will these changes persist? It's still too soon to say.

> **Class Rules**
>
> Perhaps surprisingly, the *Harry Potter* phenomenon hasn't had much of an impact on the sales of children's books generally. Take the *Harry Potter* numbers out of the equation, and sales of children's books have grown more slowly than the U.S. economy as a whole over the past 10 years or so.

New Labels for a New Century

In the mid-1990s, children of picture book age were a bulge in the population, and therefore picture books were hot. As those children got older, demand increased for books for older children, and publishers have adjusted. So far this century, most publishers' new initiatives have been aimed at pre-teen and teenage children.

Publishers know that teens have their own money to spend, and so *teen* has become the label for a hot new segment of the market. Houghton Mifflin was the first to jump, starting their Graphia imprint in 2004, but now just about every large publisher has a teen imprint, typically publishing popular fiction in series, and some nonfiction. And imprints such as Aladdin Mix or the Candy Apple line at Scholastic have carried the trend to a younger audience, known as the *tween* group.

> **def•i•ni•tion**
>
> A **teen** book is intended for teenagers, like YA (young adult) but is most likely published in paperback for teens to buy, while **tween** is a new label for books for pre-teens. Books for both age groups (and others) may be published as **graphic novels,** books set up in comic-book format.

With children living in an increasingly visual culture, it's no surprise that publishers are bringing *graphic novels* to the children's market. Graphic novels, if you have somehow missed this trend, are like comic books in real book form, using "sequential art" and text panels and dialogue to tell some surprisingly sophisticated stories. As with the teen market, just about every major publisher has jumped in, starting new imprints or lines or individual titles. Graphic novels are accepted in the library market as well, with Roaring Brook Press's First Second imprint winning the first major award for a graphic novel, the Printz Award, for Gene Luen Yang's *American Born Chinese* in 2007.

Does this growth in publishing for older children mean those authors writing picture books should try novels? Absolutely not—plenty of picture books are still being published, and it's always a good idea to stick to what you do best. In any case, it's only a matter of time before picture books become the growth area. They may already be, as noted in "Picture Books Are Back" printed in the February 26, 2007, issue of *Publishers Weekly*.

It's an Electronic World

The hype has died down from what it was, but the "new media"—the new electronic ways to publish or present material, from CD-ROMs to *e-books* and more—are a small but growing factor in publishing. The major publishers are now routinely releasing novels in e-book formats but not getting big sales. Smaller publishers are finding that e-books and digital technology are making it easier for them to get into the market. But none of the wilder predictions of the late 1990s have come close to coming true so far, and print books are not on their way out. This is a change to the business that's still mostly in the future.

def•i•ni•tion

A book that must be read in an electronic format instead of on paper is an **e-book**. These books can be set up for reading on personal computers or on special e-book readers.

Several years ago, some saw CD-ROMs as a real threat to traditional books, and even to illustrated books. Many companies invested in CD-ROM publishing, only to discover how difficult it is to make money in this area. Today, reference is the only area of publishing in which CD-ROMs have had a big impact. That's not surprising. A CD-ROM is for many people an improvement over a multivolume encyclopedia set. Publishers have yet to convince the ordinary consumer that an e-book is preferable to a paper one.

Print-on-demand publishing (POD), in which single titles of books are printed when needed, is actually a kind of electronic publishing. It uses electronic book files to quickly create printings of one book (or more) when needed. Academic and specialty publishers can use it to sell copies of their books in bookstores that can't otherwise carry them, and some companies are providing POD as a service directly to writers; you get books, but you have to pay for them. This technology can also enable publishers to keep a novel or black-and-white nonfiction title technically "in print" indefinitely, even if it's not selling lots of copies. So far, this doesn't work for books with color, and prices per copy tend to be high.

Developments will keep coming. For now, most publishers see electronic publishing as an opportunity to sell a book in another format, much like audiotapes or paper-backs, and not as a replacement for books themselves. For authors and illustrators, that means that e-books are not an area in which you have many opportunities to sell original work. But your publisher might well produce or license an e-book edition in addition to a print edition.

It's a brave new world in children's books, but also a big and diverse one. It's not the world we knew as children, but it's still a world in which dedicated and creative writers—and that means you—can find a place.

The Least You Need to Know

- ◆ Children's books used to be published mostly for sale to libraries, but that's not true anymore.

- ◆ Paperbacks are an increasingly common way to publish a children's book.

- ◆ Publishing companies are getting bigger and bigger and often are part of multi-national corporations.

- ◆ Publishers are trying to sell more books to consumers so they make them attractive to adults; they also license movies, TV shows, and products to make their books instantly familiar.

- ◆ Teen, tween, and graphic novels are areas of growth—but ours is a cyclical business.

- ◆ Electronic publishing has yet to have a big effect on children's books.

Chapter 8

Book Formats and Age Levels

In This Chapter

- A look at fiction and nonfiction
- Picture book versus book with chapters
- The lowdown on easy readers, story collections, and more
- The different kinds of books with chapters
- Who reads "children's books" (hint: adults and teenagers do, too!)

You know you want to write or illustrate for children, you've explored the classics as well as the current titles, and by now you're probably on a first-name basis with the librarians and booksellers in town. But do you know what kind of book you might create? Do you know the difference yet between *chapter books* and *picture books?* How about *collections* and *easy readers?*

In this chapter, I give you an overview of different children's book formats and how they more or less align with different age levels. I also explain why you may be writing not only for children, but for adults, too. I continue the discussion in Chapter 9, when I move on to some common subject areas.

The Main Categories

First, you need to know a couple basic distinctions between fiction and nonfiction and between picture books and books with chapters.

Tell the Truth, the Whole Truth

What you may know as *nonfiction* books from your school days are now often called *informational books.* Many different approaches and subjects fit under the nonfiction tent. Here are just a few examples:

◆ Books that present "just the facts."

◆ Biographies, or stories about real people.

◆ In creative nonfiction, writers use techniques usually found in fiction to present information.

◆ And there are how-to books for children.

def•i•ni•tion

Also known as an **informational book, nonfiction** can include writing in which the author presents information, activities, or knowledge; recounts a historical event; or creates a biography.

If you like to do research and write or illustrate what you've learned, you can work on nonfiction. Is nonfiction less creative than fiction? Not so, says nonfiction author Sneed Collard: "My first four children's sales were all fictional stories…. Once I began writing nonfiction, I loved it. It provided me with a great excuse to learn more about biology *and* could be just as creative as fiction.

Have Fun Lying

Fiction is what we make up, although it might have a basis in fact. As renowned writer Jane Yolen—author of novels, picture books, poetry, and much else—puts it, "Memory is just one more story. And sometimes not a very good one at that. It needs that sandpaper touchup, a bit of paint, a little lie here, and a bigger lie there—and so fiction is born." Although nonfiction can never be based on an entirely invented incident, fiction can find a basis in fact. Fiction is not truth, but it can hold truth within it, such as the truth of personal experience or universal themes. As you delve deeper into these two wide categories, you'll find the boundaries between them are very blurry.

def•i•ni•tion

Fiction is writing from the imagination. Fiction is "made up," although most good fiction does, paradoxically, seem real.

As with nonfiction, there are many types of fiction. You'll learn about these in more detail in this and the following chapter.

Pictures vs. Words

After you've taken in the fiction/nonfiction distinction and noted its fuzziness, move on to formats. Very generally, children's books may be dominated by pictures, in which case we call them *picture books*, or by words, in which case we call them *chapter books*.

For the Little Ones: Picture Books

When people think of children's literature, picture books often come to mind. These are the books Mom and Dad read to you at bedtime or the teacher read to you at story time. In a picture book, a line or two of text typically accompanies a page of illustration, although the amount of text can range from none to a paragraph or two.

Most picture books are pretty short, and not just because their audience—younger children—have pretty short attention spans. Most picture books are printed in full color, and that's expensive. Because books are printed in *signatures*, picture books come in lengths of 16, 24, 32, 40, 48 pages or sometimes more; 32 pages is the typical length.

def•i•ni•tion

Signatures are groups of 8 or 16 pages made by printing one sheet of paper and then folding and cutting it before gluing or sewing it into the binding. Books have been printed this way for hundreds of years, and that's why pages often come in multiples of 8.

For Big Kids: Books with Chapters

When kids move from picture books to reading books themselves—books with chapters—they've entered a new world. Here, the words are dominant, although these books may also have illustrations. Books with chapters range from easy-to-read novels with short chapters, illustration, and limited vocabulary, perhaps 48 or 64 pages long, to serious novels and nonfiction for teenagers, meaty 300-plus-page tomes with no illustrations at all. Think of the *Frog and Toad* books, *Island of the Blue Dolphins*, the *Nancy Drew* series, and *Bridge to Terabithia*. These are all different types of books with chapters.

What's for Who? How to Tell

Underlying these basic distinctions, and the following category descriptions, lies the basic truth that children are constantly changing and growing. So what works for a 3-year-old vastly differs from what works for a 12-year-old. And that makes your work as a writer or illustrator much more complicated than if you were creating books for adults. How can you know how to adjust? Although there are no hard-and-fast rules, you'll begin to learn some rules of thumb. Keep these in mind, and remember there are exceptions:

Length   The shorter the text, the younger the child, usually. A notable exception: beginning readers may start to read with books that are shorter and simpler than the picture books that were being read to them.

What you do with words   Cumulative or predictable language, using the same familiar words over and over, or using rhyme and rhythm; all of these can make a text easier for younger children to follow.

Complexity of sentence structure, vocabulary, plot, design, and illustration   All of these can get more complex for older children.

The age of the main character (in fiction)   Generally, children read about children at least as old as themselves. You don't usually find 11-year-olds savoring a story about a third-grader.

Subject matter   Are the concerns addressed in the book the concerns of the intended audience?

Now, on to some more details about certain kinds of books.

Types of Picture Books

Picture books probably account for more books on the children's department shelves than those in any other format or for any other age level. Children beg for them, parents love them as a vehicle for literacy, and people buy them as gifts for children *and* adults all the time. They can be fiction or nonfiction, and because adults read them to children and they're used in schools, they vary in length from a few hundred words to as many as 2,000. This is a very flexible format, allowing for all kinds of subject matter and approaches. You need to know about the common types, so you can understand and talk about what you're writing or illustrating. Keep in mind, though, that word count and page length are not rules. As Jane Yolen says, "Should be, what an awful concept. A book should be as long as it needs to be, not some arbitrary length."

Concept Books

Concept books are both a special type of picture book and the most common format for toddlers and younger. They explore a concept rather than tell a story; in a way, they are nonfiction for the very young.

Ruth Krauss's classic *A Hole Is to Dig* was one of the first concept books and is well worth reading. For more recent examples see Tana Hoban's *Colors Everywhere* or Suse McDonald's *Peck, Slither, and Slide.* Concept books are often but not always illustrator-created because text is minimal.

"True" Picture Books

Moving to older children—by which I mean children old enough to follow a simple story—we come to "true" picture books. The stories in these books are carried at least as much by the pictures as by the words. Maurice Sendak's *Where the Wild Things Are* is a good example of this type. You couldn't follow the story without the pictures, and you generally find illustrations on every page. The best of these books, including Sendak's book, are designed and laid out as a coherent whole.

True picture books may have only a few hundred words and be intended for preschoolers, such as John Lawrence's *This Little Chick.* Or they may run considerably longer, up to and beyond 1,000 words, as is the case with Kevin Henke's *Lilly's Purple Plastic Purse.* These two examples also show typical thematic differences for books from different ends of the picture book spectrum. Little Chick's story is one of exploring the world away from Mom, but returning to her at the end. Lilly's story focuses instead on school, dealing with rules and relationships with classmates and teacher.

> **Can You Keep a Secret?**
>
> All these types of picture books work with fiction and nonfiction. Nonfiction picture books tend to have higher word counts then their fiction counterparts, though.

Illustrated Storybooks

Illustrated storybooks, or picture storybooks, have a story that could be read on its own. The illustrations add to the story, but it would still make sense without them. Virginia Burton's *Mike Mulligan and His Steam Shovel* is a good example of this kind. Illustrated storybooks also often have more text, perhaps a full paragraph per page, or a chunk of text facing an illustration. Many classic children's books fit in this category; it's less common today.

Board Books

I've left board books for the end of this discussion, because they're really a binding format like hardcover and paperback, not a different type of story. Board books run the gamut of the picture book range. Some, perhaps specially made for board book publication, are concept books. Many others are reprintings of already existing picture books, perhaps with pages cut or condensed. Some are created as part of a licensing program.

Board books are not an area of great opportunity for writers. It's not just that board books are so often converted from an existing picture book; even the originals being made are either created by an illustrator or written in-house by a publisher. Writers and illustrators should both keep in mind that many more true picture books are published, and no matter how much they interest you, the way into board books may be through picture books.

I Can Read This: Easy Readers

Remember the thrill of reading your first book yourself? Children may start with those picture books that have fairly simple texts, but beginning readers soon crave more than books like those that relatives read to them. They want *more*—more words, more length, and more to read.

But be careful. You don't want to overwhelm this reading group. Because parents don't read these books (under various names) to children, the vocabulary must be simpler than in picture books so beginning readers can handle it. Sentences must be short and simple, and stories can't be too long or too complicated. Illustrations, although still important, are subordinate to the words.

Author Larry Dane Brimner notes these basic distinctions among books for beginning readers:

- *Easy-reading picture book*   32 pages (This is a picture book with easy-reader vocabulary and sentence structures.)

- *Easy (or early) reader*   48 to 64 pages

- *Early chapter book*   48 to 64 pages

Lengths vary from several hundred to 1,500 words. The *Arthur* books by Marc Brown are a good example of the first easy readers kids pick up. You might also want to study an entire program, such as Simon & Schuster's *Ready-to-Read* books and the careful gradations between the levels of its program.

The best thing you can do to focus your energies in this area is immerse yourself in the books. As you browse, note that series dominate in this area, unlike picture books and novels. You can find single titles, but kids just starting to read want more of the books they like. So by publishing them in series, publishers make those books easier to find and more likely to be purchased. Note, too, that many of these series aren't being added to continually, so if you want to write or illustrate early readers, you'll need to find the publishers interested in new titles. (Proposing an entire new series, for a beginner, is almost impossible.)

In most kinds of books, you can just sit down and write a story, using your judgment about vocabulary. But easy readers are one of the types of books that often must be built around a carefully selected vocabulary list. When even *Make Way for Ducklings* proves too advanced, or when the audience delights in simple rhymes and sounds, books like *One Fish, Two Fish, Red Fish, Blue Fish* appear on the shelves.

> ### Can You Keep a Secret?
>
> For more detailed information on writing early and easy readers, surf over to www.underdown. org/early_rd.htm and read "Targeting the Emergent Reader," an excellent article by Joan Broerman that examines this tricky area.

Also commonly found in textbooks, controlled vocabulary does not have to cramp your style. It inspired *The Cat in the Hat*, which Theodor Geisel (Dr. Seuss) crafted from a list of a little more than 200 words for beginning readers, using every single one of those words and no others. If a publisher's guidelines call for a controlled vocabulary, be sure to use their word list. You can assume most children's publishers don't care about this, however.

"Mom, Can I Get This?" Novels and Other Books with Chapters

Children can move from early reader books to books with chapters as early as second grade. Such books are what we think of when we fondly remember classic novels for children such as E. B. White's *Charlotte's Web*, Laura Ingalls Wilder's *The Little House on the Prairie*, and Beverly Cleary's *Ramona the Pest*. For younger readers, the first "chapter books" may have some illustrations and be no more than 64 pages long, but they can range up to 200 pages or more. These books bridge the gap between easy readers and true novels. They don't have controlled vocabularies, although writers must keep in mind their audience and not get too sophisticated (or too easy!).

More generally, "books with chapters" can be fiction or nonfiction. Here's the range of all books with chapters:

◆ *Easy readers with chapters* or *early chapter books*   48 to 64 pages (approximately 6- to 8-year-olds)

◆ *Young middle-grade*   48 to 80 pages, longer if nonfiction (7- to 9-year-olds)

◆ *True middle-grade*   80 to 160 pages, occasionally more (8- to 12-year-olds)

◆ *Older middle-grade* or *transitional*   128 to 200 pages or more (10- to 14-year-olds)

◆ *Young adult* or *YA*   Up to 300 pages (12-year-olds plus).

◆ *Harry Potter*   Several hundred pages (almost all ages) (I'm only half-joking—*Harry Potter* books need an entry of their own because they break so many rules. Be careful not to assume that you can do the same.)

> **Class Rules**
>
> I include a number of kinds of books with chapters in this category, but remember: the term *chapter books* means books between early readers and true novels.

It's difficult to make hard-and-fast distinctions between the different levels of early reader books, so until you develop an intuitive sense of them, just write, and remember Jane Yolen's warning about word counts.

For the Backpack

Want to write something similar in form to books for middle-graders but more sophisticated in content? Don't forget the *young adult* audience. Loosely, that's teenagers.

Only relatively recently did the publishing business start to target teens separately from other children. Authors such as S. E. Hinton, Walter Dean Myers, and Judy Blume started to write more challenging novels for teenagers in the late 1960s, and the young adult category was invented in response. As noted in the October 18, 1999, "Making the Teen Scene" feature in *Publishers Weekly*, the trade magazine for publishing: "From *The Outsiders* in 1967 to *Smack* in 1998, publishers have consistently released books by talented authors who speak directly to a teen audience about sophisticated, though teen-appropriate concerns."

> **def•i•ni•tion**
>
> **Young adult** (or YA) books are exactly as they sound. *YA* is the term used in library collections and by publishers to designate teens.

Teens are likely to be insulted to find their books near the board and picture books of younger children, of course. And so for years, publishers, librarians, and booksellers have struggled over where to shelve teen titles. Sometimes there's a separate YA section in the library, store, or catalogue; sometimes there isn't. Recently, bookstores and publishers have started to rename the YA category "teen." As a writer, don't concern yourself too much with these labels.

Class Rules

Don't censor your writing for a teen audience. Adults sometimes underestimate the sensitivity and self-awareness teens possess. Long before an official "young adult" genre was created, authors who respected teens were reaching them. For example, J. D. Salinger's coming-of-age novel *The Catcher in the Rye* caused controversy among adults when it was published in the 1950s but is now considered a classic.

That's a Lot of Stories!

Cutting across all the age categories are *collections*. You can find a collection of just about anything, from picture books to literary young adult stories. Some are put together from existing books—publisher-compiled collections like the complete *Curious George*. Others are new and original works, and a type of book in which some authors do well.

Folktales and Fairy Tales

Do you remember the stories of Hansel and Gretel? Sleeping Beauty? Both are fairy tales, a form of writing that developed from folktales. *Fairy tales* and *folktales* are an important part of children's literature. The only difference between the way we pass on folktales today and the way it was done ages ago is the medium. In years past the stories were passed on orally; today we use books.

def•i•ni•tion

A **folktale** is a story that's been passed down orally and may appeal to both adults and children. A **fairy tale**, although like a folktale in form, is told specifically for children and involves more literary elements or stylistic devices. Both usually feature supernatural beings, the use of magic, happiness for the good, and punishment for the bad. Some may define these terms differently, but these definitions will apply most of the time.

You'll see plenty of such stories made into picture books, but many don't work well for an audience that young. What to do if you love these? One approach is to put together a collection. But do watch out for copyright infringement. (For guidance, see Chapter 24.) Virginia Hamilton's *The People Could Fly* and Howard Norman's *The Girl Who Dreamed Only Geese* are great examples of collections of retold folktales.

Short Stories and Poetry

You can also put together other kinds of collections. Short stories can be collected for book publication, although extremely few short story collections for children are published. Those that are tend to be for older readers and include works by several writers. Look at James Howe's *The Color of Absence: 12 Stories About Loss and Hope*, for example. Howe wrote one of the stories and collected the others, meaning he had to seek permission to use them. If you want to publish only your stories, stick to magazines, at least until you're famous enough to put together a collection like Roald Dahl's *The Umbrella Man and Other Stories*.

Poetry collections are a similarly tough sell, because the few publishers that do publish poetry look for an overall theme and a distinctive style. Ironically, that's not what publishers usually receive in the mail. Publishing companies receive a surprising number of big miscellaneous collections of poems from aspiring poets—don't go there! Take a look instead at Paul Fleischman's *Joyful Noise: Poems for Two Voices*, which won the Newbery Medal in 1988. This collection not only focuses tightly on insects, it is set up to be read aloud by two people.

> **Can You Keep a Secret?**
>
> As with short stories, if you love poetry, you can also set out to create anthologies of the work of many poets. You will have to handle permissions, though.

The Adults in the Way

We're less than halfway through our tour of the many varieties of children's books, and you already might be wondering if you have to know exactly what kind of book you've written to get it published. The short answer is no; you don't need to be able to say to a publisher, "This is an early chapter book aimed at a 7-year-old reader," but you need to have some feel for what you're doing and how it fits into the established categories.

Why? Because you can write something wonderful and not get anywhere with it, if the "gatekeepers" don't know what to do with it. *Not only children read children's books.* Editors read them first. Then parents, grandparents, teachers, and librarians largely decide what their children read, although teenagers typically have some control over their own spending. These people are the gatekeepers, and it's a fact of life that you must get your book past them to the child you want to reach.

Sometimes, that can be a problem, especially if you want to write something children will handle just fine but might not be approved by every adult. Still, the best children's books appeal to both children and adults. Always have, and always will. Some appeal more to adults than others do, as noted in Chapter 7. Should you, then, aim your writing at adults? No, because if you do, you might miss children altogether. Concentrate on children, and if you do your job really well, maybe you'll reach adults, too.

The Least You Need to Know

- Nonfiction writing aims to inform readers about real things, people, or events.

- Fiction writing may begin with a real experience but goes beyond it to tell a story that did not happen.

- Picture books are heavily illustrated with little text for the younger child. Someone other than the child reads the book to him or her.

- Books with chapters have more text, and contain, of course, chapters. Other children's book formats include easy readers and collections.

- When you write, you won't only be writing for the child, but for adults, too.

Understanding Subjects and Genres

In This Chapter

- ◆ Literary fiction versus popular fiction
- ◆ A look at some children's books genres
- ◆ Children's fantasy and science fiction
- ◆ The world of multicultural books
- ◆ Historical fiction, fiction in nonfiction, and straight nonfiction

In Chapter 8, I introduced some basic book formats and examined the kinds of books written for different age groups. This chapter delves into subject matter. Almost any subject or type of writing done for adults can also be done for children—*if* you take the right approach.

In addition to giving you an overview of some of the different *genres*, this chapter offers many titles for you to peruse at your leisure; reading some of them will deepen your understanding of each area. Use this chapter to learn more about what interests you—and so you can tell an editor what you've written.

Good Books (Literary Fiction)

Not all children's books are created equal. As with anything, some books are "better" than others. *Good* usually refers to the high end of any product; more carefully crafted from better materials, the high-end products are also usually more expensive. It's the same in children's books. Some publishers aim for those book buyers who seek quality—libraries and independent bookstore customers, to drastically oversimplify—while other publishers use lower prices, bells and whistles, and movie tie-ins to attract other buyers. Quality publishers seek to please adults, while those taking the popular approach seek to attract children, perhaps children buying books for themselves.

def•i•ni•tion

The *format* of a book refers to its physical appearance—picture book or chapters, soft- or hardcover; **genre** refers to the type of writing—fantasy, historical fiction, multicultural, or nonfiction.

The following are a few examples of quality picture books:

- ◆ *Mirette on the High Wire* by Emily Arnold McCully
- ◆ *Kitten's First Full Moon* by Kevin Henkes
- ◆ *A Snowy Day* by Ezra Jack Keats

And here are some high-end literary children's novels:

- ◆ *Al Capone Does My Shirts* by Gennifer Choldenko
- ◆ *The Watsons Go to Birmingham* by Christopher Paul Curtis
- ◆ *A Wrinkle in Time* by Madeleine L'Engle

If in your discovery of children's literature you haven't read these books, you really should seek them out. When you study them, ask yourself, *What makes these books outstanding works of literature?*

They're, Like, *Soooo* Popular: Popular Fiction

How many of you adults love a really great scare and pick up Stephen King night after night? Or how many romance novels sell directly off the racks in supermarkets, gobbled up by adoring fans of lovely heroines and muscle-ripped heroes? Popular fiction appeals to just about everyone. And just as Mom and Dad may not always read Shakespeare, children don't always cuddle up to *The Secret Garden*. And why should they? You like Miss Marples; they like Nancy Drew. You like romance novels; they like *The Princess Diaries*.

Here are just a few examples of popular fiction for younger children:

◆ Any of the *Maisy* books by Lucy Cousins

◆ Any of the *Arthur* books by Marc Brown

◆ The *Magic School Bus* series

Here are just a few examples of popular fiction for the older reader:

◆ The *Magic Tree House* series by Mary Pope Osborne

◆ Matt Christopher's sport novels

◆ The *Sweet Valley High* series (recently relaunched)

Popular books and good books generally come from different publishers, or at least from different divisions within the same company. Depending on what approach you take, you need to seek out the right kind of publisher. (I go over the differences in Part 4.)

What those good or popular publishers actually publish is another part of the story, but again, whatever adults like, children like, and that goes for many of the common genres: fantasy, mystery, historical fiction, etc. Some areas, of course, are more popular with children than with adults, and vice versa. Mystery stories are an established genre for children, for example, but not as big as they are for adults.

Let's look at some of the most common children's genres.

Fantasy: Swords and Sorcerers and Talking Bunnies

Fantasy and science fiction books have long been a mainstay of children's publishing. The kind of fantasy publishers want does require some study, however.

Science Fiction

Science fiction (SF) is a kind of fantasy for a simple reason: it's shelved with it. Also, as in fantasy, things can happen in science fiction that can't happen in our world; faster-than-light travel in a way is just as fantastic as riding a broomstick. There's more fantasy for children than SF and almost no SF for

def•i•ni•tion

Fantasy is a type of fiction in which the rules of the world are different—animals talk, magic works, and strange creatures exist.

younger children, but some wonderful books are out there, such as Newbery winners Madeleine L'Engle's *A Wrinkle in Time* and Lois Lowry's *The Giver*.

If you want to write SF for children, just remember that you face a crucial challenge: making an unfamiliar world believable without overwhelming your reader with the details. That might be one reason why there's less SF than fantasy for children—children know dragons and witches and magic from folktales and the like, but not laser guns, warp drives, and force fields. A SF writer has more world-building to do.

Traditional Fantasy

One of the best-known traditional fantasy titles ever remains J. R. R. Tolkien's *The Hobbit*, and the *Lord of the Rings* movies have brought that weightier and more demanding work to a new generation of children. Besides *The Hobbit*, other classics you might want to check out include Ursula Le Guin's *Earthsea* books or Susan Cooper's *The Dark Is Rising* series.

Can You Keep a Secret?
For short histories of fantasy and science fiction in children's books, read the informative essays in Anita Silvey's *The Essential Guide to Children's Books*. For a current guide to the field, read Marnie Brook's article "Make the Impossible Possible" at www. underdown.org/sffantasy.htm.

Fantasy may be even more common in picture books. Pick up any stories with witches and ghosts in the plot, or stories that involve imaginary friends, and you just picked up a child's fantasy title. Children know at an early age that these are fantasies but still enjoy them. Moreover, fantasies can provide small children with a way of dealing with their own feelings and developmental problems. The monsters in Maurice Sendak's *Where the Wild Things Are*, for example, may be physical symbols of a child's own destructive impulses or their fear of some external threat.

Personification and Other Questionable Fantasy

If you're just starting to write, avoid certain kinds of fantasy. Bringing inanimate objects to life and giving them human qualities—*personification*—is not common in mainstream publishing (the "good" publishers), although you'll find it is popular. *Budgy the Helicopter* by Sarah Ferguson, Duchess of York, is a typical effort in this area. A mainstream publisher published this book, but celebrities sell books regardless of the content. Your average author would not have been able to.

In a similar vein, although more common, are what you might call *animal fantasy*—picture-book stories in which animals stand in for people. They dress like people do, talk like people do, and get into difficulties like people do. This technique is known as *anthropomorphism*. Often adopted by beginning writers, who may go further and give their characters alliterated names (such as Bev Beaver), this approach only earns speedy rejections.

Venture into these territories at your peril! Any book with talking beasts or happy-go-lucky silverware must quickly prove itself unique and original, or a publisher won't look twice. If you're writing more substantial animal fantasies for a much older audience, like *Watership Down* by Richard Adams and Brian Jacques's *Redwall* series, keep in mind that your tone can't be cutesy and your world must be rich and believable.

def•i•ni•tion _____

Anthropomorphism and **personification** have much in common, but they aren't the same thing. Anthropomorphism involves giving human characteristics to animals. Personification is making characters out of ordinary nonliving objects.

Stories Dressed in Facts: Historical Fiction

Stories dressed in facts—this is an unusual but accurate way to describe *historical fiction*. The most important thing to remember about this hybrid genre is this: they are *stories*, not fact. Although historical figures may appear in them, and fact weaves itself into the tale—often in great detail—the stories themselves are fiction and are shelved in that section of the library or bookstore.

Classics in the historical fiction category include, of course, Scott O'Dell's masterpiece, *Island of the Blue Dolphins*, and the Colliers' *My Brother Sam Is Dead*. Fittingly, the award for historical fiction is named the Scott O'Dell Award. And books in this genre may win even wider recognition. The Newbery Medal winners in 2002 and 2003 were both historical fiction, and the Coretta Scott King Author Award for 2007 went to Sharon Draper for *Copper Sun*, a historical novel about the slave trade and slavery. Some popular writing is being published in this area, too. See the *American Girls* books by the Pleasant Company, *Dear America* from Scholastic, and the *American Diaries* books by Simon & Schuster—kids enjoy historical fiction.

def•i•ni•tion _____

If you yearn to tell a story of a child caught up in a historical event or just living in different times, you are writing **historical fiction**. In this type of writing, the main character and often many others are invented, while the setting and other details are based on careful research.

Neighbors Next Door and Far Away

One area of children's literature has developed only recently—*multicultural literature.* What is it? Most broadly defined, it's simply literature that takes into account the fact that we live in a multicultural and multiracial world. As recently as the 1960s, very few books were published in North America that had main characters who weren't white. In response to criticism and in an attempt to reach new markets, publishers have slowly brought African American, Hispanic, and Asian American authors and illustrators into the field.

Multicultural books aren't a genre so much as an approach. As a result, many types of books fall into this category. Start with picture-book stories like the delightful *More More More Said the Baby: Three Love Stories* by Vera B. William. Move on to novels grounded in a particular culture, such as Laurence Yep's *Dragon's Gate* or Angela Johnson's *The First Part Last.* And don't forget nonfiction, such as *Black Diamond: The Story of the Negro Baseball Leagues* by Patricia McKissack and *Talkin' About Bessie* by Nikki Grimes.

Just what it is and who can write what about whom is the subject of considerable and sometimes bitter debate. On one side are writers who believe they can imagine anything without the benefit of personal experience, while on the other side are cultural guardians so concerned with authenticity they'd limit writers to writing only about their birth culture.

Realistically, there is a middle ground, but where is it? Ask yourself how much experience of a culture you need to be an insider. Visiting a country for three weeks is personal experience, but writing about it from anything other than a tourist's outsider perspective will be very difficult. Your imagination may be powerful, but it may invent details that conflict with actual reality. Working in an immigrant community as a social worker may give you personal contact with it, but only as a visitor and a caregiver, not someone part of it 24 hours a day, 7 days a week. Long-term immersion works, as one can see in Paul Goble's illustrated retellings of Lakota legends. Originally from England, he's made this his life's work and has received the approval of tribal elders.

Class Rules

If you want to write about a culture other than one you grew up in, choose one you've truly lived in, not one to which you are an outsider.

Creative Nonfiction

I've talked about taking facts and immersing them in fiction, but what about using techniques from fiction to get information across to a reader? When you take a non-fiction concept—let's say the planets of the solar system—and weave a story line or dramatic anecdotes into the facts, you're "dressing the facts in fiction," a technique sometimes called *creative nonfiction*. You're also probably making the learning process much more accessible and interesting to a child.

Putting the *Story* into *History* (or Science)

Narrative nonfiction is the most conspicuous variety of creative nonfiction. The popular television program *The Magic School Bus* started life as a book series, and it provides a great example of fiction being used as a medium for fact. In the series, the teacher, Miss Frizzle, leads her students—Arnold, Phoebe, Ralphie, and Tim, among others— on adventures in a school bus that transports them all over the world of science. The characters and the story are secondary to the lesson, but fiction that carries the lesson is a powerful tool. *The Magic School Bus* books fly off the shelves.

> ### Playground Stories
>
> You may be surprised at what you finally decide to write. Susan Campbell Bartoletti, author of the Newbery Honor book *Hitler Youth: Growing Up in Hitler's Shadow*, confesses, "Given my interest in historical fiction and nonfiction, it's hard to believe that I was one of those kids that whined about history class. I didn't like class lectures. I didn't like taking notes, I hated the textbook. But I crave stories—all kinds of stories—and history just happens to be one of the places I look for stories."

Some other titles you might want to read to get a better idea of this genre include *Minn of the Mississippi* by Holling Clancy Holling, *Cathedral* and similar books by David Macaulay, or the more recently published *An Extraordinary Life* by Laurence Pringle and *Prairie Town* by the Geiserts. In all cases, the story is fictional, perhaps with a fictional main character, but the information presented is scrupulously accurate.

Using Techniques from Fiction

Some nonfiction books in this category use the techniques more commonly found in fiction while not inventing a story. Check out the following books for good examples of factual books enlivened by dramatic writing:

◆ *The Great Fire* by Jim Murphy

◆ *When Plague Strikes* by James Cross Giblin

◆ *The Tiger with Wings* by Barbara Esbensen

Nonfiction doesn't have to be nonlively! As James Giblin notes in his book on writing, *The Giblin Guide*, nonfiction can be made more lively in a number of ways: "the overall direction of the book, careful pacing, lively quotations and anecdotes, effective chapter openings and closings." Some of your favorite nonfiction probably uses one or more of these techniques.

Straight Nonfiction

As noted briefly in Chapter 8, there are also a number of kinds of straight nonfiction books in which the author (and illustrator, if there is one) strive to present just the facts.

Straight nonfiction includes how-to books. Just as this book is a how-to for you to write and publish for children, many how-to books are written for kids. Klutz Press is one publisher that specializes in these books; you'll also find such titles as *Passport on a Plate*, which presents recipes from around the world, and *Handtalk: An ABC of Finger Spelling and Sign Language* by Remy Charlip and Mary Beth Miller. From cooking to card games, from hula dancing to sign language, kids want to know how to do it all!

> **Can You Keep a Secret?**
>
> The boundary between straight nonfiction and creative nonfiction can get blurry, so don't see these types as opposites—more like close relatives.

Some books present information. Informational books, such as Lerner's *Early Bird* series, appear in libraries and schools; this series is approaching 100 books, all in the same 48-page format and targeted at elementary-age children. They cover topics from geography and nature to magnetism and physics.

Some tell real people's life stories. Otherwise known as biographies, these make up a big part of the nonfiction section, from the highly respected *Lincoln: A Photobiography* by Russell Freedman, to the popular *Britney Spears* by Alix Strauss. Children enjoy real-life, nonfiction tales about other kids, too. A popular example of this idea is Rebecca Hazel's book, *The Barefoot Book of Heroic Children*, which brings together the lives of some of the most exceptional children in the history of the world.

In short, there are many ways to write both fiction and nonfiction. Different publishers specialize in different kinds of books, so what you want to write most likely has a home somewhere. For now, your challenge is to keep reading and figure out just what you're writing, which will help you find out where it belongs.

The Least You Need to Know

- ◆ All children's books are not created equal. As with many products, there are popular books and books seen as having quality.

- ◆ Just as for adults, different genres and types of books are published for children.

- ◆ Significant areas in children's literature include fantasy of various kinds, science fiction, historical fiction, and multicultural literature.

- ◆ Nonfiction may be "just the facts" or may use some of the techniques of fiction to be more engaging.

Chapter 10

A Guided Book Tour

In This Chapter

- What goes on the cover, jacket, and spine
- Front-of-the-book items
- Dedications, forewords, and introductions
- Interiors of picture books, chapter books, and other types of books
- Back-of-the-book material

Every book is made of many parts—parts you, the children's book author or illustrator, need to know the names of. In this chapter, I navigate you from cover to cover through all the components of a children's book. You learn where everything from the copyright information to the glossary goes. Along the way, you also learn definitions used in the publishing world for specific areas of the book. Get ready, because here comes your crash course in the anatomy of a book!

It's a Cover-Up! The Cover, Jacket, and Spine

When you walk into a bookstore and pull a book from a shelf, you immediately see the cover—the front of the book, most likely covered by a jacket.

You may have heard the saw, "don't judge a book by its cover," but most people do anyway, or they at least identify a particular book by its cover. To the publisher, the cover consists of three parts—the front, the back, and the spine. More about each part in a second, but first let's check out the whole cover.

The book's cover may either be hard (called *hardcover*) or pliable (called *softcover* or paperback). The type of cover determines what's printed on the front. Traditionally, hardcover books didn't have anything on the front and back covers, with the possible exception of a stamped decorative design. Instead, identifying elements—the first and last name of the author, the publisher, and the title of the book—were found on the book's *spine*.

def•i•ni•tion

When a book is produced with a hard, stiff outer cover, it's a **hardcover** book. The covers are usually made of cardboard, over which cloth, treated paper, vinyl, or some other plastic is stretched. When the cover of a book is pliable, the book is **softcover.** Pliable covers are usually made of thick but flexible paper or light cardboard coated with varnish or a synthetic resin or laminate. The center panel of a book's binding is the **spine.** The spine hinges together the front and back cover to the pages and faces out when the book is shelved. The book pages all connect at the spine.

Hardcovers come with jackets, glossy paper that protects the book. On the jacket, you'll find identifying elements—the title, author, illustrator, publisher, *ISBN* (International Standard Book Number), price, and promotional blurbs about the book, the latter on the jacket flaps. Increasingly, children's picture books may also have printed covers that duplicate the eye-catching jacket design.

def•i•ni•tion

ISBN is the acronym for International Standard Book Number, a number that gives the book a unique ID for orders and distribution. The publisher assigns the ISBN based on procedures set up by the R. R. Bowker Company and the International Standards Organization. You'll find the ISBN of your book in the bar code on the back of the jacket for a hardcover, on the back of a paperback cover, and on the copyright page.

Let's take a look at the hard- and softcover editions of Ursula Le Guin's *The Tombs of Atuan:*

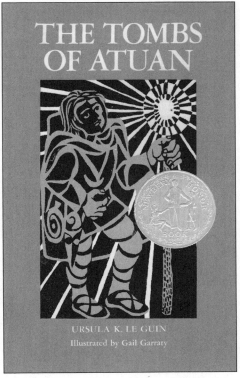
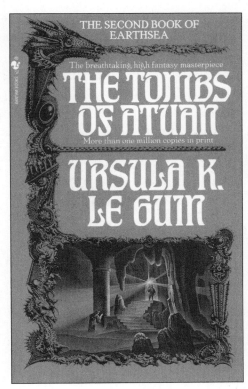

The hardcover jacket (left) and the paperback cover (right) of the same title may look different, although for picture books, they're often the same.

The hardcover version offers you a good example of what you'll see on a hardcover book jacket. The information you see on the front and spine of the hardcover jacket is also printed on the cover itself. Typically, you'll find some promotional information on the back, but not as much as what's on the jacket flaps. Some publishers also print promotional copy on the inside of the cover.

A softcover or paperback book does not have a jacket. The cover design is different from the hardcover edition, which is typical for a novel. If you compare the back covers of the hardcover and paperback versions of the same book, you'll see that the ISBN also is different.

What's in a Name—Or a Title?

When you first open a hardcover book, you see blank pages. These, including the one stuck down on the inside of the cover, are called *endpapers*. These sheets attach the cover to the interior pages. Publishers may gussy them up with maps or use fancy paper, but you don't need to worry much about them now.

Keep turning the pages. Soon, you should find the title page. The title page is home to many things other than just the book title. You'll find the author's full name (no initials unless the author goes by initials only), the illustrator, and the name and sometimes the location of the publisher. If the publisher has a logo, that appears here, too. The main point of this page, though, is the title.

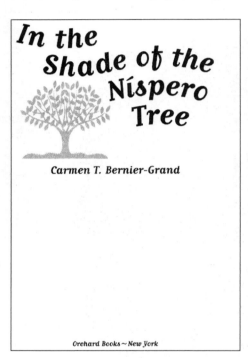

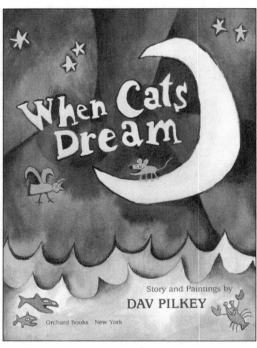

The title page in a novel (left) usually has only the title, author's name, and publisher's name. The title page of a picture book (right) is usually more elaborate.

Can You Keep a Secret?

Many of the elements of a book's design date to the nineteenth century or earlier and have been retained even though they may not be needed in a book. Title pages, for example, were much more necessary when books were published unbound, possibly in installments, to be bound and given covers by the purchaser. Half-title pages, on which nothing more than the title of the book appears, occasionally appear before the title page as another one of these traditional elements.

Legal and Other Details

The page directly after the title page is the copyright page and colophon (unless a publisher puts this material at the end of the book for design reasons). Several kinds of information are printed here. Most importantly, the publisher states that it has copyrighted the text and illustrations in the names of the author and illustrator. (See Chapter 24 for more on copyright.)

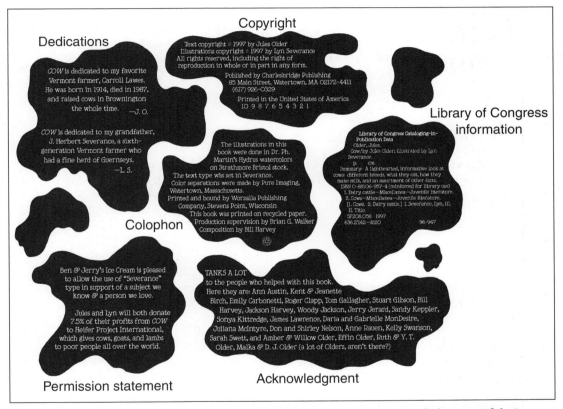

Copyright

Dedications

COW is dedicated to my favorite Vermont farmer, Carroll Lawes. He was born in 1914, died in 1987, and raised cows in Brownington the whole time. —J. O.

COW is dedicated to my grandfather, J. Herbert Severance, a sixth-generation Vermont farmer who had a fine herd of Guernseys. —L. S.

Text copyright © 1997 by Jules Older
Illustrations copyright © 1997 by Lyn Severance
All rights reserved, including the right of reproduction in whole or in part in any form.

Published by Charlesbridge Publishing
85 Main Street, Watertown, MA 02172-4411
(617) 926-0329

Printed in the United States of America
10 9 8 7 6 5 4 3 2 1

Library of Congress information

Library of Congress Cataloging-in-Publication Data
Older, Jules.
Cow/by Jules Older; illustrated by Lyn Severance.
p. cm.
Summary: A lighthearted, informative look at cows: different breeds, what they eat, how they make milk, and an assortment of other facts.
ISBN 0-88106-957-4 (reinforced for library use)
1. Dairy cattle—Miscellanea—Juvenile literature.
2. Cows—Miscellanea—Juvenile literature.
[1. Cows. 2. Dairy cattle.] I. Severance, Lyn, ill. II. Title.
SF208.O56 1997
636.2142—dc20 96-947

The illustrations in this book were done in Dr. Ph. Martin's Hydrus watercolors on Strathmore Bristol stock.
The text type was set in Severance.
Color separations were made by Pure Imaging, Watertown, Massachusetts.
Printed and bound by Worzalla Publishing Company, Stevens Point, Wisconsin
This book was printed on recycled paper.
Production supervision by Brian G. Walker
Composition by Bill Harvey

Colophon

Ben & Jerry's Ice Cream is pleased to allow the use of "Severance" type in support of a subject we know & a person we love.

Jules and Lyn will both donate 7.5% of their profits from *COW* to Heifer Project International, which gives cows, goats, and lambs to poor people all over the world.

TANKS A LOT
to the people who helped with this book.
Here they are: Ann Austin, Kent & Jeanette Birch, Emily Carbonetti, Roger Clapp, Tom Gallagher, Stuart Gibson, Bill Harvey, Jackson Harvey, Woody Jackson, Jerry Jerard, Sandy Keppler, Sonya Kittredge, James Lawrence, Daria and Gabrielle MonDesire, Juliana McIntyre, Don and Shirley Nelson, Anne Rauen, Kelly Swanson, Sarah Swett, and Amber & Willow Older, Effin Older, Ruth & Y. T. Older, Malka & D. J. Older (a lot of Olders, aren't there?)

Permission statement

Acknowledgment

This copyright page, from Cow *by Jules Older and illustrated by Lyn Severance, includes many of the items often found in the frontmatter.*

Other information besides the copyright appears on the copyright page. The complete address of the publisher, how many printings the book has gone through, the Library of Congress Cataloging-in-Publication (CIP) data, the ISBN, and any acknowledgments of use of someone else's copyrighted material are found here (although the latter can appear elsewhere). The CIP information helps get your book into the nation's libraries. The publisher submits the book to the *Library of Congress*, which assigns it its own number and creates basic cataloging information.

Picture books are reviving an old tradition in publishing—the *colophon*. The colophon provides information about the production of a book, such as the typefaces used, the names of the designer and typesetter, and the kinds of paint and paper the illustrator used. Often this appears on the copyright page, but if the information is lengthy, the colophon may get its own page.

def•i•ni•tion

The **Library of Congress** is a federal agency charged with maintaining a collection of all books published in the United States and creating standardized cataloging information for libraries; most other countries have similar agencies. A **colophon** is a page in the front of a book's that gives information about how it was produced, from typefaces to the kind of paint an artist used.

The Matter in the Front

Now that we've gotten through the business of the book, let's move on to other stuff you might find in the front of the book. Logically enough, folks in publishing call all this material the *frontmatter*.

Dedication

As an author or illustrator, you might want to dedicate your creative efforts to someone. The publisher places the dedication page after the copyright page, or, especially in picture books, at the top of the copyright page.

Table of Contents

Just after the copyright page and dedication, you sometimes find a table of contents (TOC), or simply contents. The average board book or picture book won't have one, but plenty of other children's books—like anthologies, novels, or informational works—do include a TOC. The amount of detail a publisher goes into varies, but you'll certainly find the chapter number, the chapter title if there is one, and the beginning page number of each. If the book has sections, they appear, too, and sometimes subdivisions of chapters are listed (as they are in the front of this book). Glossaries, indexes, and other material are also listed.

Contents

This table of contents from The Forestwife *by Theresa Tomlinson shows chapter titles as well as chapter numbers and starting page numbers.*

Foreword and Introduction

After the table of contents, you may find either an introduction or a foreword—or perhaps both. Sometimes the foreword may be called a prologue. Generally speaking, a prominent expert or authority writes a foreword to a book. If you write a children's book based on astronomy and John Glenn writes a few pages talking about your book and its merits, that's a foreword.

Typically an author writes an introduction to provide information integral to the understanding of the book or some background on the basis or making of the book. For a historical novel, for example, you might want to include an introduction to give your reader some background on the period of time in which your novel takes place.

The Good Stuff: The Body of the Book

After you get past all of a book's business and practical details, you get to the good stuff—the stories, the poems, the learning, the history—the content itself! Let's take a look at the *body* of the book.

In a picture book, the body of the book is the story and the pictures that accompany it, in one straightforward narrative. For other kinds of books, the setup may be a little more complicated and other elements might be included.

Chapter Books

The identifying factor of chapter books—novels for kids—is simply that the text is broken up into chapters. The chapters may or may not have illustrations. Seems easy enough, right?

But you have choices. A chapter may just have a number, or it can have its own title. Look on your own shelves for examples, and get a sense of the length of chapters. Do they vary much? Are they longer in books for older children?

Alphabetical and Other Setups

Chapters aren't the only way the body of the book can be broken up. Authors can be as creative with the structure of their book as they are with the content. Especially for picture books, the letters of the alphabet might be used to break up and organize the body of the book. Jerry Pallotta, for example, introduces a variety of types of jets and explains how a jet engine works in his *Jet Alphabet Book*.

def•i•ni•tion

The **body** of any work is the work itself without any extraneous information like the copyright page or the dedication or the index.

A chronological structure works well in books set up as diaries. Lisa Rowe Fraustino's *Ash*, for example, is written as the journal of a boy dealing with the breakdown of his older brother, while Patricia McKissack's *A Picture of Freedom* from the *Dear America* series follows the life of an enslaved girl on a Virginia plantation.

Other Elements

Chapters and other ways of putting the body of the book in order aren't all that can appear there. You can also find these elements:

- Pictures with captions and labels

- Tables

- Special elements like pop-ups

- Running heads (These go across the top of the page and help you know where you are in the book.)

- Headers and subheaders (You'll see these throughout this book, as a way of breaking up the chapters.)

Go to the Back of the Line—The Back Matter

Children's books, especially nonfiction ones, may include what we in the industry call back matter. Basically, back matter includes anything of informational purposes other than the text—a glossary, recommended reading lists, an index, information about the book, games to play based on the book, and other material. The author writes much of this, but the publisher might add some as well.

 **More About Bugs for Lunch**

There are more insects in the world than any other kind of animal. More than 800,000 insects have been studied and named, but scientists believe that there are probably millions that nobody knows about yet. It's a good thing that insects are food for so many creatures, or the world might be overrun with them.

 The NUTHATCH is called the upside-down bird because it walks headfirst down tree trunks as it searches for food. With its strong beak, it pries out insects, caterpillars, and insect eggs that are hidden in cracks in the bark.

 SPIDERS catch insects in webs and traps made of silk. Each species of spider has a distinctive design for its web or trap. When they catch more than they can eat at one time, most spiders wrap the leftovers in silk to save for a later meal.

 BATS fly from their roosts to look for food as the sun goes down. But even in total darkness, they can catch insects. Bats send out a constant stream of sounds that are pitched so high that people cannot hear them. As these sounds hit objects, they echo back to the bat. When an insect flies across this beam of sound, the bat can tell exactly where the bug is and can swoop down to catch it in flight.

 A GECKO is a small lizard that lives in warm climates. Many people like to have geckos in their gardens and backyards. They know that geckos will come out of hiding at night to eat moths and other insects that people find pesky.

Back matter in a picture book may include additional information, as in this page from Bugs for Lunch *by Marge Facklam, and can include recommended books, sources, a glossary, or even an index.*

Can You Keep a Secret?

You're more likely to see back matter in nonfiction for older children, but picture books have back matter, too, especially non-fiction picture books or books based on folktales.

Just what's in the back matter varies enormously. The back of the paperback edition of the novel *A Wrinkle in Time* doesn't contain much back matter: Yearling Books includes descriptions of four other books by Madeleine L'Engle as well as a short biography with her picture. In contrast, *The 20th Century Children's Book Treasury* contains a more extensive back matter. In this anthology of picture books, the reader will find "Biographical Notes" about each author, a "Guide to Reading Ages," and an "Index of Titles, Authors, and Illustrators."

Back matter in a chapter book can be lengthy. This is the first page of the back matter in James Giblin's When Plague Strikes.

SOURCE NOTES AND BIBLIOGRAPHY

So many books, magazine articles, and newspaper reports were part of the research for *When Plague Strikes* that it would be virtually impossible to list them all. Here I'll single out those that contributed significantly to the planning and writing of the book.

OVERALL

Four books stimulated my thinking when I was deciding how to treat the subject of plagues in history. They were:

Plagues and Peoples by William H. McNeill (New York: Doubleday, 1977). This fascinating book describes the decisive role that disease has played in the historical development of the human race. From it I gained a much clearer notion of how plagues like the Black Death could travel from one continent to another.

The Doctor in History by Howard W. Haggard (New York: Dorset Press, 1989). A history of medicine and its practitioners from prehistoric times to the early years of the twentieth

197

To learn more, browse books, specifically looking at the back matter. Pull several books from different age categories and pore over the back pages. See what other authors and publishers have included. Do you think it adds to the book? Do any of the books seem to have something missing?

To learn more about the parts of the book, consult *The Chicago Manual of Style;* its sizable first chapter is all about "The Parts of a Published Work." Keep all this in mind when working on your own book. A book can be put together from a large grab bag of components in many different ways, and you can be as creative with those components as you are with any other part of your writing.

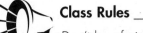

Class Rules

Don't be afraid to mention your ideas for back matter in a proposal for a book. In fact, keep notes on all your ideas for any back matter and list those possibilities in the proposal with examples. You'll give the publisher a more complete vision of your work.

The Least You Need to Know

◆ A book contains many elements, each of which has a name and a purpose.

◆ Hardcover books have a jacket that details specifics about the book; softcover books must fit all the information on the cover.

◆ Business aspects of the book—copyrights, publisher information, and dedications—occur at the front of the book.

◆ The body of the book is your work—the good stuff!

◆ Many books, even picture books, contain back matter, which might include anything from a biography of the author, to suggested games to play, to an index or glossary.

Finding a Good How-To

In This Chapter

- ◆ What to look for in a writing how-to
- ◆ How to find a how-to that suits you
- ◆ Tips on deciding what kind of guide you need
- ◆ Stocking your how-to library

I've always said that a writer or illustrator needs three books to get started in children's books: a guide to the business, like this one; a market guide, such as *Children's Writer's and Illustrator's Market;* and a book to help learn the craft. You've got the first one, there aren't many to choose from for the second, but what about the third? If you're a writer, you'll find many books, of many different kinds and approaches, to consider. In this chapter, I show you how to find the right how-to for you.

What Do *You* Need?

As I wrote this chapter, I really wanted to avoid mentioning any specific book titles at all because what's right for one person might not be right for another. And my thoughts were confirmed when I asked writers I know for suggestions. Although a few books were mentioned several times, and I'll tell you which those were, I kept being surprised by a writer who passionately supported a particular title that no one else even mentioned!

Can You Keep a Secret?

Barbara Seuling, writer, editor, and author of a well-known how-to, had this to say about what writers look for in a how-to: "Some will want non-threatening titles that guide them gently, some will want a book with meaty chapters and tough questions at the end, others will want philosophical and inspiring guides and still others need practical advice. All are looking for magic: something to turn them into writers. I think we all offer some of this magic to beginning writers when we share our knowledge and experience with them."

My goal is to help you figure out which book or books would work best for *you*, not someone else. I'll give examples and discuss what you can find in a particular book, but please don't assume that you should jump for the first book I mention. Take some time to think about what you want or need in a how-to:

◆ Consider your personality. Are you looking for encouragement? Challenges? Or just information?

◆ How do you learn? Are you a right- or left-brain person? Do you like examples or explanations? Exercises or reading lists?

◆ How do you write? If you're highly organized and go one step at a time, you'll want a how-to with the same approach—unless you're trying to change your ways.

◆ Has a writer you admire written about writing? Don't assume their advice will work for you.

◆ Are there specific problems or issues you want to address?

◆ Are you writing or planning to write in more than one genre?

You might not be able to answer all these questions, and that's okay. If you're not sure what you're looking for, read on for some possibilities, and get your hands on a half dozen or so. Take all of them home and try them out. Read at least a chapter or two and do some sample exercises, if the book has them. You might find that you feel most comfortable with one or two; if you've been gentle with the binding and not marked up pages, you can return the others.

Begin at the Beginning

If you're just getting started as a children's book writer, you've got a bewildering variety of titles to choose from. There are a larger number of people in the "beginner" group than any other, and more coming in every year, so it's no wonder publishers target you and your colleagues. When considering books for beginners, two specific questions will help you make choices:

◆ How much of a beginner am I?

◆ Do I want a general guide or help with a particular genre?

I refer to these points when I survey *some* of the titles available.

For Real Beginners

If you're just getting started, meaning you've written only a few stories, or you aren't sure what you want to write and aren't familiar with the current landscape for children's books (which this book is showing you, of course), be careful that you don't buy a book that's too advanced for you. A book that doesn't speak to you where you are will just leave you frustrated or discouraged. Spend some time browsing the general guides, and be sure to look into three particular books.

The first is Barbara Seuling's *How to Write a Children's Book and Get It Published*, which not only provides general guidance but includes chapters on writing picture books, easy-to-read books, early chapter books, fiction, nonfiction, verse, and even plays. She gives practical writing advice, including "checklists" of key points to remember when writing a particular genre. Her book is a good choice if you aren't sure what you want to write or are already writing in more than one genre.

On the other hand, if you're particularly interested in picture books or are an illustrator wanting to move into writing, Berthe Amoss and Eric Suben's *Writing and Illustrating Children's Books for Publication* might be for you. This book does go into other types of writing, but picture books are a constant theme. The book is more heavily illustrated than other how-to's, perhaps because Amoss is an illustrator. This is also

> **Class Rules**
>
> Beginner guides usually include information about children's literature, the submissions process, and the business of publishing—which I already cover in this book! So focus on the material on writing, and if you just don't think it's what you need, don't be afraid to consider a more advanced book that does concentrate on writing.

a good choice if you learn more from writing exercises and case studies than from straight explanation.

If you find the preceding two titles a bit daunting and want something more concise and less costly, consider Aaron Shepard's *The Business of Writing for Children*. Don't be misled by the title! This book is as much as about writing as it is about the business side, and it could be the right match for you. He writes folktales, so his book is a good source for help in that area, but he provides useful tips for other areas, too.

Beginner Plus

What if you've been working in the field a little longer? Say you've been to a few conferences, you've actually started submitting manuscripts (and getting rejected), and you not only know a Newbery from a Caldecott but have read several recent winners. You might find a somewhat more advanced but still general how-to beneficial. You have a number of books to choose from. Here are some you might consider, but look at others, too.

> **Can You Keep a Secret?**
>
> Find more information on all the books for beginners I mention in this chapter, and many others I didn't have room for, on my website at www.underdown.org/writing-guides.htm. I've organized the list in categories, and each title is linked to the book's page at Amazon.

Jim Giblin is both an editor and a writer, so *The Giblin Guide to Writing Children's Books* has a unique perspective on the writing process. As an editor, Jim has seen writers take different approaches, so he doesn't assume there's only one way to write. And as an editor, he's a good source for help with editing and revising. As a bonus, Jim writes nonfiction, so his guide is a good choice for someone writing nonfiction for children.

Anastasia Suen's *Picture Writing: A New Approach to Writing for Children and Teens* is one of the more unusual how-to's I've seen. Anastasia talks briefly about her "picture writing" approach, which essentially uses visualization to enrich writing. But the bulk of the book is taken up by guided analyses of existing books to learn about plot, character, and setting. This is a good choice for someone who likes a structured approach to learning and has the time to do some homework.

Moving Up or Narrowing the Focus

You'll reach a point when general guides don't solve all your problems; *when* you reach this point depends on you. Some writers never need more than a few books, a writer's group, and a friend to talk to when they get stuck; one writer I heard from has more than 100 books on or connected to writing on her shelves.

When you reach this point, you'll find a wide variety of books to choose from. This can be confusing, but fortunately, what's out there can be grouped into three categories.

Writers Writing About Writing

At some point in their careers, many successful writers produce a book or two (or three) about writing. It might be a sort of autobiography of their writing, it might be philosophical or inspirational, it might take a very practical how-to approach, or it might combine elements of all of these approaches. Many writers find such books helpful when they're stuck or need inspiration. And don't limit yourself to books by children's authors; books by writers for adults can be just as helpful.

Here are some recommended reads:

◆ *Bird by Bird: Some Instructions on Writing and Life* by Anne Lamott

◆ *Gates of Excellence* by Katherine Paterson: a collection of essays on writing and children's books

◆ *On Writing* by Stephen King: often recommended, and not just by horror fans

◆ *On Writing for Children and Other People* by Julius Lester

◆ *Steering the Craft: Exercises and Discussions on Story Writing …* by Ursula LeGuin: more of a how-to than many books by famous writers, by a writer for children as well as adults

There are many others! As you look at them, don't let someone's strongly worded advice persuade you to write in a way that doesn't come naturally to you.

Class Rules

Don't assume that a book by your favorite writer will necessarily help you with a structure problem you're having with an easy reader. If you need specific advice, look at the books that address your issue.

Specialized or Advanced Books

Do you write in a specific genre, such as poetry or nonfiction? Are you wrestling with a particular problem of technique, such as point of view or plotting? Or are you looking for more advanced help than you can find in your general how-to? It may take some time to find, but most likely there is a book for you.

Playground Stories

> Help with a writing problem may not come from a writing guide. Karen Romano Young had been struggling with her approach to nonfiction in *Across the Wide Ocean,* which as she puts it, she wrote, "not in the traditional linear style, but in one that is more of a mosaic. ... You can start with one piece (such as the black story in David Macaulay's *Black and White*) and go with that, then come back to other pieces, and it doesn't much matter." She didn't have a name for this until she read *Radical Change* by Eliza Dresang and realized she was part of a relatively new approach in children's books (and books generally), in which writers may present several narratives. Now that she has a name for what she's doing, and how it works, she can pursue it more effectively.

As with books by famous writers, you might not find help addressed to children's writers, and that's fine. A novelist is a novelist, whether he or she is writing for 12-year-olds or 42-year-olds. If you write nonfiction, William Zinsser's *On Writing Well: The Classic Guide to Writing Nonfiction* is one title to consider. Poetry? Take a look at *Poem-Making: Ways to Begin Writing Poetry* written by Myra Cohn Livingston, one of the great poets for children. If short stories or science fiction and fantasy or fiction is more your style, you can find books for those, too; see my online list for titles.

If you're having difficulties with a particular aspect of your writing, there might be a book out there just for you. Do you struggle to edit your own writing? Fiction writers may turn to *Self-Editing for Fiction Writers* by Renni Browne, Dave King, and George Booth. Do you have problems with characters and point of view? Turn to Orson Scott Card's *Character and Viewpoint.* Are you uncertain about the vocabulary to use in a book for a certain age group? Consult a book like *Children's Writer's Word Book* by Alijandra Mogilner.

Books About Creativity

There are two sides to writing, as you've probably learned already: the hard work and the ideas that drive it. Everyone needs help with ideas, whether it's solving a particular problem in a story or finding something to put on a blank sheet of paper.

Books in the area of creativity may have a practical focus, as is the case with *Story Sparkers: A Creativity Guide for Children's Writers* by Debbie Dadey and Marcia Thornton Jones. Or they may address themselves to nurturing your creative spirit more

Can You Keep a Secret?

These more advanced books, and many others I didn't have room for, can be found on my website at www.underdown. org/writing-guides.htm.

generally, as does Natalie Goldberg's *Writing Down the Bones*, along with other books she's written.

Beyond My Lists

The books I mention here and list on my website represent only a fraction of what's available. If you're looking for something specialized or something different and can't find it by browsing in a bookstore or online, seek help from your fellow writers.

Writers love to talk about books about writing. Go to the Society of Children's Book Writers and Illustrators (SCBWI) discussion boards, or the even livelier ones on author Verla Kay's website (www.verlakay.com), and you'll most likely find a recent discussion on this very topic. If not, you'll certainly get suggestions if you ask. Don't forget to ask writers you know for their personal recommendations.

Don't be afraid to try out new titles or older ones no one's mentioned. Just keep a few things in mind:

- Check copyright dates and be wary of books that haven't been recently revised, as "best practices" in children's book writing do change.

- Be skeptical of books that make exaggerated promises, saying, for example, that they'll help you write a publishable manuscript in 30 days.

- Check qualifications and think twice about a book that focuses on an area in which the author apparently has no experience.

Class Rules

Will the right how-to solve all your problems? Rukhsana Khan, picture-book author, told me this: "I think how-to books are excellent stepping stones for understanding how to structure and format a story. They of course can't teach originality or even creativity. That's what you have to provide."

Above all, keep your needs in mind and find the how-to that works for *you*.

The Least You Need to Know

- Books for beginners are not all alike. Find the right one for you.

- Choose from books about specific genres and writing problems when you need advanced help.

◆ Books on creativity or by famous writers about writing can help you find inspiration.

◆ Help with your writing can come from unexpected sources.

◆ Keep your eyes and ears open and investigate books I haven't mentioned.

Part 3

Reaching Out

Is your manuscript ready to go? First, you need to learn how to check to see if it is—that's the first chapter in Part 3. When your manuscript is ready to go, you need to know just how to send it. Or if you want to get work as an illustrator, how do you do that? How do authors and illustrators work together? And who can help you in the publishing jungle … an insider? An agent? Find how to make contact in Part 3.

Chapter 12

Is It Ready to Hand In?

In This Chapter

◆ Determining if your manuscript is ready to send to a publisher

◆ Well-meaning friends and relatives

◆ The skinny on critique groups

◆ The best ways to get good feedback on your work

◆ Children's writing programs and classes

You've learned about children's books and the publishing business, and you think you're ready to send your manuscript to a publisher. Are you?

Okay, you've heard fabulous things about your writing abilities, but you need more than your neighbor's sister's opinion. You need to learn how to obtain useful criticism that will help you improve your manuscript and make it publisher-ready. That's what this chapter is for; I give you several options for improving your writing and discovering just when the time is right to hand in your manuscript.

Rabbit's Friends and Relations

If you're a fan of Winnie-the-Pooh, you might remember that Rabbit had a horde of friends and relations, none of whom were much help in getting Pooh unstuck from Rabbit's hole. Like Rabbit, you might tell your closest and dearest friends and relations about your aspirations to write a children's book. And hopefully they will support you and your creative side. Show them your first effort, and they'll invariably exclaim, "Fabulous!" "We loved it!" "It'll sell a million copies!" Sounds encouraging, doesn't it?

In reality, your relatives and friends—although well meaning—aren't the best choice for honest and educated responses to your work. It's wonderful to have the support of your mom or your hubby, but in most cases, they don't have the skills and experience needed to evaluate your manuscript. So go to them for support, but go to others—experts—for criticism.

Ugh! *Criticism.* It seems like such an ugly word. However, criticism helps you become a better writer. Let's begin the process.

Reading Aloud

I know many writers who use the simple but powerful feedback tool of reading their work aloud. When you do this, you hear things you won't notice when reading a manuscript silently. An awkward construction jumps out at you; a missing transition reveals itself. Try it for yourself, and you'll see.

One Is the Loneliest Number

The first person to whom you should read your book aloud is none other than you! Stand up, pick up your clean, typed (or printed) sheets of creative genius, and begin to read out loud. Although this might feel funny at first, you'll soon become comfortable with the sound of your own voice and begin to perceive and hear where changes need to be made. If you hate being alone, call your dog into the room and read to him.

Guided Responses

After you've listened to your own words and made any changes from your review, pull in an audience to hear your words. Now is the time to gather sisters, brothers, uncles, neighbors, and co-workers for a reading, singly or in a group.

But don't ask them to listen and tell you what they think. Instead, give them specific tasks. Ask them to tell you how the story makes them feel or if they can catch any problems, such as an awkward word or a confusing phrase. You might even want to give your audience a *response sheet* to fill out while you read. Or you could let them read your story silently first and then respond after your reading.

On a response sheet, you want to be as specific as possible with your questions, to help focus the attention of your listeners. Here are some examples of the types of questions you can include on a response sheet. Change them as you see fit or make up others:

1. Did you feel any emotions while reading it/listening to the story? If so, what did you feel?

2. Are there any awkward breaks in the text? If so, where are they?

3. Please note any word choices you think are wrong or not precise. Is there a different word I could have used? What?

4. What age group do you think would most enjoy this book? Why?

5. What do you like best about this story? What don't you like about this story?

def•i•ni•tion

In the writing process, often a writer relies upon a peer editor to improve the manuscript. For writers or peers with little editing experience, sometimes a **response sheet** is useful. On the sheet, the writer lists certain ideas, devices, or grammatical points for listeners to consider when listening to or reading the manuscript to help clarify the writer's problems or strengths.

The Director's Chair

This may sound strange, but another way to get a different perspective on your writing is to have someone else read it to you. You'll hear it fresh and because that person won't be familiar with it, you'll notice problems more easily than if you were reading it yourself. When you read the story, you can juice it up with drama and fix its rhythm, but someone coming to it cold won't be able to do that. Sit with a copy of the text and make notes as your mouthpiece reads.

Apples of Your Writing Eye: Children

Now comes the true test of your skills: reading to children. You want to write for them, so why not read to them? Children may not provide you with expert grammar advice, but what they do provide is even more valuable: a direct emotional response to your story.

A word of caution, though: because children love being read to, don't take an enthusiastic response as a sign that your book is ready to go. And above all, don't offer it as a sign of the quality of your work when you write to a publisher. Any writer sending a manuscript to a publisher can claim that kids love it. If you want to use children as critics, you have to learn to interpret their responses and even guide them.

Class Rules

Be careful when reading to a room of kids. You'll want to read expressively—but not with over-the-top dramatics. Kids naturally gravitate toward drama, and they might appear to love your book when they actually loved the way you read your book. Choose short selections from your work and from two published books, and watch their reactions. To which were they most attentive? Where did they react spontaneously to the action?

Start with children who don't know you. Your own children or your neighbor's children are hopelessly biased, and you wouldn't want it otherwise. Instead, gather a junior focus group.

How do you go about wrangling a group of kids to listen to your work and provide unbiased feedback? You go to where the kids are. Depending on the age your book targets, seek an audience either through a day-care center or preschool, elementary school, or middle or high school.

Set up your reading group as thoughtfully as you can. It should be fun for the children, but also useful to you, a market researcher. Find two published books with stories of the same type and of similar length as yours. Type them out like yours, and practice reading all three of them so you can spend as much time as possible with your eyes on the children.

When you're in front of your group, just read and don't tell them which work is yours. Watch their reactions. Note their body language. Listen for spontaneous "aahs" and "oohs." Listen for whispering

Can You Keep a Secret?

Another great way to get feedback from kids is by reading your story at a neighborhood bookstore. Offer to read your piece, mixed in with similar selections from published books, and lead a story-time session in the store. Or you can approach a teacher at a local school, though you may have to fill out some forms and get approvals before being allowed into the school.

and other signs that you've lost their interest. Did they react differently to each story? How they react may tell you more than what they say afterward, but do ask them questions about each story when you are done reading. Ask them if they had a favorite part and why, or ask questions to help the children make comparisons. Don't "coach" them with hints about what you expect them to like.

Know-It-Alls: Critique Groups

Every writer, from the novice to the expert, knows the merits of joining a writer's group and receiving critiques on her work. I highly recommend that you seek out a local writer's organization or club and join. If you can't find one, create one! And if there aren't enough writers in your area to sustain one, look into online writer's groups or consider exchanging critiques by e-mail with people you've met at conferences and classes.

You'll find the experience and keen eyes of other writers a tremendous asset to your own writing. You, in turn, can also provide an invaluable service to your fellow critiquers: your keen observations about their work. Generally, club members all bring their work "to the table" where a read-around occurs. Each member reads another member's work and responds to it. Sometimes, you need to provide a copy of your work for each member. They take them, read them, and report back at the next meeting on what they thought of your story.

Beyond the great instructional feedback you receive, the camaraderie among members extends beyond the meetings and the critiques. It's comforting to know that there are others with aspirations like yours, learning the ropes, writing, hoping one day to publish their books. The group can serve to keep you focused toward your goal and intent on attaining your dream. Of course, classes may not be your cup of tea. Says Charles Ghigna, author of more than 25 books, "The only way to learn to write is to write. There is no other way. Workshops and conferences can only take you away from the real work—the real world of writing."

Critique groups can be tremendously helpful, but they can also err in two very different ways. If the group is too supportive, with most comments being along the lines of "What a wonderful story," everyone will feel great about his or her writing but won't be pushed to improve it. On the other hand, if the group nitpicks every line or is never satisfied with anything, its members won't know where they stand. Strive for balance in your group.

Another valuable aspect of critique groups is that the right kind of information seems to naturally gravitate toward them. One person in the club might know where to find that information you need about moose behavior. Another member might tell of a writer coming to town and orchestrate a meeting. A third might have news of changes to a publisher's editorial staff. The "brain trust" within these groups is wonderful. It's like having several personal trainers for your creative spirit.

So what are you waiting for? Grab your manuscript and join a writer's group!

Writing Classes

Here's something you'll hear over and over from experienced writers: you should never, never stop learning. Being a writer (or an illustrator) means always trying new things and attempting to improve on what came before. Writing classes, seminars, conferences—all these improve your writing and help hone your craft. Each year, all over the United States, writers meet for workshops and classes, usually taught by experienced authors. These are great settings in which to learn and get objective and often skilled feedback on your writing.

Beyond the workshops and classes, you can find specialized programs in writing and even writing children's literature. And if a college degree in writing isn't what you envisioned or want, local colleges, universities, and extension campuses typically showcase a host of composition, writing, and English classes for those who just want to improve their writing skills. See what's available in your area. (And when considering teachers, apply the criteria I suggest for writing consultants later in this chapter.)

> **Can You Keep a Secret?**
>
> Several universities offer specialized programs in writing for children. Two that offer MFAs in writing for children are Simmons College in Boston (www.simmons.edu/gradstudies/liberal-arts/academics/childrens-literature/writing.shtml) and Hollins University in Virginia (www.hollins.edu/grad/childlit/childlit.htm). Others offer summer writing workshops. You can probably find a workshop near you.

Playground Stories

Not all authors dive into classes. Says Charles Ghigna: "Stop attending workshops. Read other writers if you must, but for heaven sakes save your soul and stay away from how-to workshops and conferences. At worst, they'll drain you of your creativity. At best, they'll have you writing like everyone else. Keep what little originality you have left from childhood. Protect it. Nurture it. Let it run wild. That's all you have. That's all you need. The only way to learn to write is to write. There is no other way. Workshops and conferences can only take you away from the real work—the real world of writing." The perspective works for Ghigna, who has authored more than 25 books, including *Tickle Day: Poems from Father Goose.*

Professional Critiques

What about critiques from professionals, such as freelance editors or published writers? Your writing group might include a few professionals who already are offering you advice without charging you, so why pay a fee? Or if you've got money to spend, why not use it on a class? Because good writing consultants can provide you with the insight and detailed criticism that will most improve your writing. Working with a good one can be like working with a good editor.

Your challenge is to find the good professional and not just some fraud who poses as a professional and charges a fee to make money. There *are* people out there who prey on writers desperate to succeed—even at great expense. Be wary of those people who call themselves "agents" and want to charge you a "reading fee" to evaluate your work. You are not likely to get useful feedback for that fee—or any help finding a publisher. Also be wary of consultants who approach *you* or who advertise their services on hard-sell websites.

So how do you go about finding an honest and learned writing consultant? You act like a detective and do your research. As you come across possible candidates, ask yourself—or them—questions like the following: Who recommended this person? If it's someone you know personally or respect, that's a good sign. Has the consultant actually published any writing or worked as an editor for a publisher? Ask for a resumé, or list of published books. Who else has the consultant helped? If she can't provide any references, walk away. What does the consultant charge? Don't automatically run from a substantial fee. Many good professional writers must charge a fee to weed out the less serious and allow themselves time for their own work.

The key to finding a professional is asking questions. Just as all law-enforcement agencies run background checks on future cops, you need to run your own background check on anyone who charges to look at your work. If you don't want to do this, you're better off working with people you know—the people in your local children's writer's group, the staff at the local college, and even your own friends and relations—with some guidance provided by you, of course.

The Least You Need to Know

- Although well meaning, relatives and friends are not the best choices for critiquing your work.

- Read your work aloud or have someone read it to you. Hearing your work read aloud is a good way to find the trouble spots.

◆ Kids want the straight scoop about your story. Observe their reactions to your work carefully.

◆ Join a writer's group, take a class or two, and seek out professional perspectives on your work.

◆ When seeking the help of a professional, thoroughly investigate the individual's credentials.

Chapter 13

Play by the Rules

In This Chapter

- ◆ Preparing your manuscript
- ◆ What you must—and must *not*—include in a submission
- ◆ The all-important cover letter
- ◆ Tips for not putting a manuscript reader to sleep

You've finished your manuscript and you're ready to send a copy to dozens of publishers to see how many of them are interested. If that's your plan (or something like it), stop—you're already breaking two of the basic rules. Following the rules won't guarantee that you get published, but it may save you some time, spare you some grief, and help you come across as a professional.

In this chapter, you learn how to prepare your manuscript and a letter to go with it, untangle the mysteries of unsolicited manuscripts and multiple submissions, gain tips on writing cover and query letters, and discover some alternative ways to get in the door at companies that have closed theirs.

Manuscript Submission Basics

It's hard not to obsess over the treasured story or nonfiction work you're about to send off into the world. You want it to be just right. Should you type it double- or single-spaced? Should you write a letter to go with it? What else do you need to send? Fortunately, what you need to do is pretty simple.

Setting Up and Formatting Your Manuscript

Getting your manuscript ready to go is straightforward. First of all, type it, using double-spaced lines. Editors don't read handwritten stories. On the first page, either upper right or upper left, put your name and full address. That's important in case the manuscript gets separated from your letter and envelope. Skip a few lines and then put the title. Skip a few more and start the story. You can skip straight to a second page and start the story there, but that's not necessary.

Class Rules

ALL CAPITAL LETTERS MAKE A STORY MORE DIFFICULT TO READ, and although *the fancy typefaces that come ready to use with word processing programs are tempting, don't use them either.* A designer might use a fancier typeface in the finished book, but right now, your goal is to make your manuscript as easy on your editor's eyes as possible.

Be sure the manuscript is easy to read. Type it using both capitals and lowercase letters in good old Times Roman or `Courier`. White—not pink, neon yellow, or textured—paper is your best choice.

Break the manuscript into paragraphs. Start a new page only when you come to the end of another one. Don't try to type it out in book form. That's particularly important if you've written a picture book; 32 pages, each with one line on it, can be frustrating to read. Editors are used to imagining how a book would be laid out and prefer a standard format, whether that means the manuscript is 1 page or 200 pages long. If you want to, you can put a double line break wherever you imagine a new page, but that's not necessary.

SASEs (Self-Addressed Stamped Envelopes)

If a publisher doesn't like your manuscript, you'd rather not know about it. But to keep track of who has seen it and who hasn't, enclose a *SASE* (pronounced *say*-zee), a *self-addressed stamped envelope*, for the publisher's response and the return of the manuscript. This can be expensive, especially if a novel is involved, but don't take a shortcut and include an envelope "for response only," as some writers have started to do. This sends a message that you don't care enough about your work to get it back. Sure, it's saved on your computer, but can you bear to imagine your work being thrown out or recycled? Don't let a publisher think so.

Some of the larger publishers have created a new approach to submissions that saves time and stress—for them. They don't respond to submissions unless they're interested, even if a SASE has been enclosed. With such publishers, you obviously don't need to send a SASE. Publishers that follow this procedure do publicize it.

def•i•ni•tion

The envelope a rejected manuscript is returned in is a **SASE**, which stands for **self-addressed stamped envelope**. It carries your complete address in the space where the address belongs, and it must be large enough and contain enough postage for your manuscript.

Pack It Up and Send It Off ...

You might not know the individual to whom you are sending your manuscript, or even his or her name, but experienced writers always include a brief cover letter addressed to the Submissions Editor. (You learn what you need to write in it later in this chapter, and some samples are provided in the back of the book.)

Put your manuscript, SASE, and cover letter in an envelope. If the manuscript is only a few pages, you can fold it neatly and put it in a standard business-size envelope. Don't jam it into something smaller. If the manuscript is longer and you need to send it unfolded, use a plain manila envelope. You don't need to bind or cover it. Type or neatly write an address label and send it all by the good old U.S. Postal Service.

Why Can't I E-Mail Them?

I can hear people whispering in the back of the room, "Why is he telling us about the right kind of paper, the envelope, and SASEs? I'm just going to e-mail my manuscript to the publisher!" It would be nice if it worked that way, but so far, it mostly doesn't. Publishers are slow to change, and making their submissions process electronic is not a high priority. So find out what a publisher wants. Some companies, especially e-publishers and magazines, do accept queries by e-mail, but few accept submissions that way.

... And Then Wait

As a submitting writer, you need patience. Most publishers take a minimum of three months to read through their submissions, and some take much longer than that. If you want some assurance that the publisher received your manuscript, use the inexpensive "Delivery Confirmation" option from the U.S. Postal Service, or include a

SASP (self-addressed stamped *postcard*) and request that it be returned to you when your package is opened. But don't be surprised if that postcard doesn't come back to you right away—some publishers don't even open manuscript submissions until they read them.

That's it. Letter, manuscript, SASE, envelope, and patience are usually all you need to make an unsolicited submission to a publisher.

What's an Unsolicited Submission?

Some of the thousands of manuscripts a publisher receives each year come from authors who are already working with that publisher. But many manuscripts are *unsolicited*, meaning that the publisher did not request them. Some publishers still read these in the hopes of finding the next Margaret Wise Brown or J. K. Rowling. Maybe that's you.

def•i•ni•tion

An **unsolicited submission** is one a publisher didn't ask for from an author. You send solicited or requested manuscripts in response to a letter or phone call from a publisher, and if you are doing so, you should write that on the envelope.

Although the odds are long, the unsolicited manuscript is your foot in the door. You have to find out which publishers read them (learn how in Chapter 19) because not all do. Thanks to this policy, children's books are one of the areas of publishing in which you don't absolutely have to have an agent or a friend in the business, because if you follow the rules and have chosen the right kind of publisher, you've got a chance of finding a home for your work.

When your manuscript arrives at a publisher, the envelope is opened, probably by an intern or an editorial assistant. He or she may read it herself or leave it for a junior editor to read. You had hoped it would be read by Mr. Bigshot or Ms. Children's Publishing Wonder? Don't be discouraged. Mr. Bigshot and Ms. Wonder are so busy with their current authors and illustrators that even if they read your manuscript and loved it, it's unlikely they'd publish it anytime soon. Editors at their level see many more "publishable" manuscripts over the course of a year than they can actually publish.

def•i•ni•tion

The **slush pile** consists of all the manuscripts a publisher has received from writers or agents the publisher doesn't know. They will be read … eventually.

Fortunately, the junior editors and assistants reading the unsolicited manuscripts are exactly the people you want to reach. They don't already have well-known writers to publish. They can rise up in their company by discovering writers with promise, so they spend as much time as they can mining the *slush pile*.

Some publishers, of course, don't accept unsolicited submissions. Simply put, if you aren't a published author or don't have an agent, they won't read your manuscript. This seems terribly unfair, and your natural response might be to try to find a way in through a back door. There *are* ways to do that, and you read about some of them later in this chapter and in Chapter 16, but it might not be worth the effort. The companies that have closed their doors just don't need to find new authors. You can spend a lot of time and energy making contact with editors at those companies only to discover that they don't "have room on their list"—they've already got enough books signed up for the next few years. Instead, spend that time finding out about companies that really want your work. Start with them, and you may in time move on to a "closed" company.

Simultaneous Submissions—Are They Worth It?

Why bother to find the right company to send your manuscript to? After all, it can take six months or longer to hear back from a publisher, and even the "fast" ones don't promise a response in less than three! You know the first editor to read your work might not fall in love with it, and it could be years before you get it to the right person. So why not send your manuscript to a bunch of publishers at the same time—say 20 or 30?

It's tempting to resort to *simultaneous submissions* and send copies of your manuscript to several publishers at once. You keep track of whom you sent it to, and if one of them offers to publish it, you let the others know. Think twice before you do this, and keep your list short if you do decide to go this route. After all, you might be helping to kill the goose that lays the golden egg by overloading those publishers that still read the slush pile, causing even more of them to close their doors. And you might be wasting paper and postage on mailing 37 copies of your manuscript when further research would have helped you target three or four publishers. And some publishers are keeping their doors open by only reading manuscripts that are clearly identified as *exclusive* to that publisher.

What to do? National organizations, such as the Society of Children's Book Writers and Illustrators (SCBWI), suggest allowing a publisher three months to respond to a submission. If you haven't heard by the end of that time, you write to the company and

def•i•ni•tion

A **simultaneous submission** is a manuscript sent to two or more publishers at the same time. Many people, including editors, use *multiple submission* as a synonym for simultaneous submission, but properly it means sending several manuscripts to one publisher. An **exclusive submission** is a manuscript sent to only one publisher.

withdraw your submission. You might still hear from that company, because it might not be able to match your letter of withdrawal with your submission, but you can then send your manuscript elsewhere with a clear conscience.

In the case of "no-response" publishers, don't bother to write; just consider it rejected. With any publisher, following up to find out about the status of a submission usually doesn't work, so just wait or move on.

> ### Can You Keep a Secret?
>
> You've sent your manuscript to a publisher that receives 6,000 manuscripts every year and publishes only 60 books, most by its current authors. You may wonder if someone will even read your manuscript. But many of those submissions disqualify themselves by being badly written or sent to the wrong publisher. So don't despair: yours might be one of only a few hundred, or a few dozen, truly worthwhile manuscripts.

Whether you choose to submit your manuscript exclusively or to a short, targeted list is up to your own sense of ethics, but do not resort to scatter-shot multiple submissions to dozens of publishers. No week goes by at Charlesbridge, the publishing company where I used to work, without the need to return something the company just doesn't publish, such as a novel for adults. This is a waste of time for both staff and authors.

Dear ... *Somebody*

You're ready to launch your manuscript into a sea of many other manuscripts. With your name and address on your manuscript, no publishing credits to cite, and no specific person to write to, why should you bother to write a letter to accompany the manuscript? Why not just put the manuscript in the envelope and send it off? Because a letter is the polite and professional thing to do, even though the envelope says "Submissions Editor" and your letter's salutation is *Dear Editor*.

def•i•ni•tion

A **cover letter** is the letter that accompanies your manuscript to a publisher.

What to Include in Your Cover Letter

Check Appendix C for some sample *cover letters*. The absolutely necessary elements of a cover letter are few: business-style set-up, including your address, the address of the publisher, and a date; a salutation such as *Dear Editor*; the title of your manuscript; a brief and tempting description of it; and your signature.

What *Not* to Include in Your Cover Letter

The most important items not to include, unless a publisher specifically says otherwise, are also few: your resumé; a marketing plan; inflated claims, such as "a surefire Newbery winner"; endorsements—from children or adults; an apology for your lack of experience; or a lengthy plot summary.

A good cover letter is simple and business-like. It contains the necessary information and no more, and it does not distract the editor from the business at hand—reading your manuscript.

Class Rules

I've heard some authors say that a Post-it note with a brief greeting is all you need to send with a submission. If you know the editor, that's fine; otherwise, you're assuming a degree of acquaintance by being so informal. Write that letter instead, and let your professionalism and personality shine.

When to Send a Query Letter

Sometimes you'll find another hurdle to simply sending off your manuscript to a publisher. Some publishers, particularly for novels or longer works of nonfiction, require a *query letter*, in which you ask them if they want to see your manuscript.

This procedure has advantages and disadvantages. On the one hand, it may save you postage and copying costs. It's also completely acceptable to send out several query letters for the same manuscript simultaneously. On the other hand, it gives the publisher the opportunity to say no before even seeing your manuscript.

def•i•ni•tion

A **query letter** is a letter you send to a publisher to ask, or query, if it is interested in seeing your manuscript.

If a publisher doesn't require a query first, and your manuscript is short, it's usually better to just send the manuscript. That saves you the time you would have spent waiting for a response to your query, and it lets you put your best foot forward—your manuscript.

If you must query, or choose to do so to avoid sending out your 500-page fantasy epic, remember that your letter is meant to intrigue the reader so he or she will want to read your manuscript. If your manuscript is fiction, including a paragraph or two from it can be effective; choose a passage that displays your style to good advantage. If you have a nonfiction piece, think about what it is that makes your subject interesting, and be sure to include sample chapters or an outline if the publisher's guidelines request them.

Can You Keep a Secret?

Editor and writer Jackie Ogburn has written a thoughtful and funny guide to cover letters and query letters, complete with sample letters showing what to do and not do. Read it online at www.underdown.org/covlettr.htm.

That's a No-No!

The quality of your writing will get noticed in the end, but be sure to avoid the common mistakes that might mean no one actually bothers to read your manuscript, or dismisses it quickly when he or she does read it.

Neatness and Spelling Count

You thought you could stop worrying about spelling and punctuation when you left school, right? Wrong. Presentation counts in publishing, and you'll lose points for spelling mistakes, bad grammar, and even bad style. An editor is learning about *you* as she reads your cover letter and manuscript. If you come across as a sloppy typist or a careless speller, she may expect that to continue if she were to work with you.

I've seen amazing things in cover letters, starting with authors who get the name of the publisher wrong or get my name wrong. And I've seen plenty of bad grammar, poor style, and even almost illegible photocopies. Does the cover letter have to be perfect? No, but publishers do assume that the appearance of your submission says something about how much care you put into your writing. If you care enough to ask your friend who knows grammar and spelling to check over your cover letter and manuscript, you're the kind of author with whom many children's book editors want to work.

Pink Envelopes and Other Horrors

Feverish visions of the swaying heaps of manuscripts that make up the slush pile understandably drive many to desperate measures in an attempt to make theirs stand out from the rest. "If they read mine first, maybe they'll appreciate it better." Actually, you're more likely to come across as naïve and attention-seeking, so avoid the following ploys and variations on them:

◆ Express delivery of any kind—your wait will be just as long after the manuscript arrives.

◆ Pink, neon yellow, or decorated envelopes.

◆ Fancy covers, folders, or binding.

◆ Enclosures of food, stuffed animals, or toys—they won't fit in the files.

◆ Faxing your manuscript—you can't send a SASE and it's harder to read.

A plain envelope, white paper, the right postage, and a SASE are all you need.

Too Much Information!

What would you think of a building contractor who put more time and energy into a sign announcing the work he was doing than he did into the simple ground-level patio he was constructing for you? You'd wonder about his sense of priorities and worry that the effort he put into the sign took time away from his work on your patio.

That's how editors react when someone sends a five-page marketing plan to go with a three-page picture book manuscript. The marketing department will take care of that aspect of the book, if your book is published. Editors feel the same when they see a plan for a lengthy series if they work for a publisher that prefers to sign single titles. And they react the same way when someone tells them about his life at great length, or encloses a detailed resumé, when nothing in his experience relates to the piece he has written.

These kinds of things happen too often. When I was an editorial assistant at a large company, a group of us assistants developed an irreverent rule of thumb: "The quality of a manuscript decreases as the amount of other material enclosed increases." Put your effort into your manuscript. An editor cares about that, and nothing else.

The Wrong Kind of Bedtime Book

The time-honored tradition of parents putting their children to sleep by reading them a book should not extend to your reader's reaction to your manuscript. Any editor or other reader of manuscripts sees hundreds of manuscripts a year and will be put to sleep quickly by certain kinds of submissions. Although you'll find exceptions, most editors at trade publishers—the ones you're targeting—become very sleepy when they encounter the following:

- Cute, fluffy animals

- Writers imitating a popular author and claiming they are the next *(fill in the blank)*

- Stories that contain thinly disguised moral lessons

- Memories of someone's childhood

I could give other examples, but you need to find from your own experience what gets a reaction (even if it's just a personal rejection letter) and what doesn't. Imagine that poor assistant, slumped in front of a stack of 100 manuscripts to read by 5 P.M. And then imagine her jumping up and running into her boss's office, and saying, "Hey, this one's got something different about it." That's the reaction you want to provoke. In fact, an unusual, unconventional, difficult-to-publish, but wildly creative manuscript is more likely to get a response than one that plays it safe, follows the rules, and just isn't that different from anything else.

So go for it! Write your best, not what you think someone wants to see, and send it the right way.

The Least You Need to Know

- Manuscripts need to be typed, double-spaced, on plain paper, with your name and address on the first page.

- A submission to a publisher needs a short cover letter, the manuscript, a SASE, and a stamp.

- Simultaneous submissions are multiple copies of the same manuscript sent out to more than one publisher; avoid them if you can.

- A good cover letter is short and doesn't get in the way of a manuscript, while a good query letter makes an editor want to see your manuscript.

- Be sure your manuscript has what it takes to get noticed.

Chapter 14

The Rules for Illustrators

In This Chapter

- ◆ Portfolio basics
- ◆ The importance of a dummy
- ◆ Working with publishers
- ◆ Marketing yourself

If you're ready to start marketing yourself as an illustrator, you've come to the right place. In this chapter, I explain what a portfolio is and what to put in it, outline what else you need to prepare to show prospective clients, and give you tips for contacting publishers.

Take a Peek in My Portfolio ...

You might think a *portfolio* is just a big carrying case with a zipper into which you can stuff art you want to carry from one place to another. Well, that's one definition, but in publishing terms, a portfolio has a more specific meaning: it's a thoughtful selection of no more than 15 samples of your best work, aimed at the needs of a particular publisher.

If you're approaching a publisher of novels, choose individual pieces that grab the eye because that publisher needs jacket illustrations. For a publisher of picture books, be sure to show a few sequences of illustrations because a picture book is much more than a collection of individual illustrations. You need to have your portfolio ready to take or mail in when a publisher expresses interest in you; it may lead to your being offered a contract, if it confirms that you can do the job the publisher has.

The samples should not only show your best work, but be of good quality. Do not include original art, but do include *tear sheets* or good-quality color copies. Do not use smudgy printouts from your color printer. Do not send slides. Do not send black-and-white copies unless your work is done in black and white.

def•i•ni•tion

A **portfolio** is a large, sturdy folder-type case, usually with handles, ideally with pockets inside the covers, and some means of closing it. It's also a careful selection of illustration samples, chosen for a specific publisher. Originally, **tear sheets** were work an illustrator (or writer) had done that had been torn out of a magazine or other source. Now a tear sheet can also be a photocopy of such a sample.

Can You Keep a Secret?

Chris Tugeau notes some essentials in samples for children's publishers: "character development, interaction, real space, and a narrative feeling." Find out what she means by each of these items online at www.underdown.org/cat_advice.htm, and see also "Getting Out of the Art File" at www.underdown.org/artfile.htm.

What should the samples show? At a minimum, as artist's representative Chris Tugeau reported of a conversation with an art director, you need "good drawing, good composition, good color." *Good drawing:* do the figures, objects, and structures look real? *Good composition:* do the different parts of it work together? *Good color:* are the colors you use compatible and appealing? Keep in mind that you're showing what you would do with an illustration assignment. You don't want to include your wonderful fine art work, for example, if those pieces don't function well as illustrations.

Creating a Dummy

For work on picture books, one of the most important areas in children's publishing, you will help your cause greatly if you can also include a *dummy*. This is a stand-in for an actual book and a necessary stage in creating a picture book.

To prepare a dummy, break up the text as you would in a book, remembering to leave a title page, a copyright page, and any other necessary pages outside of the main text. (Reread Chapter 10 if you aren't sure what to include in a book.) Tape or glue the pieces of text onto separate pages, and generally set up the book as if it were a full-size finished book, with a title page, copyright page, and so on. Put sketches where you intend to have illustrations. You don't have to complete all the illustrations, but do two or three finished pieces. Make color copies of the finished pieces, and put the color copies in place in the dummy.

def•i•ni•tion

A **dummy** is a manuscript laid out in book form, with sketches of all the illustrations and at least two or three finished pieces.

Tuck your dummy into your portfolio's front pocket, along with a letter and resumé. Tuck some samples for your viewer's files and a SASE (self-addressed stamped envelope) into the back pocket, and you're done. Of course, you'll have to redo it every time you send it out or show it to a different publisher.

Where the Work Is and What It's Like

Where should you look for illustration work? You'll find a wide variety of work at the publishers discussed in this book. The following sections explain what to expect from different publishers.

Trade Publishers

Contact trade publishers if you're looking for work on picture books and jackets. Some chapter books have interior illustrations, and an illustrator might be hired to do the jacket and a dozen black-and-white illustrations for the interior, but these assignments are less common than they used to be. When you work with a trade publisher, you're typically paid a royalty for picture books and a flat fee for a jacket. You have considerable artistic license, and you usually have plenty of time to work.

Mass-Market and Educational Publishers

Mass-market and educational publishing are big markets for illustrators. Lots of individual illustrations are needed for textbooks—and on tight deadlines. This work can by cyclical, as textbook publishers only do new programs every three years or so. Mass-market publishers need illustrators, often for ongoing picture-book series based on popular characters, or for workbooks, activity books, and many other kinds of products.

I put these two publishers together because both expect illustrators to work to their schedule and specifications, and both usually pay fees rather than royalties. Many illustrators make a living from their work in educational publishing, so don't ignore these areas if you want to illustrate full-time.

It's difficult to get work in these areas unless you have an artist's representative. And watch out for the dangers of "work-for-hire" contracts. It can be okay to be paid a fee, but if the fee gets the publisher the right to keep your original art and to reuse it indefinitely, put your foot down. You deserve to get your art back, and ideally you want to give the publisher "single use" only. Failing that, push for limits on what the publisher can do with your work, such as restricting them to a particular market. (I discuss this more in Chapter 17.)

Contacting Publishers

Getting work as an illustrator requires that you spend a good bit of time marketing yourself. It's not enough to find a dozen publishers you like, send them each a sample of your work, and sit back and wait for the assignments to come in. Having a good portfolio isn't enough either, if you don't first get publishers interested enough to ask to see it. There are some settings in which you can show a portfolio cold, but mostly you need to have it to show to people after you've contacted them in some other way.

What do you need to do? First, be aware of how most publishers keep track of illustrators. There's a favored group of illustrators who the art director or an editor already works with regularly, and who they will always turn to first when a manuscript needs an illustrator. They may also have a small file of people they would like to work with in the future. If a manuscript doesn't work for one of the regulars, they'll open that file. Then there are the samples that came in recently and are still sitting on their desk. After that they may browse through some catalogs or look at the files they have from artists' reps they like. They're likely to turn to the art sample files, which are probably overflowing and badly organized, only as a last resort. If you're in the art files, you may never get out.

Consider any or all of the strategies discussed in the following sections to enhance your chances of being both liked and remembered.

Playing Well Together with Others

Before you even think about the specific strategies you're going to use to market your abilities to publishers, think a bit about your personal style. This time, I don't mean your art style. I mean how you relate to others.

Are you shy? Are you thoughtful? Are you assertive? Whatever your style is, don't let it become a liability. If you know you get quiet when meeting new people and you have to meet with a publishing staffer in person, plan some questions you want to ask ahead of time (not asking questions can be interpreted as not being interested). Make some of the questions personal, but not too personal: ask what their most recent project was, or what their favorite childhood books were. Just don't go to the other extreme and become a pest.

> **Class Rules** _____
>
> Your personality and approach to your work are as important as the work itself. A colleague told me about one person "who was so overly aggressive in seeking work (calling more than once a day and having me paged out of a meeting). Those people got none of my attention, as I thought that if they were going to annoy me that much without work, they would certainly annoy me if I gave them work."

When you contact an art director, designer, or editor, they don't just evaluate your illustration ability. They evaluate, perhaps subconsciously, how you would be to work with. Don't come across as someone who does great work but would be a constant energy drain—someone who resists making any changes, responds slavishly but unimaginatively to suggestions, or needs constant and unreasonable amounts of encouragement. Strive to be the positive, problem-solving person with whom anyone would like to work. Publishing is still a personal business, so remember you are marketing yourself.

This Is Me: Mailings

In Chapter 13, I went into some detail about how a writer can contact a publisher. As an illustrator, much of what you should do is similar. You should send away for illustrator guidelines or find them on the company's website, before contacting a publisher. When you send a publisher a small selection of color samples, include a cover letter and a SASE if you want them returned (but don't expect them to be—illustration samples, typically, are either filed or discarded), and take some care to get them to the right companies.

When contacting publishers, illustrators do some things differently from writers:

- Send samples to the art director, not the editor. If you don't have a name, that title or "Art Department" should get your work to the right place.

- Contact as many companies as you want to at the same time, because you are hoping to be put on file for future projects, not to get a job right away.

- Send color postcards as reminders to publishers who you've contacted before. Include your address, phone number, and e-mail so a publisher can request more samples if they're interested.

> **Can You Keep a Secret?**
>
> The Picture Book Artists Association is an organization for published children's book illustrators. Its website, where members can post samples, features links and resources for all: www.picturebookartists.org.

Mailings are often just a first step, but they can be a very useful one. If you do a mailing to 30 publishers and 2 art directors contact you and ask to see more, you've done well.

Mailing Your Portfolio

Before children's publishing got to be big business, most illustrators lived in the New York City area and could come in and leave a portfolio off at a publisher. Some publishers still have "drop-off days," but the industry is more scattered now, and it's often possible to send in your portfolio by mail. If you're asked for your portfolio by mail, do not send in a full-size portfolio with large samples. You need to have something ready that you can send in a small package, such as a ring binder with your tear sheets in clear plastic pockets.

Personal Contact

If you can arrange a meeting with an editor or art director, great, but look also for portfolio showcases in which dozens of artists show off their work to browsing publishing staff. I've been to such showcases, organized by local chapters of such groups as the Graphic Artist's Guild or the Society of Children's Book Writers and Illustrators (SCBWI), in both New York and Boston, and I believe that they happen in other parts of the country. People do get discovered at such events, so if there's one in your town, consider taking part.

Directories

If you've ever visited a publisher of any kind, you might have noticed the bookcase with the big heavy illustrator directories, also known as sourcebooks. In these annual tomes, you can find hundreds of illustrators, all seeking work in some area of publishing. At children's publishers, with one exception, these books gather dust and are consulted only in desperation because 95 percent of the illustrators and photographers in them are seeking work from magazines and the like and don't work in a style that suits children's books.

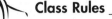

Class Rules

The only illustrator directory worth buying a page in is called *Picturebook*. Find out more about them online at www.picture-book.com.

There is an exception: *Picturebook* (www.picture-book.com—be sure to put the hyphen in the web address!), a relative newcomer, was started by some children's illustrators and it caters specifically to them. It has gotten considerably thicker and is now the directory of choice for people looking for illustrators. Buying a page in it also costs considerably less than the other, general-purpose directories, and you get 1,000 reprints of your page to use in mailings and space in their online portfolio.

Think carefully before buying a page in a directory. Every year, I see some pages in *Picturebook* with work that just isn't good enough or that's presented in an amateurish way. Those illustrators have wasted their money. Wait until you have a few publishing credits—a sample from a magazine will be looked at more carefully than an unpublished presentation piece.

When you do jump into a directory, build the rest of your marketing around it by mentioning it in every mailing you send out and using the tear sheets they gave you.

Website Do's and Don'ts

On first glance, a website might seem to be the ideal way to market yourself as an illustrator. Web space is cheap, your website is accessible to all, and you can put up some scans of your best work. Then you wait for the assignments to come. It's not so simple.

Just because you have a website, you can't be sure anyone is coming to it. Imagine putting up a huge mural in your living room. It's impressive, but you're the only person who sees it. To get visitors to your site, you have to register with search engines, contact directories of illustrator sites, and generally make sure that people looking for sites like yours will find yours listed in the places where they start their search. Even with this effort, you might not get many art directors coming to your site.

Ironically, a website can be most useful to you as a supplement to more traditional marketing. Include the website address in all your samples and mailings, and if someone wants to see more of your work, he or she can go to your website instead of waiting for you to send it. That convenience factor could help you land an assignment from an art director facing a looming deadline. Even for a less urgent project, the easy availability of more samples is a plus.

Can You Keep a Secret?

I've put up a brief list of some personal author and illustrator websites at www.underdown. org/topsites.htm. The sites listed give you an idea of what's possible in a personal site and may provide inspiration as you build your own.

If you do build a website, put up a variety of work and include at least a few samples that display at a large size on a monitor, at higher resolution, to really show off your work. The files will be larger, but most publishers have high-capacity Internet connections, so this won't be a problem. Try to develop a special feature that will help people remember you, such as a series of pages showing the process you go through from rough sketch to finished piece. And as with all your marketing efforts, your website should reflect who you are as a person, so put some thought into the overall presentation and design.

However you decide to market yourself, remember that it can take years to break in, so keep at it. Try different things, follow up contacts, and don't give up.

The Least You Need to Know

- A portfolio is a careful selection of your best samples, aimed at a particular publisher's needs.

- Individual illustration samples aren't enough; you may also need to create a complete book dummy to send out.

- Different publishers have different kinds of work available to illustrators.

- Mailings, directories, personal contact, and websites can all be part of your campaign to market yourself as an illustrator.

Chapter 15

Who Draws the Pictures?

In This Chapter

- ◆ Who is responsible for illustrations and why
- ◆ What instructions a writer can expect to give to an illustrator
- ◆ Some notes on photo research
- ◆ Enjoying the magic of illustration

Today, children's books have better illustrations than ever before, printed to exacting standards, in a wide variety of styles. Visual riches can be found in any decent children's bookstore or library. This treasure trove can be daunting—and sometimes misleading. Books are published as a package of writing and illustration, which can give beginning writers the idea that they are somehow responsible for all of it.

Writers, I want you to relax. Whether writers like it or not—and some people don't like it at all—publishers are almost always in charge of choosing and overseeing illustrators. Writers are best off sitting back and letting it happen. Often enough, the results are magic.

But I Can't Draw!

Looking at the end of the publishing process and seeing a gorgeous picture book, it's easy to assume that the beginning of the process must be more than just a manuscript. You obviously also need the illustrations that go with it. And so when submitting their manuscripts, many aspiring authors apologize for not including illustrations, send sketches or computer art as a substitute, or even get a complete set of illustrations done by someone the author knows.

In fact, in just about every case, a publisher does not want or expect an author to include illustrations when sending a manuscript. After all, why should a *writer* be responsible for *illustrating* a story? A writer's skills are in working with words, not paint or pastels.

My Brother-in-Law/Daughter/Husband Is an Artist

As a writer, you know and like an artist and think this person is just the right match for your story. The artist completes some illustrations, you make careful color photocopies of some of them and send them along with your manuscript, and you are confident that the two of you are doing the right thing. Unfortunately, you aren't.

Publishers almost always choose—that is, hire and pay—the illustrators for their illustrated books. And let's face it, they know more illustrators than any individual writer does and have experience matching texts with artists. Therefore, the publisher most likely won't like the illustrator you set up. As a result, you might reduce the chances of their responding to your manuscript the way you want them to. Those illustrations might not show the manuscript to its best advantage, or the publisher might not like feeling like they're being told what to do.

Playground Stories

Published illustrator and occasional author Megan Halsey says: "I believe there are 2 types of storytellers in the children's book field …. A writer tells their story using words. An illustrator tells their story using pictures. There are some people who do both successfully but that is a *rare* occurrence." She goes on to say that especially when you're getting started, it's best to stay with the one thing you're good at.

Here's a simple rule of thumb to follow: if you're a writer, don't include illustrations done by someone you know, unless that person is Maurice Sendak. And if you're an illustrator, don't agree to do illustrations for a friend's manuscript unless your friend is

Jane Yolen. To rephrase a popular bumper sticker: "Friends don't ask friends to illustrate their stories."

I Hired Someone

It doesn't happen too often, but there's another scenario worth mentioning, to head you off in case you're considering it. Sometimes writers hire an illustrator in the hope that this will increase the chance that they'll get a story published, or perhaps so they can have more control over how it's illustrated. (As explained later in this chapter, publishers normally don't let an author have too much to say about how a story is illustrated.)

If you're an independently wealthy writer and can afford to hire a designer, an editor, and a copyeditor and pay to have a book printed and distributed, this could be an effective strategy. For submissions to publishers, though, this strategy is no more likely to succeed than hiring your brother-in-law is. In such circumstances, any good illustrator will (and should!) charge a writer thousands of dollars to do the work. He or she will want this money up front, because there's no guarantee the book will ever be published. And even if a writer does find a good illustrator, there's also no guarantee that a publisher will have the same aesthetic tastes.

> **Class Rules**
>
> If you're the illustrator in this scenario, don't even consider it unless you're paid in advance, you can use the work as a way to build your portfolio, and you have a written contract that grants you ownership of the art. Traveling to a national children's book conference or taking a class is a better use of your time and money.

Why Don't You Get Dave Caldecott?

So you've accepted that you can't hire your brother-in-law, but you'd still like some say in how your book looks. Maybe you've heard that a beginning writer is better off if her story is matched with a famous illustrator.

If you're offered a contract, there's no harm making suggestions to your editor. Just don't get too attached to your preferences. Illustrators whom a writer is likely to know—unless you're a children's librarian or reading teacher and spend your days immersed in the latest children's books (lucky you!)—are the top-of-the-heap people, the Caldecott winners, the professionals who've been around for a long time. Even if a publisher agrees that a particular illustrator would be a wonderful choice, these well-known artists are the ones who are least likely to be available.

It's the Publisher's Job

Simply put, the publisher chooses and hires the illustrator. For the writer, this is a blessing and a curse. The writer isn't responsible for finding an illustrator but also can't insist on a particular illustrator.

Many writers see the story as theirs and want the book to follow their vision. If that describes you, try to step back a little. Yes, the story is yours, but turning it into a book is a true team effort, and one that's coordinated by the publisher. In addition to the illustrator, perhaps a dozen or more people are involved in taking what could start out as a 2-page typed manuscript and turning it into a sturdily bound 32-page, full-color book. You'll learn more about some of those people in Chapters 25 through 28.

For now, understand that so much of the time and expense that makes the magic happen is the publisher's responsibility, so it's no wonder the publisher wants to be the one deciding who illustrates a book. And after all, they've got more experience than you do in making that kind of decision.

But I *Want* to Illustrate!

Forget about brothers-in-law and famous illustrators—you want to illustrate your book *yourself*. You've always had some talent, and you don't see why you should split the money you'll be paid with someone else.

For Professionals Only

If you are a professionally trained illustrator, or an unusually adept self-taught one who has taken some classes, you can realistically hope to be considered as the illustrator of your own manuscript. Take one of a few different approaches.

The simplest is to include samples of your work with the manuscript, and mention in your cover letter that you would like to illustrate the manuscript. These samples could be related to the story or not, but in any case, they should be color photocopies or printed samples, sometimes called *tear sheets*. Don't send slides, which are a hassle to deal with, and *never* send original art.

To push even harder for consideration as an illustrator, the best way to show your abilities is to send a *dummy*. Both tear sheets and dummies are defined in more detail in the previous chapter, so refer to Chapter 14 if these options interest you.

Doing all the art for the book won't do more to convince an editor that you're the right person for it. After all, editors usually choose an illustrator before any art for a particular book is done. Doing all the art will just take you extra time—time that could be wasted if another illustrator eventually does the book. Even if you are chosen, you might find that after you start working with the professionals at your publishing company, you have to take a new approach and jettison some or all of the work you already did. In this and all these other scenarios, be prepared to be flexible.

Class Rules

If your illustration abilities aren't up to professional standards, do yourself a favor and don't include them in a submission to a publisher.

Your Best Foot Forward

If you're an illustrator and a writer, as far as a publisher is concerned, you're really two different people. One of you might be the author of a book, and the other might be the illustrator. You might end up working on the same book, but you might not. In this situation, you've got to put your best foot forward—or it might end up firmly in your mouth!

Class Rules

With the exception noted previously, if you want to write and illustrate, you should follow separate paths when contacting publishers.

Often the best way to do that is to have the publisher consider your ability as an illustrator separately from your ability as a writer.

Instructions to the Illustrator?

Okay, you're a writer who accepts that you're not an illustrator and that your job is to write. But you have some instructions you'd like to pass along to the illustrator, or you'd really like to see what he's doing and make sure it fits in with your vision for the book.

Be prepared for a shock. Although policies vary from company to company, many publishers do not allow the author to have contact with the illustrator while he or she is working. If you're an illustrator, you're probably relieved to hear this. You like the freedom to develop your own vision. So what can both of you expect? Some publishers may show the writer the illustrator's sketches, but some won't even do that. How can a writer expect to have an influence? You have a few different paths you can take.

Keep It Out of the Manuscript

Many authors, particularly those who have written a book with very little text and proportionally more reliance on illustrations, want to include guidance for the illustrator for the manuscript. This can range from general instructions as to how the characters "should" look to page-by-page advice on what to illustrate, where to have page breaks, and so on. Including this attempted guidance in a manuscript is a bad idea, however.

Editors and illustrators alike are experienced at reading unadorned manuscripts and envisioning how they would turn into picture books. Experienced authors know this and happily cede control of this area to them. So if an editor sees notes to the illustrator in a manuscript, he or she may assume the author is inexperienced or would struggle with letting the illustrator do his or her job. The editor is likely to remove such notes and is less likely to put the writer in contact with the illustrator.

What's Okay—And What's Not

The writer's voice is heard. A writer's advice may not be followed, of course, but it will be heard. Writers must simply provide their guidance in an appropriate manner. For example, if your story relies on surprise elements in the illustrations, or a page turn at a specific point, you have justification for saying so in a cover letter when you submit it. But if you just have ideas about the color of someone's hair or how a house should look, keep these to yourself until your book is underway, and even then, be prepared to accept that your editor or illustrator may have different ideas. Offer your ideas in a letter or phone call, but don't expect them to be followed.

Can You Keep a Secret?

As you obtain more experience either writing or illustrating, you may have opportunities to work with your counterpart—but don't expect it. At least at the beginning of your career, you'll work separately and the editor will mediate. Just remember that your common goal is to produce the best possible book.

Be Flexible

Writers need to be flexible. If your story is based on childhood memories, offer snapshots as reference materials, but don't expect every detail to be kept the same. The illustrator needs to find an independent vision. If your story calls for characters with different hair colors and you see one as blond, one as brunette, and one black, don't be surprised if the illustrator makes different choices.

Both writer and illustrator must understand that they each bring unique talents to a book's creation. Just as an illustrator cannot expect a writer to revise a manuscript to suit the illustrator, a writer can't expect an illustrator to revise his or her work. These kinds of revisions do happen, of course, but not routinely.

Laying Out the Book

Sometimes it can be useful for you, the author, to lay out the book as it would appear in print. This helps you get a sense of whether you've provided what's needed—sort of the reverse of the exercise of typing up a published picture book text into manuscript form. In this case, you're looking to see if you've created enough different scenes, some of which can be set in the same place, as long as something new happens.

See what happens when you spread out a copy of the manuscript across 28 pages, which are the usable pages in a picture book. In some places, you might put text on every page, while in other places you might put text only on one page of a 2-page spread. Is there enough? Too much? What happens when a page turns? Does the story just continue, or is there a new direction or a surprise? Compare it in your mind to books you've read.

You'll find that you get a better sense of how your manuscript might work in book form with this exercise. Do not, however, send this to an editor as part of a submission. She won't want to see it. Use it, learn from it, but keep it to yourself.

The Exception: Photo Research

In one notable area, publishers not only allow the author to contribute to the illustration process—they sometimes insist on it. This is when the book being created is photo-illustrated. This type of book spans the age ranges, from the photo essay, a nonfiction picture book with minimal to a considerable amount of text, to the photo-illustrated book for middle school or high school children.

When making a submission of a book that is to be photo-illustrated, either because that's the only kind of book the publisher does, or because that's the way you want to see it published and you know that this publisher is open to it, it's okay to include samples and lists of possible sources. You may be required to do the photo research, so the publisher wants to see that you are ready to do the job.

Playground Stories

Nonfiction writer Ginger Wadsworth advises that researching photographs can be just as important as researching information. Find out who controls the right to reproduce a photograph you'd like to use in your book; it could be a private photo agency, a government agency, a historical museum, or an individual. Have a tentative budget ready for the photographs you suggest using, and in many cases publishers will pay the fees or help you pay them. If you're clever, even high fees can be okay, she notes: "Do you want to spend $300 on a picture (the price for the black-and-white cover photo of my book, *Rachel Carson, Voice for the Earth*)? My publisher said yes after I had obtained the right to use several family photos for free."

Let the Magic Happen

Can you imagine *Goodnight Moon* without its familiar and charming bunny family? Of course not. And yet it didn't have to turn out that way—in the early stages of the book's development, the characters were to be humans. The idea of them being bunnies developed later. Almost all books go through changes, of course. The illustrations can really transform a story and make it much more than it was when it was just a manuscript. Noted picture-book author Tony Johnston was pleasantly surprised when G. Brian Karas showed the characters in *Three Little Bikers* as sheep. She hadn't imagined them that way, but they were fun.

So relax. Work on your writing and let that magic happen when it's the illustrator's turn to work.

The Least You Need to Know

- ◆ Writers don't have to provide illustrations to go with their picture-book manuscripts.

- ◆ If you want to illustrate, make sure you measure up to professional standards before sending your work to a publisher.

- ◆ Writers don't need to send all kinds of suggestions and information to an illustrator.

- ◆ The only kind of book for which an author has to work on the illustrations is a photo-illustrated book.

- ◆ Illustrators add unexpected and magical things to a writer's words.

Chapter 16

I Know Somebody Who Knows Somebody ...

In This Chapter

◆ Why calling editors can be a bad idea

◆ How and how *not* to drop names

◆ The value of conferences

◆ Contests as a way to a contract

Many children's publishing companies, particularly the larger and better-known ones, have closed their doors to unsolicited submissions, as explained in Chapter 13. They might accept samples from illustrators but just not turn to them very often. Primarily, they work with people they already know. After spending years honing your skills, reading the latest books, and learning about publishing companies, you are frustrated because you're not one of those "already known" people.

Maybe you think you've got a solution to this problem. Knowing someone is *the* only reliable way to get someone to look at a manuscript or peruse a portfolio, and that's all you need, right? After he does, he'll recognize your brilliance. Or maybe you've come to believe that your work doesn't even have to be brilliant to be published, as long as you have a friend in the business.

There's some truth to all this, but the truth is a little more complicated than you might think. This chapter sorts through the various strategies people have used to finagle their way into the inner sanctum and shows you what might work for you … and what won't.

Closed Doors: How to Pick the Lock

If a publishing company won't read an unsolicited manuscript, it's reasonable to think that the way to get someone to read it is to get someone else to ask for it. If you don't know anyone with connections, what better way to do that than by making a phone call and asking for an editor? Or if you're an illustrator, why not call the art director?

Sounds good, but most editors and art directors just don't like getting calls from people who are eager to sell themselves. These calls are time-consuming, and so many companies instruct receptionists, company operators, and assistants to do everything they can to avoid putting through calls from writers and illustrators they don't know.

Such a call is just another opportunity for an editor to say no, because it's impossible to evaluate a manuscript on the phone, and so sending a letter and a manuscript is a better choice.

You might be wondering if a personal visit to a publishing company might be more effective than a phone call. Unfortunately, if you show up at a publishing company without an appointment, you won't get past the receptionist. You may not even get past the security desk in the lobby. Want to visit *with* an appointment? You'll have to call to make one, and even if you get through to someone, he won't want to take the time to meet with you unless he's already working with you.

Cold calling and knocking on doors, tough techniques in just about any sales job, are not at all effective in children's publishing. Some other ways of making personal contact can be, however, so read on.

> **Playground Stories**
>
> Read a funny and foot-noted version of an imagined phone call to an editor in Wendy McClure's "Let the Mail Prevail! A Guide to Etiquette, Status Calls, and More" at www.underdown. org/etiquet.htm.

A Friend in the Business

Maybe you know someone in the business—another author or illustrator or, best of all, someone who works at a publishing company. Understandably, you want her help, and if you believe in your manuscript as much as I hope you do, you probably believe she'll be happy to give it.

As your friend, she may feel obliged to pass your work on to someone she knows, or perhaps let you mention her name in a cover letter. That might not do much for you if the person she refers you to doesn't know her. You're more likely to get a personal response if you write with a *detailed* or enthusiastic personal endorsement from someone the editor or art director knows—but she will still evaluate your work just as stringently. A friend can help you get a foot in the door, but you won't get through the door unless your work merits it.

Go ahead and use a contact like this if you have one. But don't be a pest to your friend, and realize that she is more likely to be useful to you if you ask her about her experiences. She'll enjoy talking about herself (who doesn't?) and you'll get to increase your knowledge.

> **Class Rules**
>
> When you mention someone in a letter who suggested that you contact an editor or art director, be sure it's someone she actually knows or will recognize the name. I've often received letters proclaiming "so-and-so suggested that I send you the enclosed manuscript. He thinks it would be just right for your list," but I had no idea who that so-and-so was.

A Name on the Envelope

If you don't have an agent (see Chapter 17), does it help to send your manuscript to a specific person, have someone such as your lawyer send it on your behalf, or proclaim your affiliation with a professional organization? Let's examine each scenario to see.

To a Particular Person

Some people believe it helps to have an editor's name on an envelope and go to the effort of calling publishers to get the names of editors if they haven't been able to find them out in other ways. (*Literary Market Place*, among other books, lists staff by name, but gets out of date and doesn't include everyone.) But if the editor doesn't know you, the manuscript is likely to be shunted to the slush pile anyway.

If you do put a name on an envelope, be sure you've spelled it correctly. Be sure that editor still works there—don't rely on 3-year-old writer's guides. And don't put a letter to one publisher into an envelope that's addressed to another. (I've seen it happen.)

> **Can You Keep a Secret?**
>
> Who reads their own mail? Who needs to find exciting new authors so they can move up? Assistant and associate editors, that's who. If you have the name of someone at this level, because it was mentioned in a newsletter or at a conference or someone you know knows the person, use it. The less-established editors want to hear from you.

Some folks take what looks like a creative approach and contact the head of a division or company, or even someone in the marketing department. In the first case, the hope is that the big boss will pass the letter on, and that because the letter comes from him or her, it will then be treated with more care. Sorry, but those manuscripts and samples are treated like everything else and sometimes sit around for weeks in the head honcho's office. In the second case, you might be trying to excite someone in the marketing department, who will then send it along with an endorsement. This is not a good idea. People in marketing have their own jobs to do, and these just get passed along, too—if they aren't simply thrown out.

I'm a Member of ...

Some writers and illustrators mention their membership in professional organizations and may even note them on their envelopes. This tactic can help in some cases, particularly if you belong to the Society of Children's Book Writers and Illustrators (SCBWI) in the United States or the Canadian Society of Children's Authors, Illustrators, and Performers (CANSCAIP) in Canada, the two national children's writers and illustrators organizations (see Appendix B for information on how to join).

A few publishers with closed doors actually open them to members of these organizations, on the reasonable assumption that someone who belongs to one of them has been working on his writing and learning about the market for a little while and so is more likely to be sending something interesting and well targeted. If you belong to another, less-relevant organization, such as the National Writer's Union or the Graphic Artist's Guild, it may not hurt to mention it, but it won't earn you any credibility.

Conferences and Schmoozing

Perhaps the best way to make contact with an editor (and less frequently, an art director) is to go to a conference like those sponsored by the SCBWI and other organizations and actually meet someone.

> ### Playground Stories
>
> Marilyn Singer's first three books were signed up and published in quick succession. Her fourth, *It Can't Hurt Forever*, was not: "If there's one thing a writer must have, it's perseverance. And luck. And *contacts*. I went to my first SCBWI conference and met Liz Gordon, then an editor at Harper & Row (later to become HarperCollins). I introduced myself and asked if I could send her some stuff. She said yes, and off went the novels. Back came a note. Was I was willing to do extensive revisions on *It Can't Hurt Forever?* ... I revised my novel and Harper published it."

Meeting Editors at Conferences

Meeting editors at conferences really can work for you. But there are ways to do this, and ways not to do this. Understand from the beginning that editors do not enjoy being besieged by eager authors. They do expect to meet people at conferences, but they don't respond well to pitches or to manuscripts thrust in their hands (or slid under the door of their bathroom stall, as has happened). They particularly don't like it when someone relentlessly promotes himself, badgers them for advice about his 300-page story about his puppy, or plunks down next to them at lunch and attempts to lock everyone else out of the conversation.

There are always one or two people like that at conferences, and they may succeed in getting the editor's attention, but not his respect. Be polite, and don't expect someone to take your work home with him; write to him after the conference.

Remember, too, that a conference is not an opportunity for a one-time smash-and-grab raid. In the long run, you'll do even better to get involved with the organization sponsoring the conference. You'll get to know more editors if you help plan a conference than if you only attend one, and you're more likely to impress them with your professionalism, too. Most editors have published writers they met at conferences, but they are usually the folks who've been in it for the long haul, not the ones who show up at just one conference.

Trade Show Tips

Editors also may attend trade shows at which publishers show off their books to booksellers, librarians, or other organizations of people interested in children's books. These shows are a great place to go to find all the latest children's books under one roof, all organized by publisher. They are *not* a great place to go to meet editors, with the possible exception of the American Library Association (ALA). Even at the ALA convention, editors may be looking after their published authors or attending meet-ings, and although they may be polite and listen to a pitch if they aren't busy, they'll have forgotten it by the time they leave for the day.

If you go to a trade show, don't try to share your manuscript or art samples with people in the booth. They are very busy dealing with customers, and even if they do accept your materials, they are likely to be lost or discarded when the show closes. Take catalogs and guidelines, if available, and use the show to find out about pub-lishers you didn't know, but a show is not a place to sell a manuscript or leave an art sample.

Faking a Contact

I mention the option of faking a contact—claiming you met an editor when you didn't, pretending to have been referred by a famous writer, or some other ruse—in a cover letter only to urge you *not* to do this. If you're found out, you can forget about working with that publisher, or, if you are found out later, you'll destroy the trust that had built up. Even if you're not found out, you'll be worried that you will be, and you'll never be entirely comfortable. And of course, making up things like this is just wrong.

Win a Prize!

Some companies sponsor contests, which you can find out about in *Children's Writer's and Illustrator's Market* and similar guides. For example, the small but respected mul-ticultural publisher Lee and Low sponsors the New Voices Award for picture-book fiction. Delacorte offers a similar prize at the other end of the age spectrum: the Delacorte Press Prize for a First Young Adult Novel. This award allowed Christopher Paul Curtis, winner of the 2000 Newbery Medal, to get his foot in the door. Even if you don't win in a contest like this, if you enter, your manuscript will be read and you may hear from someone.

In addition to publishers' contests, organizations like the SCBWI offer grants, some of which unpublished authors can win and use as a credential in a submission.

Useful but Not Essential

In the end, all these ways to find or create or make use of a contact can be useful, but it's possible to get yourself discovered without a contact, too. To some extent, the way you choose to submit your manuscripts or sample illustrations should suit your personality.

Do you think there's a right way to do things or there's one right publisher for you? Can you be stubborn in going after that? After you find that one right publisher and start to correspond, keep at it.

Are you a people person? Do you enjoy meeting and getting to know people? Then spend some time going to writer's conferences and other events. Don't try to hand a manuscript to every publishing insider you meet. Talk to them and find out what they do. Keep in touch with them. Later, when you have the right kind of manuscript for them, you can send it to them. Or if it's not right for them, maybe they can tell you who it's right for. I know several authors who got published this way.

> **Playground Stories**
>
> It took Bruce Balan a year and a half to convince Green Tiger Press (a small company now gone in a merger) that his submission was right for them, but eventually they accepted his manuscript.

Are you systematic? Then do your research. Set up lists of publishers to contact and go down the list. Keep at it until you make a contact or decide you need a new system.

There are as many ways of getting published as there are people. Just stick with it, and don't be discouraged by initial rejections.

The Least You Need to Know

- ◆ Phone calls and office visits don't help you make contact with an editor or art director.

- ◆ Putting a name on the envelope or in your cover letter is only useful in certain circumstances.

- ◆ Attending conferences and contests are good ways to make contacts.

- ◆ Faking a contact or going out of your way to create a contact isn't worth your while. It's possible to be published without knowing someone.

Chapter 17

I Need an Agent!

In This Chapter

- ◆ Understanding what literary agents and artist's representatives do
- ◆ Do you need—and are you ready for—an agent or rep?
- ◆ Why it's difficult to get an agent or a rep
- ◆ How and where to find agents and reps

At some point in your career as an author or illustrator, having an agent in your corner can look like a very good thing. In this chapter, I show you what agents do, help you decide whether or not you really need one, and give you info on how to find one.

Secret Agents

Not too long ago, children's book agents were pretty uncommon. I'm talking about the 1960s, when authors and illustrators generally represented themselves. Those children's book agents who did exist typically worked for a larger agency and may have handled clients in other areas, too. Not enough money was being paid to children's book illustrators and writers to support more than a few agents.

def•i•ni•tion

A **literary agent** acts on your behalf, selecting and writing to publishers with your manuscript, negotiating with the publisher, and generally going to bat for you. Some also work with you to help you develop your career. An **artist's representative,** or *artist's rep*, gets your samples out to publishers and otherwise acts much like an agent.

But oh, how times have changed. Publishers have grown busier, our genteel little business has become more profitable, and now people can make a living as agents for children's book writers or *artist's representatives.* On hearing about all the closed doors in children's publishing, in fact, many authors and illustrators decide they need to get a *literary agent* or an artist's representative. After all, they reason, the rules against unsolicited submissions some publishers have don't apply to agents. Provided that the agent is someone a publisher knows (which isn't always the case because anyone can call himself an agent), submissions from an agent are treated with respect.

What's in It for You?

Of course, an agent doesn't only help you get your foot in the door. What does an agent do? Agent Jennie Dunham of Dunham Literary notes three main functions:

◆ *Submit material to publishers*   Agents can submit manuscripts to any publisher and know who to submit to from their full-time, firsthand experience.

◆ *Negotiate contracts*   Agents understand the terms and may have the clout to get a better deal than an individual author can do.

◆ *Collect monies and distribute them*   Agents handle payments from multiple publishers and check royalty statements.

Artist's reps do similar work. They typically make sure the right publishers see your work with several sample mailings per year and annual personal visits with art directors and editors. When asked, they follow up with more print samples and books or suggest possible artists for a manuscript or program need. They also negotiate your contracts and handle invoicing and payments from publishers.

An agent may withhold some of the rights associated with a manuscript, as explained in Chapter 23, but rights to illustrations are more likely to stay with the publisher because they can't easily be sold independently of the text.

What's in It for Them?

For this work, an agent or a rep gets a commission from you. Agents typically charge 15 percent, although a few still charge what used to be the standard 10 percent.

Artist's reps receive higher commissions of 25 or 30 percent because their expenses are higher. (They share in the cost of buying directory pages and pay for printing and postage on mailings.)

With the exception of the commission, all this sounds great, doesn't it? The question is, should you take time out from sending manuscripts and samples to publishers to send them to agents so you'll have someone who will be sending your work to publishers for you?

To Agent or Not to Agent?

Indeed, agents open doors. But first you must open theirs, and that's a challenge, too. Finding someone to represent you can be more difficult than finding a publisher, because the established, reputable agents and reps are as selective about new clients as publishers are with new authors, if not more so. They have to be selective because usually they represent all of your work, while you might work with two, three, or even more publishers over the course of a few years.

> **Playground Stories** _____
>
> Agent Sandy Ferguson Fuller of the Alps Arts Co. says: "I think the decision whether or not to contract with an agent is a very personal one. In today's market, it is probably advantageous to have an agent to 'get in the door' if you're able to convince a reputable, experienced agent to take on your work. ... That is *not* to say that a writer can't tackle the market without an agent. If an individual has the time, desire, and savvy to research potential publishers, make the contracts, and submit in accordance with guidelines, many publishers still can be approached without an agent."

In fact, many of the best reps and agents admit to having a "referrals only" policy on new clients, meaning their doors are closed as tightly as the doors of the publishers you want them to open for you. They'll only look at someone who comes to them with the endorsement of an existing client or publisher. These same agents and reps often go on to insist that they're still open to someone with unique qualities—if you can get that referral or personal contact.

Before you start to feel irritated with this apparent lack of helpfulness, consider the sad fact that most agents and reps have as many clients as they can handle and may receive thousands of contacts annually, partly the result of closed doors at publishers. People often try to use agents and reps as the entry point to publishers, even when they're not ready for one. One agent I know tells me that she gets about 200 queries from possible clients per week—and she'll maybe take on a handful of new clients a year. Agents can't do their job for the existing clients if they don't close their doors; they'd end up spending all their time dealing with their mail and e-mail.

The situation is somewhat different for authors and illustrators, so consider the following before you decide what to do.

Now or Later?

Your ability to find an agent might depend on the kind of writing you do. Nonfiction, especially for the institutional market, does not earn large advances and get high sales numbers, so many authors in this area represent themselves. Picture-book authors, because they split royalties with an illustrator, are also less likely to have an agent. Conversely, good fiction writers are relatively more attractive to an agent, especially if their work is strong enough to garner interest from multiple editors—possibly leading to an auction, which agents love. (You'll love them too, if one of your books is auctioned!)

Class Rules

Don't even bother to contact an agent if you don't have a good backlog of unsubmitted material.

Before trying to land yourself an agent, it's important to ask yourself if you're ready for one. Do you have several publishable manuscripts complete and ready for submission? Agents want to represent someone with a career in front of them, not a one-shot wonder. They particularly don't like being offered a manuscript that's dog-eared from making the rounds.

Are you ready to commit to working with an agent over the course of several years? Unless you're a bad personality match or have conflicting ideas about what approach to take, expect to work with your agent for some time. Don't expect an agent to take you on a trial basis. They want to help you build a career and to share in the fruits of that effort.

Info for Illustrators

Illustrators might need to be represented more than authors do, and more published illustrators do seem to have reps. The main reason for this is the overall market for illustrators is different from the market for writers. Both work on trade books, but the textbook market is a much larger one for illustrators than it is for writers. Writing in textbooks is often done in-house or by teachers on a for-hire basis. And sometimes, excerpts from existing trade books are used. However, textbook publishers, when working on a major new textbook program, may want literally hundreds of pieces of new, high-quality illustration, done to often quite precise specifications, in a short period of time. They can't take the time to sift through the samples of individual illustrators, so they tend to turn to artist's representatives, either directly or via the design studios doing the basic design work on the books. When this work is available, it keeps a lot of illustrators busy.

For the most part, though, you can't get this work unless you have a rep. A rep, when contacted by a textbook publisher, can suggest illustrators for a large number of different illustrations and can vouch that each of them will deliver on time, and deliver work that's as good as their samples promise. The textbook publishers like this because they know what they'll be getting, and they can take care of a batch of illustrations more quickly than by contacting illustrators one at a time.

So much textbook work is available that even reps who spend most of their time marketing their clients to trade houses tell me that more of their income—meaning more of their clients' income, too—comes from educational projects than from trade ones. Educational illustration not only pays well, it can also be a good training ground for the more time-consuming (and, let's face it, prestigious) work needed to create picture books.

So illustrators are well advised to seek out a rep, and you'll be pleased to know that they will mostly be prepared to work with you, even if you're just getting started. Do not contact them, however, unless you are ready for them. Here are some questions Chris Tugeau asks in an article on her firm's website:

◆ Can you draw and paint well? (I regularly see many who don't!)

◆ Is your work quality truly professional and competitive with what you are seeing in good picture books and educational program books?

◆ Do you have a style that reproduces well and easily?

◆ Are your characters uniquely yours, but also potentially appealing to the art buyers *and* the public?

◆ Can you afford to do your style for industry-norm pay scales? (If your approach is too time-consuming, you may not be able to make a living with it.)

◆ Do you have published work to show? (We don't make a dime if we don't get you work, and having *had* work is of practical interest.)

◆ Do you have at least 10 to 15 wonderful pieces for a portfolio, duplicates to send out, printed "keeper" cards/pages, and money to spend on pages in industry promotional books? (Reps get discounted prices and contribute something as well.)

◆ Do you have a fax and e-mail (essential) and can you send JPEG samples to the agent or buyers? (This is becoming more essential.)

◆ Are you good with specs, directions, and deadlines?

◆ Can you really listen to and accept criticism and revisions of your work and concepts?

If you can answer yes to all those questions, you may be ready for a rep.

Can You Keep a Secret?

Some illustrators have an agent, not an artist's rep. Why do they do that? As one of them told me, "I write as well as illustrate. Agents deal with editors, reps often deal only with art directors .... Second is the potential for secondary rights and reversions to be sold through an agent. Most artist's reps do one-time sales, [and] do not follow up on other markets." She notes, too, that she's not interested in textbook or other for-hire work, and that she's a bit too "artsy" for most reps.

Whatever you decide, remember that the time you spend trying to find an agent or rep, a search that may not succeed, could be time spent on trying to find a publisher. For this reason, even if you do decide to try to find someone to represent you, don't stop contacting publishers directly yourself.

Getting to Solla Sollew

Looking for an agent or a rep can be like the Dr. Seuss book *I Had Trouble in Getting to Solla Sollew*. In that book, a very determined and angry character overcomes enormous obstacles to get to a place where there are no problems, "or at least, very few." When she does get there, she discovers that in fact the only problem is that she can't get in.

It's easy to believe that if someone is representing you, all your troubles are over. They aren't. Your agent may not be any more successful at placing your manuscript or finding you illustration work than you are. You may not agree with the approach the rep is taking, or the rep may offer you too little guidance with your work, or too much.

It's best to go into a relationship with an agent or a rep with your eyes wide open and your expectations reasonable. Be sure to have a written contract with them. (Most will offer this as a matter of routine.) You are entering into an important professional relationship, one that's potentially closer than with any one publisher. You can work for several different publishers, but you're only going to work with one agent at a time.

Where *Are* They?

If you decide you want to have an agent, use resources such as *Children's Writer's and Illustrator's Market* or Ellen Shapiro's *Writer's & Illustrator's Guide to Children's Book Publishers and Agents* to locate them. Do your homework before you contact them and be prepared to ask questions.

It's reasonable for you to ask them about what they will be doing for you, but only after they've expressed interest in representing you. Nothing turns off an agent faster than someone calling them and asking questions that they could have found answers to in a standard reference book or on the agent's own website. The Association of Author Representatives (AAR) has a list of questions you can use.

Find out not only their commission structures but what costs they pass on to you. If they want to charge a reading fee before they'll look at your manuscript, run, do not walk, to the nearest exit. Agents can legitimately pass on some expenses, but those charging reading fees are not living on their commissions, which is what you want them to do.

Can You Keep a Secret?

When looking for an agent, ask about fees, other clients, and if the agent belongs to the Association of Author's Representatives (AAR)—although some reputable agents do *not* belong. AAR's website (www.aar-online.org) includes several useful resources including its Canon of Ethics, suggested questions to ask of an agent, and member's list.

Illustrators can visit the website of the Society of Photographers and Artists Representatives (SPAR), at www.spar.org/index.html, and find lists of artist's representatives.

Of course, you should also talk to other writers and artists, attend conferences, and follow other paths that may lead you toward finding the rep you want. That may be the only way to get in touch with an agent whose doors are otherwise closed. But just remember that having a rep won't land you in Solla Sollew.

The Least You Need to Know

◆ Agents and artist's representatives send your work to publishers and negotiate contracts on your behalf.

◆ Artist's representatives charge higher commissions due to higher expenses.

◆ Carefully consider whether you need or are ready for an agent before trying to find one.

◆ An artist's representative can get an illustrator work in educational publishing that he or she could not otherwise get.

◆ Use book and Internet resources to help you with your search for an agent or rep.

Part 4

Understanding Publishers

The publishing world, the world you want to enter, is a complicated one. In Part 4, you learn about various types of publishers and the difference between books for series and books that work best as individual titles.

Part 4 also explores some publishers and their catalogs and then looks beyond them to some areas within the children's market that aren't so well known. Finally, this part explains just how important *you* are to publishers.

Chapter 18

Apple, Orange, or Banana? Just One or a Bunch?

In This Chapter

- Getting to know mass-market, trade, and institutional publishers
- Series versus single titles
- Why these differences matter to you

You can tell a picture book from a novel at 20 paces. You've polished your manuscript or sweated over your illustration samples. But do you know what kind of publisher you need to target?

Different publishers have different needs, and those differences do matter—and some publishers don't even want to hear from you at all! In this and the rest of the chapters in Part 4, I show you the different kinds of children's publishers and the books they publish.

Apples and Oranges—and Bananas? Kinds of Books

Children's publishers don't all sell their books to the same customers. Different customers want different kinds of books, and different kinds of publishers produce books for all those customers. As you learned in

Chapter 1, the three basic kinds of publishers are trade, mass-market, and institutional (sometimes called educational) publishers. The names come from the market areas in which they sell their books.

You know the saying "That's comparing apples and oranges"? Well, comparing trade, mass-market, and institutional books is like that ... although you have to add bananas.

Apples: Trade Books

When publishers talk about "trade" books, they're talking about books for a general readership. These books are usually higher quality, usually more expensive, and usually sold in bookstores (the book trade), with some also going to schools and libraries. Take note of the *usually*s because there can be overlap. Trade publishers are the "quality" publishers.

Trade books aren't just published in hardcover. Trade paperbacks are usually larger, better quality, and more expensive than their mass-market cousins. It's even possible for the same book to be published in a trade paperback and a mass-market paperback. You'll usually find the trade version in a good bookstore and the mass-market one in a drugstore or supermarket rack.

Generally, trade publishers seek the "good" books I mentioned in Chapter 9. And in general, they and the institutional publishers are the ones you want to contact because they need original work. Although they're quite successful, mass-market publishers don't need originality.

Oranges: For the Masses

To find out what mass-market publishers do need, look at the other end of the book-publishing spectrum. You can find mass-market books in budget retail establishments like Wal-Mart and Target, as well as in supermarkets. The big difference between mass market and trade is cost. This is not the world of the $24.95 hardcover. This is where you find pocket-size paperbacks for $7.99.

Welcome to the world of mass market. These books are low-end, high-volume titles. No frills. No fancy book jackets. They are oranges, in short, and very different from those trade apples.

These are some of the books commonly found in the mass market:

◆ Less costly versions of books originally published in trade

◆ New books based on well-known characters, such as Curious George or Peter Rabbit

- Books with tie-ins to TV shows, movies, even websites, such as *Dora the Explorer* or *Shrek* or Neopets

- Brand-name spin-offs, from Cheerios to Barbie

- Betcha-can't-read-just-one series books, from Berenstain Bears to Gossip Girls

Opportunities for creative types are limited in this area. Mass-market publishers do produce original books, especially novelty books, but they usually do the writing themselves. And whether they're putting together the latest series of stories based on a Nickelodeon hit or repackaging acclaimed hardcovers in inexpensive editions, these publishers don't want your original work. They might hire you to turn out a dozen stories featuring their characters.

Illustrators might do better, although you may find you can only get work through an artist's rep and that your creativity is strictly limited. The companies controlling the characters being licensed usually have the power to approve how they're depicted, and they aren't going to let a character from *Sesame Street*, for example, look or act differently in print from the way he or she does on the screen.

Bananas? The Institutional Market

As if the apples and oranges of trade and mass-market publishing weren't complicated enough, you also need to take note of publishers that concentrate on schools and libraries, or the institutional market.

Institutional publishers typically produce books that sell almost exclusively to schools and libraries, and often come in special sturdy bindings, without jackets. Just to make things more complicated, you may occasionally find their books in bookstores, too. You'll find clues to a publisher's identity in their catalog, so be sure to study how to read one in Chapter 19.

Institutional publishing are those series of biographies, country profiles, and the like that children turn to for good, solid information. These are the books published by companies such as Lerner or Enslow. Browse a library's children's nonfiction section and you'll find many examples.

Can You Keep a Secret?
The institutional market is sometimes also called the educational market. I don't use that name, though, because these companies aren't just selling to schools, and textbook publishers are the true educational publishers

So needs and interests vary among these three types of publishers. Before I move on to those needs and interests, you need to get a grasp of series and how publishers handle them.

Series: One Book or a Bunch?

Like fruit, books can come singly or in a bunch. Institutional and mass-market publishers are more prone to publish in *series* than trade publishers are.

What's the difference between writing a single book and developing a series? Consider a bunch of bananas. Each banana is different in some ways but similar in shape, color, flavor, and so on. Books in a series are no different. Each book contains new content yet continues with the same overall approach—style, setting, theme, format, characters, or purpose. The books hang together like bananas in a bunch.

def•i•ni•tion

Books linked in theme, purpose, characters, style, setting, or content are part of a **series**. Each subsequent book in the series continues one or more of these elements. Often the series also has a title, just as a book does. For example, this book is part of the *Complete Idiot's Guide* series.

Many writers see series in stores and libraries and think they'd like to publish that way, which might explain why editors at trade publishers continue to receive letters and manuscripts from authors who have written 1 story—or perhaps who just have an *idea* for 1 story—and are proposing a 24-book series. Editors may reject those proposals because the author doesn't actually have a good idea for a series. More likely, the author sent the idea to a publisher that doesn't publish *any* series.

Class Rules

Editors at trade publishers don't like to see manuscripts proudly presented as the "first book in a series" because they primarily publish single titles. If a book is a phenomenal success, they might want to do another; however, at the beginning, publishers prefer for authors to put their energy into 1 book instead of planning the first 12.

Series or Single Title?

Every series begins with one book but not every book is part of a series, nor can it be. In fact, the vast majority of titles published for children are single titles, and so they should remain.

Many authors write only this kind of book, and many fine children's books started as one book and remained so. Consider such Caldecott Medal–winning titles as *Mirette on a High Wire* by Emily Arnold McCully, Peggy Rathmann's *Officer Buckle and Gloria*, or Allen Say's *Grandfather's Journey*. Each have compelling characters, but they were published as single titles and, in spite of their success, have not spawned a series.

Don't assume that a book with one or more sequels is part of a series. Although sequels may feature many of the same characters as the first book, a series goes on much longer. The five books in Lloyd Alexander's *Prydain Chronicles* are more of a set than a series.

I Didn't Mean to Do That: The Unintended Series

Say you wrote a book and never even considered that it would evolve into a series. But what if that one book becomes so "tickling" that kids yearn for more? What if the concept is so engaging that the public wants more? That's exactly what happened with Laura Numeroff's delightful picture book *If You Give a Mouse a Cookie*. Kids loved the idea of "if, then" that Numeroff explored. Finally, after many antics, the mouse comes full circle and returns to the beginning and the cookie.

Children immediately embraced the simple concept and funny actions of the story's little mouse and child and wanted more. Numeroff responded with *If You Give a Moose a Muffin*, *If You Give a Pig a Pancake*, and *If You Give a Cat a Cupcake*. The author's single title resulted in a short series—an unintended series. Of course, this doesn't happen very often. When it does, it starts with one book, done well.

Okay, Time to Get *Series*

Where are the series, if not in trade publishing? Mass-market fiction is home to one kind of series. Consider one of the most popular children's book series of all time: the *Nancy Drew Mystery Stories*. In the series, our sleuthing teen unravels tales of the unknown and uncovers mysteries. Each story involves a different plot and scenario, but two common elements—Nancy and a mystery—remain throughout the series.

Style, format, and length also do not vary. For lengthy series such as *Nancy Drew*, which are developed by independent companies called *packagers* or *development houses*,

def•i•ni•tion

A **packager**, or **development house**, is much like a publisher, except its work stops with the completion of a manuscript, or in some cases with the printing of the books. A publisher puts its name on the books and handles the sales and marketing.

there might even be a "bible"—a notebook detailing all the character quirks, dress guidelines, history, and other information—to ensure consistency from book to book. Other well-known fiction series such as *Goosebumps* or *Sweet Valley High* have similar characteristics.

Mass market is a very different world from the more prestigious trade-publishing world, and the kind of writing an author does for a series is different from writing for single titles. Single-title books can stand on their own. Books written for a series, especially for a planned series, often don't stand alone. Or all the books tell essentially the same story, providing comforting and satisfying familiarity by rerunning the same plot, with minor variations, over and over again. To learn more, look in industry magazines such as *Publishers Weekly*, which run occasional features on the latest series.

Back to the Bananas: School and Library Publishers

Not all series books fit into the fun category like the *Animorphs* or *The Boxcar Children* books. Some series books are downright bookish—almost *text*bookish! Nonfiction series titles that publishers develop specifically for schools and libraries are the bread-and-butter of institutional publishers. Not surprisingly, some knowledge of school curriculums comes in very handy if you want to publish in this area.

These series come in different forms. Some are short and focus on a specific subject area, such as 12 books on 12 different habitats. Others are identified by a specific design, length, and vocabulary level, such as Children's Press's *True Books*. This series consists of hundreds of titles, grouped into subseries on subjects such as national parks, continents, and transportation. Or one subject area, such as biographies, will be the focus of an ongoing series that continues to add titles.

Series nonfiction generally doesn't pay well, but it can be a training ground. Noted writers like Seymour Simon started out writing series books for Franklin Watts, an institutional publisher. Now he publishes with top-level trade publishers.

The writing experience itself may also be different from writing for trade publishers. When asked whether he found writing for publishers like Children's Press different from or similar to writing for trade publishers, Larry Brimner, the author of *Brave Mary*, *Dinosaurs Dance*, *E-Mail*, *A Migrant Family*, and many others, first pointed out a difference that's not as great as it used to be: "There was a time when one could look at books published by educational publishers and identify them by their appearance. They looked 'text-bookish,' as if they belonged in schools. Today, thankfully, this is largely no longer the case." However, he says that any manuscript that doesn't fit into an existing series or serve to launch a new one will be a very hard sell. Also, the publisher's focus on the school market might limit what an author can do, in terms of both subject matter and artistic expression. Trade publishers generally allow a wider range of writing style than publishers that must meet curriculum guidelines. Writing for institutional publishers can be different from working with trade publishers. Keep this in mind, and you're less likely to be disappointed.

Getting Your Idea to the Right Publisher

If you've concluded that you do indeed have a viable idea for a series, you next need to take care in getting it to a publisher. Choose the kind of publisher carefully, of course, by researching their program to be sure they publish the types of books you envision. For the more mass-market fiction series such as *Goosebumps*, look to packagers rather than publishers. You'll find information about specific packagers and publishers in market guides such as *Children's Writer's and Illustrator's Market*.

Then you probably need to send in a proposal. The following chapters discuss in more detail how to write to publishers and send them manuscripts. Sending a proposal isn't too different, but a proposal is more than just a letter and a manuscript. Check the publisher's guidelines to find out what they want in a proposal; you'll probably need to include a plan for a number of additional books in the series, a statement about the overall focus of the series, and some evidence that this particular idea will succeed.

Previous experience writing similar books is almost a necessity, and not just as something to mention in your letter. If you haven't written for a previously existing series, which gives you insight into how a series is put together, you'll find it almost impossible to propose and execute a new series successfully.

> **Playground Stories** _____
>
> Bruce Balan, author of the *Cyber.kdz* series, notes that there are always exceptions to the "rules": "A fiction series requires a proposal that will sell your idea to an editor. As editors see thousands of these proposals, yours must stand out. ... I sold 'Cyber.kdz' with a proposal that was written as a series of e-mail communications between myself and the fictional kids of the books .... I was told repeatedly that it was impossible to sell a series without prior series-writing experience as well as middle-grade fiction experience (for a middle-grade series). I had neither."

If you're an unpublished author, you might not get anywhere, no matter how good your idea. You need credentials, so if you want to write a series, your best bet may be to develop your chops as a writer by writing other books first—perhaps single titles or contributing to existing series. Many packagers hire writers to actually write the books in a series after the series author outlines them. Many institutional publishers extend some of their series with new books from other authors. Look around and learn about the world of series before jumping into it, and you're more likely to succeed.

The Boundaries Are Blurring

You've got it all figured out, right? You know about institutional, trade, and mass-market publishers, and you know that you need to account for their very different needs when you deal with them.

Don't hold on to those distinctions too tightly! Things change in publishing, and the boundaries are continually blurring. Lately, publishers are producing "high-end" mass-market books, also known as "mass with class," which can just as easily sit in Borders as in Wal-Mart. These books, although still softcover, are made from high-quality materials.

At the same time, trade publishers are creating inexpensive versions of their books and reaching into the mass market. Perhaps not as inexpensive as a generic coloring book, but certainly less than the $15 price of a hardcover, these books run the gamut from classics like *Goodnight Moon*, priced reasonably at about $6, to *Blue's Costume Party*, a $4 stapled softcover based on the popular Nickelodeon character.

As a result, it's not as easy as it used to be to get a sense of what a publisher's doing, because it might be doing a lot of things at once. You need to work harder to find the right home for your manuscript.

The Least You Need to Know

- Books may be published as either a trade title, a mass-market book, or an institutional title.

- Series are usually published by mass-market and institutional publishers, not by trade publishers.

- You have to approach different kinds of publishers differently.

- Lately, the lines are blurring between trade and mass market.

Chapter 19

The Publishing Maze

In This Chapter

- ◆ The difference between a publishing house and its imprints
- ◆ Why you must submit manuscripts one at a time, not simultaneously
- ◆ Choosing an imprint that's right for you
- ◆ Analyzing publishers' catalogs

Once you've learned about kinds of publishers (see Chapter 18), it's time to choose ones that interest you. But publishing houses come in many sizes, shapes, and structures. Some have one simple name. Others have different divisions. Still others not only have divisions but also may have several imprints within each division. How can you find the right part of the company?

In this chapter, you learn how the larger publishing companies group different minipublishing houses under the umbrella of the overall company. You also learn about the books major and smaller independent publishers put out from an examination of their catalogs.

Companies, Divisions, and Imprints

It's overwhelming enough to think about the hundreds of publishing companies to learn about, but you'll quickly notice that many of them seem to contain separate entities with their own names.

So where do you send your manuscript or illustrations? To the company as a whole? To its children's book division? Or to even smaller parts of the company, which, strangely enough, all have their own names? It can be enough to make you want to turn to the self-publishing chapter!

What's an Imprint?

The smallest subdivisions in a publishing house are usually called *imprints*. An imprint is literally the name that appears on the title page and spine of a book, such as Dell Yearling or Viking Books. Both of those are parts of larger companies, in these cases Random House and Penguin, respectively. Each imprint usually has its own editorial staff, and sometimes its own marketing staff, but shares all the other resources of the company. Still, the company hopes that each imprint has a separate, recognizable identity, kind of like a brand name. When you think of Pepperidge Farm Goldfish, you think of a tasty crunchy snack. When you think of Atheneum Books for Young Readers, what do you think of? Maybe nothing in particular, but a bookseller or a librarian might have a distinct idea.

def•i•ni•tion

An **imprint** is a part of a publisher with a distinct identity, name, and staff, usually concentrating on a distinct type or mix of books.

Sometimes an imprint is started from scratch and given a name intended to reflect its identity. Sometimes it carries a name that used to exist as an independent company, now absorbed into a larger one. Other times, it has the name of a noted editor, making it a "personal imprint," with books that reflect that editor's taste. In all these cases, the imprint has a name that is meant to give it an identity and its books credibility.

An imprint is not a division, which is usually a larger administrative body. Several imprints might make up the children's division of a larger company. Nor is it a "line." A line is usually a part of an imprint, such as the easy-to-read line of Typical Children's Books, which also has a picture-book line and a nonfiction line. And a line is not the same as a series; several series might be grouped together as a line. For writers and illustrators, it's the imprint that matters.

Confused? Don't worry. It'll start to make sense as you get to know the companies, and the in-depth look later in this chapter into two catalogs will help.

One at a Time, Please

You need to understand what an imprint is because you send your work to individual imprints, not the company division (too general), or line (too specific). Blue Sky Press and Cartwheel Books, for example, are two imprints at Scholastic—and very different, as you'll see if you look at their books or catalogs. You'd usually send your work to one of the imprints, not Scholastic. If that imprint isn't interested, it will return it to you and usually won't share it with other imprints at the same company.

There are limits to the independence of imprints, however. Most companies don't want their imprints to compete with each other. It's okay to send a manuscript to several different *companies* at once, but don't send it to two *imprints* at the *same* company at the same time.

There are also exceptions to the general rule that imprints have separate staffs, and that's another reason not to send manuscripts to multiple imprints at the same publisher. Smaller publishers, such as Charlesbridge and Boyds Mills Press, may set up imprints that share staff or have a system of passing manuscripts to a suitable imprint. Check on this. It's a waste of your effort to send a manuscript to more than one imprint when that's the case.

Class Rules

Never send the same manuscript to two imprints at the same company. They can't both acquire it, and management at the company will prevent them from competing for it. On the other hand, it may be okay to send art samples to different imprints within the same company, if they don't share staff. Always check the imprint's guidelines.

Door Number One or Door Number Two?

You might be inclined to send your manuscript or art samples to any imprint that publishes children's books, but slow down. One reason a publisher sets up imprints is to specialize and narrow the focus of each. Imprints typically have tight guidelines about the type of books each produces. (Although in some cases, that type might be a carefully designed mix, from young picture books to YA novels.)

Say two imprints at one company both produce children's books with historical themes. You just wrote a young adult novel based on a boy serving in the Civil War. Your book contains historical facts woven into an edgy, realistic tale. At first you think, *Hey, I'll send my manuscript to both imprints—one at a time, of course!*

Unfortunately for you, you didn't dig deep enough. One imprint only produces books for the institutional market, with an emphasis on historical fact. The other only produces picture books based on history. Your young adult title, although extremely good, doesn't fit either imprint, and sending it to either of them wastes your time and theirs.

For illustrators, different art styles suit different publishers. If you work in a more painterly, fine-art type of style, your home is likely to be in trade publishing. If your style is cute and cartoon-y, you might find that mass-market or textbook publishing is the place to be. Investigate before sending out mailings, and you'll save money and follow-up time by not sending materials to companies that just won't be interested.

> ### Can You Keep a Secret?
>
> A publisher's guidelines will tell you a little about the imprint and how to submit manuscripts or art samples to it. And they may tell you how to get a copy of a catalog. Or try searching for the publisher online; many companies now make their guidelines and complete catalogs available on the web.

To be sure you choose the right imprint, you have to do research. Get the imprint's guidelines, which usually start with a short statement about the kinds of books it publishes. Go to a bookstore and browse for books with that imprint's name on them.

Even better, take a look at the imprint's catalog, which might be part of a larger catalog for the company to which the imprint belongs. You'll find more useful and specific information there than if you call and query some assistant about the kinds of books they publish. The busy assistant will give a brief and general description of the program. But the catalog will be full of information you can use to put together a detailed profile, as you're about to learn.

The Big Guys

As you learned in Chapter 7, publishing mergers and consolidations have created several large publishers in New York. In one way, this has narrowed the market for you, but fortunately, because imprints are independent and all these publishers have several children's book imprints, you can still submit your manuscripts and art samples to each of them.

Of course, you can only send them materials if their doors are open. Writers often complain that they can't send manuscripts to these companies unless they have an agent or are published. Illustrators might find that their samples seemingly vanish into a black hole. Fortunately, not all the doors are closed. Look for the open doors, and don't let the closed ones frustrate you.

What Are the Big Guys Like?

You'll find that the big guys have a surprising variety of imprints. Some are personal imprints run by one well-known editor; others are general-purpose imprints covering the gamut from board books to young adult novels. Some are known for solid nonfiction for the library market; others are known for innovative picture books that get snapped up in bookstores.

They all tend to be slow to respond to submissions, however, so try to target your submissions. You'll spend less time waiting. How? Study their catalogs.

Introducing Simon & Schuster

Let's start with the S&S Children's Publishing catalog for Fall 2007. (If you try this, get the current catalog if you can, but note that not much will change at most companies from year to year.)

The S&S catalog represents a large, corporate publisher with more than a dozen imprints. At 256 pages, it's substantial and needs to be browsed carefully, because some imprints don't get their own section. When I open it, I notice a fold-out *Spiderwick Chronicles* promo piece, detailing the books, boxed set, floor display, and tie-in books timed to go on the market around the release of an upcoming movie. This is a strong clue that S&S is focused on the consumer market and will push to get its books into bookstores. In the catalog itself, the hardcover imprints come first, and because they're most likely to publish new, original titles, I'll look most carefully at them.

> **Can You Keep a Secret?**
>
> I've addressed writers in the following studies, but illustrators can do a similar analysis of a catalog to find out what types of books a company does, what range of art styles they use, etc. Count titles, leaving out reissues or books labeled "now available in paperback" and the like to find the new books. Look also at how the publisher presents the books.

Atheneum Books for Young Readers (sometimes BFYR) has a list of about 20 titles. It opens with a spread promoting a new *Olivia* title and consists mostly of picture books and novels. I notice that the novels are labeled either "middle-grade fiction" or "teen fiction" here and throughout the catalog; the company does not use "young adult" or "YA." Some get a designation of "Ginee Seo Books" or "Richard Jackson Books." I research these personal imprints a bit further and learn that Richard Jackson has retired, so his must be books that were "in the pipeline." I'll want to find out if

Ginee Seo's imprint has separate submissions from Atheneum. I see only three non-fiction titles, one of them a high-class pop-up about dinosaurs, and the other two for teens. The Atheneum list includes a number of award-winning authors and illustrators (David Small, E. L. Konigsberg, and Nancy Farmer, among others). The imprint seems to concentrate on the library market, with some marketing push for bookstores with selected titles.

Simon & Schuster BFYR has a similar mix of books, mostly picture books and novels, but also one easy reader and two highly visual nonfiction books. There's a different feel here: the S&S flagship imprint seems more focused on the consumer market, opening with six pages about Spiderwick items and including a picture book by Frank McCourt and novels by Tiki and Ronde Barber and Marlee Matlin. Still, most picture books or novels could be submitted to either one.

Playground Stories

Look in the section under the price and ISBN for each book in many catalogs, and you'll see who owns and can license the subsidiary rights. If it says the publisher's name and "all rights," that book either came in as an author's submission direct to the publisher or was commissioned. Some rights may be held by an agent, a foreign publisher, or a book producer. Checking this information helps you get a feel for how many books have come as author submissions and how many came from agents or from other companies.

Margaret K. McElderry Books used to be a personal imprint and now stands on its own (you'll learn more about it in Chapter 26). It's a smaller imprint, with a focus on picture books and novels, including a couple from abroad. As was the case in 2000, when I first analyzed the S&S catalog, there is less of the flash and promotional push seen elsewhere. All the books give the impression of being aimed quietly but firmly at children and seem likely to sell well in the library market and in bookstores that care about quality.

Several imprints remain, publishing paperbacks, novelty books, tie-in titles, and are worth investigating to see if they publish originals or might be sources for writing assignments. The large Aladdin Paperbacks imprint includes many reprints from hardcover editions, which I can tell from the write-ups or from information given about the hardcovers. However, it does publish some original easy readers and novels, both single title and series, and Aladdin Mix, a new imprint dedicated to "tween fiction," is included within the main Aladdin list. Exactly what Aladdin wants is worth further investigation.

Following Aladdin is Simon Pulse, a relatively new paperback imprint dedicated to teen fiction. Some of their titles are reprints, but some originals are included, too, so a teen fiction writer will want to dig deeper.

Then come imprints that publish few if any originals, but might hire writers and illustrators for specific assignments:

◆ Simon Scribbles, with coloring and activity books tied mostly to TV series and to Spiderwick.

◆ Little Simon, a mass-market imprint with lower-priced board books and books with pop-ups and other novelty features.

◆ Simon Spotlight, where we find movie and TV tie-in books of many kinds, from sticker books to novelizations.

Other imprints are listed, but none of them seem like likely markets.

I've found three imprints that seem likely to take submissions (but I'll have to find out if their doors are open), and three others that might be sources of freelance writing or for-hire illustration. That's not bad. The bad news is that the hardcover imprints seem to be publishing fewer titles than they were in 2000, when I did a similar analysis (60 versus 75). I could dig even deeper into the exact kinds of books that each publishes, and I'll show how to do that in the following section, which looks at a smaller publisher.

The Little Guys

Look at any market guide and you'll find a lot of publishers that aren't part of larger companies but are pretty large on their own. For the most part, these companies are more open to unsolicited submissions than the "corporate publishers." Those that are open are usually quicker to respond to submissions (by quicker, I mean one to three months), and more likely to make personal comments on your work.

What Are the Little Guys Like?

Smaller, independent publishers are more diverse than the larger ones. Some companies publish for specific religious, cultural, and racial groups. You'll find companies with a regional focus; publishers for children with special needs; and publishers specializing in folktales, arts and crafts books, and the American Girls dolls. You'll also find companies publishing for the general market, going head to head with the big guys—sometimes with considerable success.

Why should you bother with these companies? They don't pay as well, and they might not have as much marketing muscle as the bigger companies. But you're more likely to get personal attention at a smaller company. You may also find that, unless you're lucky or have a potential best-seller on your hand, a smaller publisher is more likely to take the risk of publishing an unknown, or the risk of publishing something a little different.

Introducing Boyds Mills Press

For our case study of a smaller and independent publisher, I looked at Boyds Mills Press. Based in Honesdale, Pennsylvania, this respected publisher is part of the company that publishes *Highlights for Children*. And as you'll see in the catalog, that magazine is the source of some of their books. I have the Fall 2007 catalog, and I'll discuss the books in more detail than in the S&S comments; you could do the same kind of detailed investigation, going imprint by imprint, in a larger company's catalog.

The 40-page catalog includes 27 titles, has color illustrations throughout, and emphasizes awards and starred reviews its authors and illustrators have received. And that tells you Boyds Mills sees teachers and school libraries as a good chunk of the market it's trying to reach, if not the most important chunk. I don't see the emphasis on promotional support I saw for the Simon & Schuster imprints.

The books are grouped by type, with picture books followed by fiction, poetry, and nonfiction. One complication I notice is that each book's imprint—Boyds Mills Press, Wordsong, Front Street Books, or Calkins Creek—is listed in the book details. However, the guidelines tell me "all submissions will be evaluated for all imprints," so I can ignore the imprint labels.

> **Can You Keep a Secret?**
>
> Use catalogs to find out about the *kinds* of books an imprint publishes, not to study specific subjects. If a catalog includes a book about the death of a pet or an unusual summer vacation, that does not indicate a strong interest in that particular subject. Stories with such subjects could be published by any general-purpose imprint because they address common childhood experiences.

Because Boyds Mills is interested in the school and library market, I'm not surprised to find a good amount of nonfiction (four picture books and photo-essays, and five titles for older readers), seven picture books (including one folktale retelling), five (!) poetry titles, and several novels, including one graphic novel. From research I've done elsewhere, I know that one of their imprints, Lemniscaat, publishes books under an agreement with the Dutch publisher of that name, so I don't consider its titles in my analysis.

I see more variety, and certainly more nonfiction, at Boyds Mills Press than I did at the larger Simon & Schuster. If I wrote poetry, I'd be encouraged by Boyds Mills' poetry titles, which are for both picture-book and older readers. I also saw activity and craft books, but they seem to be connected to *Highlights*, so before shipping off a manuscript of *101 Popsicle Stick Activities*, query to see if it accepts these materials or just reuses them from the magazine. There's even a graphic novel. And I'm pleased to see submissions are not closed, and that the company has grown since I last checked, partly by merging with Front Street and partly by starting Calkins Creek, which specializes in books with historical themes.

If you don't have access to catalogs (you can send away for them or pick them up at conventions), you can use JacketFlap's (www.jacketflap.com) database of publishers to investigate a particular publisher's titles, subjects, age levels, and more. The system uses data from Amazon but presents it in a more useful way and often includes contact information and comments.

Could you divine all I did from a catalog? Possibly not. I knew what to look for and knew what it meant. But as you learn more about today's children's book market, and as you spend time reading catalogs, you'll become better able to get useful information from them. Once you've learned from a catalog, you can use the methods introduced in the next chapter to continue to investigate publishers.

The Least You Need to Know

◆ Publishing companies may have many different parts, but imprints are the ones writers and illustrators want to get to know.

◆ Imprints are independent units within companies, and each has its own focus.

◆ Choose your imprint carefully, especially at large companies where different imprints have very different programs.

◆ Analyze catalogs to figure out the kinds of books each imprint publishes and how a publisher approaches its market.

Chapter 20

Deeper into the Maze: Other Kinds of Publishers

In This Chapter

- ◆ Picking the right publisher
- ◆ A tour of the magazine market
- ◆ Learning about educational publishers
- ◆ Regional publishers, niche publishers, and those outside the USA
- ◆ Check out new publishers, online and off

So you've been knocking on doors at the big guys as well as the smaller guys, and you're still not getting anywhere. Don't give up. There's more out there than you might think. After a quick reality check to ask whether you've been knocking on the right doors, this chapter opens even more doors—the doors to the magazine world, educational publishers (they don't just publish textbooks!), regional and niche publishers, and new publishers.

Try Next Door

You learned in Chapter 19 how to analyze a catalog to figure out what a publisher does and what books they might want to see. As I said in that chapter, be careful what you do with what you've learned. If you learned that Publisher Q publishes picture books, but you didn't notice that all of them feature contemporary children, you might send them your poetically retold Middle English folktale, to no avail. Larry Dane Brimner sent what became his first published book to Clarion, only to have it be returned by an editor praising the manuscript but urging him to "find the right publisher." He did some more research, and ended up at Franklin Watts. If you do what Larry did, nine times out of ten, you won't hear from an editor that you simply chose the wrong house. You'll just get a standard rejection letter and be none the wiser.

So dig a little deeper before you throw up your hands—but not too deep! Sometimes at conferences, I have heard authors complaining that they wish they knew exactly which editor published which book so they could send that person their book, which happens to be just like it. But an editor who happened to publish a farcical story about a dog who learned the importance of good manners might not want to see another farcical dog story. If that editor went to another publisher, that company might not want to publish such a story. But either publisher could be open to a story with an animal as the main character, so it's more important to get the publisher's general focus and approach correct. Editors come and go, but unless they're sufficiently influential to change a publishing program, few change the company's focus.

Should you be concerned about a publisher's focus just because you don't want to waste their editors' time? In these times of overwhelmed editorial staffs, maybe you should be, but let's not forget the purely selfish and practical point that you waste your own time if you send a manuscript to a publisher who isn't going to be interested in it. Yes, the publishing maze is confusing, but you'll save yourself time in the long run if you do enough research that you can target your submissions carefully and follow the publisher's latest guidelines.

Class Rules

Every editor has stories about wildly inappropriate submissions—novels for adults sent to picture-book publishers, picture-book stories sent to publishers of library nonfiction for teenagers—and their mantra is "Find out more about us!" Emma Dryden of Margaret K. McElderry Books confirmed this point by heading a list of things she wishes beginning writers knew with these two items:

- I wish more beginning writers were familiar with our backlist and current titles before submitting their projects to us.
- I wish more beginning writers submitted their materials according to our specific submission guidelines.

Magazines

So you've followed my advice and tried every single one of the publishers that might be interested in your piece on bee behavior or your story about two children learning to take care of a puppy. What now? Either it's time to put it aside or it's time to try elsewhere. To start with, try magazines. Actually, depending on what you write, you might start with the magazines before the book publishers.

Hundreds of magazines are published for children in North America. Some, like *Highlights for Children* or *Cricket*, publish for a general audience; others focus on a very specific interest or audience. Some are for preschoolers; others are for teenagers. Magazines can be pretty specialized, such as *Chess Life for Kids* and *Young Rider*, which cover the subject you might think they do from their titles. Whatever your interest, you are likely to find at least one magazine that matches up. In fact, given that magazines can more effectively target a small market than book publishers can, you'll find a wider and more varied range of opportunities among magazines than among book publishers.

> **Can You Keep a Secret?**
>
> To learn more about what magazines want from writers, go straight to Kid Magazine Writers, an online journal run by Jan Fields, at www.kidmagwriters.com.

Writing for magazines *is* different from writing for book publication. If you mostly write for younger children, you'll see that a magazine piece needs (or demands!) fewer illustrations than a story for a picture book. If you write for older children, here's a market for short stories, mostly not published by book publishers. Or if nonfiction is your bag, there's great demand for short pieces or longer essays, quite different in form from what you'd do for a book.

To understand the difference, immerse yourself in it. Get your hands on some children's magazines in an area you think interests you. If you write picture books for five-year-olds, for example, check out *Ladybug*. Type up a story from the magazine and compare it to yours. Is the length all that's different, or does the story develop differently? How about the vocabulary? Try reading several issues of a magazine and then several books intended for children of the same age, and reflect on the differences you notice.

Magazines work differently from books, too. Many magazines pay per word, or pay a flat fee per article. You can expect to receive anywhere from $25 for a very short piece to hundreds of dollars for a longer article. That doesn't sound like much, but it's a credit you can cite, and experience, and usually magazines only buy one use of your work, so you can sell it elsewhere. Check their guidelines carefully—some accept submissions generally, others want material for specific theme issues, while others commission work from you on the basis of your writing samples and stated interests. Magazines also specify how many words they want for certain kinds of pieces, where book publishers will ask for "long enough to tell the story." Follow those guidelines carefully.

> **Playground Stories**
>
> Sneed Collard writes for both books and magazines: "For a long time, I viewed magazine writing as a way to break into books, but magazine writing has its own rewards. First, you can write about a topic without spending as much time on it as a book requires. Second, I enjoy the more journalistic, 'snappy' approach that magazine articles allow. Third, magazine articles provide great 'spin-offs' from books—and earn you additional income. Last, especially with the 'testing fever' these days, several companies are gobbling up magazine reprint rights like crazy. I've now made more money from some of my magazine articles than I have from my books!"

Magazines are a big market and a great place to get experience. And who knows? You might decide this is the place for you, or at the least a great complement to what you want to do in books.

Educational Publishers

Educational publishers are another market worthy of investigation. They don't just publish textbooks; schools today want all kinds of supplementary materials, from activities to poems to stories, in all curriculum areas. To meet this demand, educational publishers may buy the right to republish a book already sold in bookstores for their school audience. Or they may seek out original work.

When you're just getting started, it will be difficult to make headway at the really big companies such as Harcourt, Macmillan/McGraw-Hill, and Houghton Mifflin. Look instead for companies that produce supplementary materials. Companies such as Continental Press, Frank Schaefer, Mondo, the Wright Group, and Carson-Dellosa are producing series of "emergent-reader" books, grade-by-grade anthologies of stories to read, and poems, activities, and even games to go with math, social studies, and science curricula.

How can you find out about companies like this? If you're a teacher, you already know about them—they're the companies publishing the books you use. You'll find them listed in some market guides, but to really learn about these companies, you should go to a national or regional convention of such teacher's organizations as the International Reading Association, the National Science Teacher's Association, or the National Council for Social Studies. You'll get a catalog listing all the attending publishers and their addresses, and you'll be able to go from booth to booth to look at the books, gather brochures, and take notes about what they publish.

Educational publishers won't all want original material, and some only work on commission. (They hire you to write or illustrate something specific on a for-hire basis.) But there is work if you look in the right places. For example, the Education Center, a teacher-resource material publisher, puts out calls for such things as "short-short" stories (525 words) for anthologies. This is a relatively unknown market, and one that might be just right for you.

> **Can You Keep a Secret?**
>
> How do you find out about the smaller educational publishers? If you can't go to a teacher's convention, Rozanne Lanczak Williams, who has built a career working with such companies, suggests your local teacher supply store. Browse through the aisles and make notes on books similar to what you write. Contact those publishers and request guidelines.

Regional, Niche, and Non-U.S. Publishers

The publishers you're most likely to know are the ones that publish for the U.S. market. You'll find their books from Florida to Alaska (and probably in British Colombia and Newfoundland, too). They publish general-interest books for a wide audience.

But what if you want to tell a story about a local hero or explain how the tide affects the bay outside your window? You might do well to find a local or *regional publisher*. What if you want to reach a child with a specific problem or background? Try a *niche publisher*. Both of these kinds of publishers do not try to reach every child in every part of North America; rather, they try to reach specific children.

def•i•ni•tion

> A **regional publisher** specializes in subjects relevant to a particular part of the country, such as deserts in the Southwest or the Everglades in Florida, and sells its books locally. A **niche publisher** specializes in a subject that's of interest to a small group of people and sells its books nationally, but only in specialized outlets.

And what if want to look beyond U.S. borders, or if you're living beyond them your-self? Then you have an entire world in front of you.

Your Neighborhood Publisher

How do you find a regional publisher? Find them in the market guides (including a "Guide to the Small Press Market" available to members of the Society of Children's Book Authors and Illustrators (SCBWI)—see Appendix B), or online, but that might take some sifting and sorting.

> **Can You Keep a Secret?**
>
> A great online source for infor-mation about independent publishers—not all of which are niche or regional publishers—is John Kremer's list of "101 Top Independent Publishers" at www.bookmarket.com/101publishers.htm.

Perhaps the most direct way is to go where the cus-tomers are. In your community, where would you go to buy a book like the one you've written? Go there, and look through the books on display. Note the publishers. Call or write to them and find out if they accept submissions. If you live in Oregon and want to write a book about the art of the American Indians of the Northwest coast, you'll come across Sasquatch Books. If you live in Maine and want to do a story about life as a Maine fisherman, you'll find that Down East Books is the place for you. Every U.S. region has one or more regional publishers.

Finding Your Niche (Publisher)

To find a niche publisher, again, go where the customers are. In this case, that's not necessarily a bookstore. I frequently receive questions from the authors of stories about children overcoming emotional problems or dealing with a physical disability. In the larger children's bookstores, you may find a special section for these books. But it might also be worthwhile to ask a child psychologist or school counselor to let you look through his or her shelves. If they do any "bibliotherapy," or offer children books that are tailored to particular problems, you might find a sizable collection.

Christian, Jewish, and other religious publishers also fall in the niche publisher category. In this case, their market is parents seeking books that speak to their par-ticular faith or that more generally support values with which they feel comfortable. You'll find Christian bookstores in just about every community, and the Christian Booksellers Association has conventions where you can investigate this market.

What other niches are there? There's one for just about every interest or lifestyle, although not always for children. Some publishers specialize in environmental themes, some specialize in craft books, and some in New Age values. Whatever your interest, there's likely a niche you can call home.

There's More out There

English-language markets outside the United States include Canada, the United Kingdom, Australia, and New Zealand. A useful starting point for all of them is *Children's Writer's and Illustrator's Market*, which recently began to cover publishers outside the United States.

If you have a publishing home outside the United States, or want to seek one, the information here can get you started; however, you'll need to do some digging. For example, look into the Canadian market. If you're Canadian, be sure to consider Canadian publishers because many of them give precedence to Canadian authors and illustrators. Always look to your own country's publishers first. If you reside outside the United States, you might also consider the U.S. market because it is, of course, the world's largest English-language market.

New! New! New!

It's easy enough to get the idea that publishers are closing down and merging, and that the number of outlets for your writing is decreasing every year. The big publishers are certainly bigger than they used to be, but new publishers and imprints appear every year. Watch for occasional "New Hats in the Ring" articles in *Publishers Weekly* or articles on new imprints in *Children's Writer's and Illustrator's Market*. If you do, you'll find out about new imprints such as these:

- ◆ Publishers interested in the teen market have launched imprints such as Graphia at Houghton Mifflin, Razorbill at Penguin, and Amulet Books at Abrams.

- ◆ Feiwel and Friends at Macmillan and Robin Corey Books at Random House are new personal imprints, although of course the editors bring favored authors and illustrators with them—and are immediately besieged by agents.

- ◆ Smaller companies such as Boyds Mills Press launch imprints such as Calkins Creek Books, and new companies such as Gryphon Press go out into the world.

Opportunities exist at companies like these but are not necessarily an opportunity to clear out your drawer-full of already-rejected manuscripts. New companies may be just as selective as old ones, so send them what they want. Keep your eyes open, read *Publishers Weekly*, read your favorite newsletter, and update your market guide every year.

E-Books and the Internet

In Chapter 7, I mentioned electronic publishing. However, so far not many new opportunities for writers to publish books electronically are emerging. Rather, much of this type of publishing consists of new editions of books already available in print form. And so far, those books are mostly novels and technical books because those translate more effectively to onscreen versions. It's more difficult and expensive to convert color picture books into electronic form. Small presses publishing e-books, either on their own or alongside print versions, also exist, but are only beginning to find an audience.

You can find plenty of freelance writing with online companies, but this is usually for short online articles, and earns you no more than a small fee. If you do work with an electronic book publisher, expect to be paid royalties, and do not expect to pay "listing" or "production" costs. (Companies that ask you to do that are just another kind of vanity publisher, as discussed in the next chapter.)

The publishing maze is large and complicated. Carry a ball of string, and don't lose track of the different ways out of it.

The Least You Need to Know

- There are magazines for every age level and interest, and they can be great markets for writers.

- Educational publishers can be an opportunity—teachers' conventions are a good place to find out about them.

- Smaller publishers focusing on regional and specialized subjects may be the home you need.

- New publishers come along every day. Read the fine print to determine how new they truly are and what their needs are.

- There is a lot of heat and noise over electronic publishing, but so far few new opportunities.

Chapter 21

The Self-Publishing Conundrum

In This Chapter

- ◆ What self-publishing is … and isn't
- ◆ Why self-publishing usually isn't a good idea
- ◆ When self-publishing *is* a good idea
- ◆ How some authors have fared with self-publishing

With traditional publishing so difficult to break into, and the brave new world of electronic publishing not much help, you might be tempted to turn to publishers who don't pay you. These range from old-fashioned vanity presses to big online companies to your local printer. In this chapter, I show you what self-publishing is, when it can be a good idea, and what to watch out for.

What Self-Publishing *Is*

What many people call "self-publishing" really isn't self-publishing. In true self-publishing, you act as a publisher. You take care of all the things a publisher does, and your book comes out with the name of your company on it, with an ISBN that you control. There are many ways to produce a book that aren't actually self-publishing, and that's not to say they're bad, but there's a lot you have to do if you want to self-publish in the true sense.

As a self-publisher, you have to compete in a national marketplace, head to head with the big publishing companies. It's possible to do that, but it takes time, money, knowledge of the market, and a carefully crafted strategy. Here's a list of just some of the things you have to do as a self-publisher (find additional details on each item on my website at www.underdown.org/publisher-expertise.htm):

- Acquisition
- Planning
- Editing
- Designing
- Art directing

- Copyediting
- Production managing
- Distributing
- Selling
- Marketing/promoting

If you find this list intimidating, good, because that was my intention! Better to be intimidated now, when you can still do something about it, than after you've already made a commitment to self-publish a book and then don't know what you need to do.

You could use this as something of a checklist in figuring out what you need to do to get a book on the market, but please note that it is not exhaustive. Nonfiction books may need to be carefully fact-checked, for example, in more detail than a copy editor would do (and not just by looking things up in Wikipedia). Permissions may be needed for photographs, quotations, or song lyrics. You might even need to consult a lawyer over potentially libelous material. There's a lot to do if you want to do it well.

If you don't want to do all of that, then stop reading this chapter and go straight to the next chapter to learn more about traditional publishing.

What Self-Publishing *Is Not*

What do all those companies that say they help with self-publishing actually do then? Well, with a few exceptions, they're just new kinds of *vanity presses*. They may use electronic and *print-on-demand* (*POD*) technologies and write clever contracts, but the bottom line is this: *you* pay *them*, and most people never make back what they've paid these publishers. There are several different kinds of these companies operating.

A Lot of Work in Vain

Vanity presses are called that for a very good reason—they rely on the vanity of those who want to see their work in print, even at considerable cost. With a traditional vanity press, you typically pay several thousand dollars for a print run of a few thousand copies.

You have to market that stock of books, printed to uncertain standards, yourself. No vanity press in existence will even try to get your book true national distribution or be able to do the marketing needed to get the books sold.

def•i•ni•tion

A **vanity press** produces books for you from your manuscript, usually without much editing and with no marketing, for a pretty sizable fee. **Print-on-demand** (**POD**) and some electronic publishers create a book file for you, which can be printed one copy at a time or sold as an e-book, for a modest fee. That's all they do.

One Copy at a Time

Now that publishing has become an electronic business, a new kind of vanity publishing has emerged. It's possible to take a manuscript and convert it into an electronic form that's all ready to be printed. Instead of going to the expense of printing and warehousing a few thousand copies of a book, a company can use print-on-demand technology to quite literally print one copy of a book at a time. Per-copy prices are reasonable, although the technology allows only for good black-and-white printing at this point. This system can be used to prolong the life of books that would otherwise go out of print.

POD can also produce books for aspiring authors, for a fee lower than charged by traditional vanity presses. Another option is to use the electronic file as the basis for an e-book and not create a physical book at all. Or a company may offer to do both. The company providing the service pays the author for each copy sold, and you can recoup your expenses if you sell enough copies. If you'd like to see how such a business works, explore www.xlibris.com and www.iuniverse.com. But please keep in mind that I'm *not* endorsing what they do.

Class Rules

Investigate the costs of self-publishing carefully. Don't accept what a company tells you at face value. Always ask what you're going to have to pay for what you want. It may be more than you had assumed.

Such companies tell you that your book will be available to bookstores and on Amazon. That's true so far as it goes, but only as one item on a list of hundreds or thousands of titles produced by those companies. No one will know about it; bookstores won't order it. As with traditional vanity presses, you'll have to market the book yourself or pay for "marketing services" at inflated rates.

Nothing Up Front

Be wary of companies I'd call no-advance, no-marketing publishers. These companies claim to pay royalties, but they don't pay advances, and they typically print a very small number of copies of a book. Authors are expected to market the books themselves and may have to commit to selling a certain number ahead of time.

One company known to be following this business model is PublishAmerica, which calls itself a traditional publisher but is notorious for not rejecting *any* manuscripts. Authors working with PA must sell enough copies of their book to cover PA's costs … and many end up buying them themselves.

Going Solo

If you just want a book for family and friends, or to sell in your local community, the best option might be to shun the big national companies completely. Work directly with a local printer, and hire all the other services needed to put a book out on the market. This will be less expensive than working with the big companies, and quite possibly more satisfying.

If you want to do more than that, you have a challenge. A publisher does a lot. If you are to replicate that and self-publish, it will cost you a lot of both time and money. Trying to reach a national market might not even be something an individual can do, as some stories later in this chapter show.

And Why Not?

What if you're really desperate to get a book out there? Maybe the costs seem worth it to you. It's your decision, but there are reasons to be cautious other than the money and extra time you'll have to put into a self-published book. For one thing, the book won't turn out as good as it would with the help of a traditional publisher's editorial and design staff, and it won't reach as many people as it would with the help of that publisher's marketing staff. Perhaps even more important, you'll damage your credibility with editors at traditional companies.

If that doesn't matter to you, if you just want to publish a particular book or a few books and don't want a career as a writer, it might be worth it for you to work with one of these companies. But do your research. Be sure you look beyond the well-known companies to reputable companies like lulu.com, where you might find better service at lower costs.

But keep this in mind: if you hope to become a traditionally published writer, one who gets an advance and royalties, stay away from all self-publishing outfits. Keep your eyes on the prize, and keep moving forward. If you try the traditional route and get nowhere, you can still come back to self-publishing in the future, and you'll know much more about the business.

> **Can You Keep a Secret?**
>
> Websites such as Preditors and Editors (anotherealm.com/prededitors/peba.htm) and Writer Beware (www.sfwa.org/beware) keep track of vanity presses and self-publishing "providers" and are a great resource to use to check out a company.

Stories from the Self-Publishing Trenches

So far I've been talking in general terms about self-publishing, giving you the lay of the land. Now I'm going to give you some case studies of actual people who chose to self-publish. As you'll see, they went about it in different ways. I don't include any stories about people who self-published a national best-seller. That happens, but even less often than people win the lottery. What follows should give you an idea of more typical experiences.

Typical Self-Publishing

Most people going into self-publishing don't know what they're going to have to do to sell their book, and so it's not surprising that the *average* self-published book sells fewer than 100 copies, or maybe even fewer than 50, according to some studies I have seen.

I worked with Gary Lusson, an author who had already decided to go with a division of BookSurge, one of the big companies. He wanted to produce a quality book, hired editors, and paid an illustrator for full-color illustrations. BookSurge charged $1,300 to create the book and do a press release, and he also paid $3,200 to the illustrator and about $500 to me and another editor. Gary is happy with the book and has sold some copies locally, but he has a long way to go before he reaches the 1,100 plus copies he'll need to sell to break even. He'll have to do that selling himself, as he can't hope for reviews or much in the way of bookstore sales.

Would he work with them again? He would, and in fact has started on a second book. He had this to say about the process: "An unexpected pleasure was working with editors and illustrators and the publisher. It is a fascinating process with frustrations, and yet satisfaction of accomplishment. The cost was well worth it also." I was surprised to hear him say this, but perhaps I shouldn't have been. His goals were met, and he enjoyed the process.

You can succeed, in a limited way, while working with one of the big self-publishing providers. On another occasion, I worked with Mary Carpenter, who managed to sell about 1,000 copies of her self-published biography of Temple Grandin over the course of four years. As this story shows, nonfiction with a clear niche audience can be easier to sell, but even so, she says she would not do another book this way: "Trying to promote a book without a 'real' publisher is so much trouble."

Targeted Self-Publishing

Self-publishing when you can tie what you do in your "day job" into selling the book might work better, but be sure to plan carefully and to have realistic expectations.

I helped Lucas Miller, a performer in schools, when he self-published his second picture book. He had to invest a sizable amount of money. He does not sell the book nationally other than to promote it on his website at www.lucasmiller.net. Instead, he sells it when he performs. He not only earns a little money but becomes a more attractive performer for a school because he's offering a book.

Playground Stories

Lucas Miller makes his living writing and performing science-related songs and stories, mostly in schools in his area. He sells CDs and his books when he performs. To self-publish *Dr. DNA & the Anaconda Invasion*, he invested about $15,000, most of that spent on printing 2,000 copies of the full-color hardcover picture book. After six months of selling the book, he had already come close to break-even point at around 1,000 copies. He worked with a printer, professional illustrators, and a designer and editor and was able to produce a high-quality book. For an interview with him, see www.underdown.org/lucas-miller.htm.

Of course, not everyone performs in the schools, but if you already run a business of some kind, or do something into which you can fit the promoting and selling of a book, then you might be able to do what Lucas did.

Self-Publishing After Traditional Publishing

In my experience, the best time to self-publish is after you are published. Provided that you have the time and money to invest, this may be a viable option, although even with the experience and contacts you'll have gained, you can't be sure of success.

The process is a little easier if you have a book that's already been published, and for which you have not only gotten the rights back but have bought or been given the film used to print it. You'll already know about the people who are likely to be interested in your book, and you'll have some idea of how to reach them. The film should only need small changes to places like the title and copyright pages. Creating this film can costs thousands of dollars, so if you have it you'll be able to save money when you go to press.

If you do self-publish, it's best to go into it with your eyes wide open, with a carefully thought-out business plan, and with the time and the money not only for a first printing but for a second printing before you've sold the first.

That was the approach that Josephine (Joi) Nobisso took when she started Gingerbread House in 2000, initially to republish three picture books that had gone out of print, but for which she believed there was unmet demand. Since then, she has added several new titles, all written by her. Joi and her daughter do all the work of a larger publisher, from art direction to promotion.

Playground Stories

Joi Nobisso says this of her decision to self-publish: "I would not have even dreamed of launching a press without strong material like *Grandpa Loved* and *Grandma's Scrapbook* in hand. I was the only author I knew of who got regular, insistent, and persistent letters from people disappointed that these two books had gone o.p. ... Maria and I launched Gingerbread House partly as a homeschooling exercise in real-life, real-time business operation. It was a risk, yes, but a calculated one. She was only 14, but we both attended small business sessions, drew up a clear and comprehensive business plan, and had a couple of exit strategies that would have recouped our investment so that we weren't 'putting up the ranch' on a fluke."

They have done well, with all their books regularly being reprinted, strong reviews and awards, and foreign rights sales bringing in additional income. How have they succeeded? With strong material to start with, top-quality illustration and production, aggressive and creative promotion, and an almost fanatical commitment to their books. The details are fascinating: read them at www.underdown.org/joi-nobisso.htm, and be sure to visit Gingerbread House online at www.gingerbreadbooks.com.

Many more self-publishing efforts fail than succeed, however. Even Aaron Shepard, the savvy author of *The Business of Writing for Children*, has found self-publishing of children's books to be a lot of work with little reward: take a look at his self-published children's books at www.shepardpub.com. Although well written and attractively produced, none have sold more than 500 copies. His nonfiction books for adults are doing considerably better.

The big successes of self-publishing are very rare, and in fact I know of only a few since I entered publishing. One was Richard Paul Evans, who self-published *The Christmas Box* in 1992; Michael Hoeye, who self-published *Time Stops for No Mouse* in 2000; and then there's Christopher Paolini's *Eragon*. It's interesting to note that in all these cases, these authors are now happily publishing with a mainstream publisher. They did not want to keep doing all the work themselves—or they knew there was more money to be made by publishing traditionally. And this isn't something you're likely to hear from a self-publishing evangelist.

Think carefully about your choices. If you want a book for friends and family, or to reach a niche market, self-publishing is an attractive option. If you've got a head for business, and time to put into a project that could take over your life, consider self-publishing, but cautiously. If you want to reach a national audience, think twice about self-publishing.

The Least You Need to Know

- ◆ Don't be driven by the difficulty of finding a traditional publisher into the arms of a vanity press.

- ◆ A self-publisher has to do all the things a publisher does.

- ◆ Many self-publishing companies are a modern type of vanity press.

- ◆ Modest success in self-publishing is possible, if you know what you're doing.

- ◆ Big success is extremely rare in self-publishing.

Chapter 22

So How Does It All Work?

In This Chapter

- ◆ Why publishers need you
- ◆ Tips for going beyond the basics and playing the game the most effective way
- ◆ Responding to an editor's interest
- ◆ The importance of persistence
- ◆ A peek behind a publisher's doors

By now you know the basics of getting your children's book published, but you need to know how to put it all together. You need to know how the system works—to the extent that it does. In this chapter, you learn why, even after recent mergers, children's book publishers still need you and how you can best approach them. You also learn what's happening behind the doors of a publisher when you don't get a response.

Publishers Need *You*

At this point, you might not believe it, but publishers still need you. Without authors and illustrators, most publishers would not exist. Your creative energy produces works that are too distinctive to be created by in-house staff, and it's these creations that the trade market, at least, demands. Some publishers do seem to have little need for fresh talent, but every one of the people whose work they publish was a beginner at some point, just like you.

Publishing works on a never-ending cycle. Every publisher must create a minimum number of new books every year or run short of income. A publisher releases two or three "lists" each year, grouping its books into fall and spring bunches, possibly adding a winter or summer group. Why? That's just the way it's always been done, although mass-market publishers tend to release books throughout the year. The publisher's business and budget are built around a certain number of books, be it 5, 10, or 50, that it must have on each list.

And that need for a full list is where you come in. Authors and illustrators leave even the most stable of lists. They get restless and move on, their editor leaves and they follow, they cut back their output, or they even die or move into another field. Every publisher needs some fresh blood from time to time. If they get it by luring someone over from another publisher, then *that* publisher needs to fill a space on their list. There's always some flux in publishing, and that change brings opportunity.

Play by the Rules

To get anywhere in this business, you need some talent, persistence, luck, and an understanding of the way things work. You provide the first three, and I hope you're finding the last one in this book.

So far, you've read a lot of detailed advice. Now it's time to pull it all together and highlight important strategies.

The Union Makes You Strong

No union of children's writers and illustrators exists, of course, but there are national organizations to which you should belong and get involved with. The occasional genius can go it alone, but the resources of the Society of Children's Book Writers and Illustrators (SCBWI) and the Canadian Society of Children's Authors, Illustrators, and Performers (CANSCAIP) are worth getting access to, and local conferences are well worth attending (see Appendix B for more information).

But do more than that. Get involved for the local critique groups, for the support of other writers and illustrators, for the opportunity to have regular contact with editors and agents. Go to one conference, and you might get a chance to talk to an editor or agent for a few minutes. Become an active member of your local chapter, and you'll get to know these folks over phone calls and letters and at the conference. That contact is valuable. Although I've met many authors and illustrators at conferences, the people I remember and keep in touch with are usually the folks who organized or helped out during the conference—not the person in the hallway who asked me if I would mind looking at her manuscript.

Playground Stories

Lisa Rowe Fraustino, author of *Ash* and *The Hickory Chair,* among other books, has this to say: "Five out of the six books I have contracted to date have been with editors I met at conferences and developed a rapport with. And the sixth book is in a series published by the same house but a different imprint than one of my regular editors, and without my prior contact with the house I doubt my proposal would have been taken as seriously." What she's not saying is that for years she was one of the organizers of a conference in eastern Pennsylvania, and that it was through that work that she met these editors, including me.

Catalogs, Conventions, and Guidelines

It's good to get to know editors; it's *vital* to get to know publishers. You've learned how to analyze a catalog, so do that for all the publishers who might be a home for your manuscript *before* you send it to them. You might end up dropping half of them from your list, saving yourself time and postage.

To get all those catalogs, you can write publishers and send the right size SASEs and wait for them to come back. Or you can go to a conference. National and regional teacher, librarian, and bookseller organizations have them every year, and in their exhibit halls, dozens and dozens of publishers set up booths showcasing their latest books and giving away their latest catalogs. For booksellers, there's BookExpo America (BEA), and regional shows like the Southeast Booksellers Association show. For teachers, there's NCTE, IRA, NCSS, NCTM and their regional variants. And for librarians, there's the American Library Association and regional conferences like the Texas Library Association convention. Often, the public can get in for the day to wander the exhibit hall; or if not, you can get a day ticket through a teacher or librarian you know.

Can You Keep a Secret?
The very best place to learn about trade publishers may be the convention of the American Library Association, where publishers display their latest books and give out catalogs. Held each year in January and June, ALA conventions move around, so sooner or later one will come to a city near you or near someone you know. Find out more at www.ala.org.

As suggested in Chapter 16, spend a day at one of these conventions. At the end of the day, you'll be exhausted, but you'll be much better informed about the latest in children's books than you were when you started.

Scope Out the Competition

Don't assume your writing is so original that no one else has ever done anything like it. Find out what other books out there are similar to yours so you can say in a cover letter how yours is different. It's not enough to say "I wrote this because I wanted to find a book on *(fill in the blank)* and there wasn't one at my local bookstore." Most editors won't believe this and may well be able to think of several books you didn't find. Anticipate them, and tell them about the similar books and the ways in which yours is different. This is particularly important for nonfiction, but you can do it for fiction, too. Careful searches on Amazon or a large public library collection, perhaps supplemented by a discussion with an experienced children's librarian, should get you the information you need.

Waiting Patiently—or Not

After you get your manuscript out there, be prepared to wait. Of course, don't just wait. Use that time to write another manuscript, to start research for a new book, or to read the five latest Newbery winners.

When you do hear from a publisher, you most likely will get a form rejection letter (more on this in a minute), photocopied, without even an individual's name. Don't be disappointed. Every author starts out getting these. But check the rejections carefully. Don't leave your returned SASEs lying around unopened because one might hold a golden opportunity inside. So open that envelope and be ready to spring into action!

Follow Up on Everything

If you keep at it, do everything right, and have a little luck, a day will come when you hear from an editor. Most likely—9 times out of 10, if not 99 times out of 100—your first actual contact will be a short rejection letter or maybe even a note scribbled on a form letter rejection. If you're an illustrator, maybe you'll just get a request for more samples. Don't be discouraged that this isn't a contract. Be encouraged that someone has taken the time to write to you. Respond, but be sure to respond appropriately.

When You Get a Nibble

The least-encouraging positive response you can get is a short note scribbled at the bottom of a *form rejection letter.* It may say "We hope to hear from you again," "Thanks for your submission," or "We don't publish this kind of story but we would like to see *[something else]* from you." Notes like this might not seem like much, but at most publishers, very few manuscripts get even this much of a response. The message? You are in the ballpark, and someone wants you to know it, even if you aren't ready to take the field as a starter. Submit work to this publisher again.

def•i•ni•tion

A **form rejection letter** is a short, anonymous letter, usually photocopied, saying something like this:

Dear Author,

Thank you for your submission. We appreciate your sharing your work with us. Unfortunately, your manuscript does not meet our current publishing needs, and we are returning it to you herewith.

Anything more personal than this is encouraging!

More encouraging is a short signed letter. Even if it's written in generic language—"Thank you for submitting XYZ. We enjoyed reading it, but are sorry to tell you that it is not right for our list"—you can be encouraged that an editor has put his or her name at the end of the letter. This is an invitation to write to that editor again, with a different manuscript. Accept this invitation!

A letter that rejects your manuscript but provides detailed reasons why should set off a celebration in your writer's heart. To write such a letter, an editor has taken a half hour or more out of her busy day (or has asked an assistant to draft a letter and then reviewed it). This editor is interested in you. If she doesn't ask to see the manuscript again, do not send a revision unless you can see ways to deal with every single one of the concerns expressed in the letter. If she asks to see a revision, do your very best to think through what she says and make changes that not only do what she asks, but also create a satisfying new whole.

And don't be in too much of a hurry to get it back. That editor isn't expecting to hear from you right away. She hopes you'll take your time and reread what you've done, mull it over, read it to your critique group, and send it back only when you're sure it's ready.

Not Too Much!

After you've made contact in this way, this isn't the time to clear out your drawer and send the editor every story you've ever written. She's not expecting it. Remember, one story drew that response. Are you confident that a new story you've written is as good? If you are, send it. Can you say the same about that story you put aside a year ago, not sure of what to do with the ending? Probably not. Read it over. Do you really want her to read it? After all, you want this editor to think highly of you, and, realistically, she just isn't going to want to publish several of your stories right away.

So unless the editor specifically asks you to send her everything you've ever written, pick and choose and send her only your best work.

Not Too Aggressive!

At the same time, remember that you're not the only author the editor's working with. She's juggling dozens of active titles and probably corresponding with dozens of other authors, on top of meetings and planning sessions and conferences. You aren't going to suddenly start to get your manuscripts back from her within a few weeks. You should not call her a day after you calculate she would have received the manuscript to ask her what she thinks. Even if she read it when it first came in, she needs a week or two to mull it over. Let *her* get in touch with *you*. Even if she takes a couple months, don't worry. There might be lots of other things going on. If you don't hear from her within the industry-standard three months, a note or preferably a phone call is a good way to get in touch.

> **Class Rules**
>
> Deluging him with manuscripts, calling him often when you don't hear from him, or e-mailing him all your latest ideas are surefire ways to ruin a budding relationship with an editor. Coming across as overeager or desperate won't get you better results and might cool his interest in you. Strive to be professional at all times.

Publishing is a people business, and acting like a professional—dedicated yet easy to work with—from the time you first write to someone through the time you see your book appear on the bookstore shelves is as important in helping you go on to another book as is the quality of your creative work.

You Can Get It, but You Must Try

Persistence leads to success. I make no guarantees—except to say that without persistence, you won't get anywhere. Most published writers will tell you that they spent years learning, and going from form rejections to nibbles to regular correspondence and finally to publication. And even after that first book, they kept learning and growing and recovering from setbacks. Breaking through to a first book is no guarantee for a second or third. You have to write new manuscripts, they have to interest an editor, and your books have to do well enough that editors (and readers) want more down the road.

> **Playground Stories** _____
>
> Sometimes persistence goes back to childhood. Writer Elaine Landau told us: "When my mother was pregnant with me, a palm reader said that she would have a girl who was destined to become a writer. And my mother did give birth to a baby girl who showed a keen interest in writing. But she felt certain that I'd never make a decent living writing and tried her best to discourage me. I continued to fill notebooks with poetry and essays. When I went to college, she insisted that I take a practical major like business. I tried but after just one term I switched to an English and journalism major. Today I'm the author of over 150 children's books. If you have that dream, don't let anyone discourage you. Just keep writing."

What's Going On in There?

Sometimes, though, you don't hear back, or all you get is a form letter. Even a form letter tells you something, if you think about it. Whoever read your manuscript decided that your submission did not warrant a personal response of any kind. You don't know if that's because the manuscript didn't measure up, or because you sent it to the wrong publisher. After trying several publishers and getting only form letters, though, you might want to go back to your word processor, or try another manuscript.

Why does this happen? Why can't publishers respond personally to *all* submissions, so authors and illustrators won't be left guessing? Let's look behind a publisher's office doors to find out—and understand why persistence is so important.

Behind Closed Doors

It is not true that editors have a peaceful job, reading manuscripts, deciding which ones they like, setting them into motion as books, and then watching them bob away on the stream. Any editor is likely working on dozens of books at various stages of completion, all of which need his personal attention, and on top of that spending time in meetings. You'll get a peek into the lives of a few editors in Chapter 26, but for now, please take it as a given that no editor has much time to spend on reading the submissions.

At most publishing companies, assistants, junior editors, or retired editors come in one day a week to read the "slush." They then pass on the 10 percent or so they feel might interest an editor. Don't worry—even if the reader is a new assistant fresh out of college, it doesn't take much training to weed out the poorly written, badly targeted, or just plain unoriginal writing and pull out only what might be good enough. The editor will still reject most of what he sees, but at least he's not spending as much time sorting through it.

Help, I'm Sinking!

Unfortunately, the system doesn't always work this smoothly. Publishers also get completely overloaded and then you might not hear from them at all, or not for a long time. The sad fact is that when people at publishing houses get busy, it's the slush pile that suffers. Editors can always read it tomorrow, or next week, but if a book is due at a printer, or a writer is waiting for comments on a manuscript, or an illustrator needs guidance, that must come first.

So manuscripts pile up on desks, in file cabinets, and in bookcases (and that's why it's called a slush *pile*). Typically a publisher has a backlog of a month or two and deals with it in batches between busy times. But it can get worse. If a company gets publicity in a writer's magazine or a staff person leaves, hundreds of manuscripts can pile up, and the publisher may resort to closing its doors to more submissions until it can get caught up.

> **Class Rules**
>
> If you don't like competing with thousands of other people, children's publishing is not for you. The Society of Children's Book Writers and Illustrators has well over 10,000 members, and plenty more who aren't members. Keep striving to do your best and most creative work so you can stand out in this crowd.

It's also true that more people are writing, and writing better. Ten years ago, a publisher might have received 2,000 manuscripts and queries in a year. That's a lot, but it's manageable. If three people each read 10 or 20 manuscripts a week, they can keep up with it. Today, that same company, with perhaps the same number of staff to deal with the manuscripts, is getting 6,000 manuscripts. That's a lot.

Do I Know You?

Faced with this situation, and perhaps not needing to find many new authors, many publishers have thrown in the towel and stopped reading submissions unless manuscripts come in from someone they know, or from someone with an agent, or someone with a previously published book. A few ask you to "query first" (send a query letter) so they have the opportunity to judge if the book you've written even sounds like something they would publish.

To many writers, it can seem that most publishers have closed their doors. That isn't true, as noted in Chapter 16, but certainly more are closed than used to be. And as more publishers close their doors, the ones who are left must deal with more mail. It's little wonder that it can be three, four, five, six months, or more before some publishers respond.

Lost in the Shuffle

A final reason that it can take so long to hear from publishers is that they are seeing more manuscripts that do not deserve an immediate rejection. Thanks to the work of organizations like the SCBWI, more manuscripts than ever are coming in that have possibilities. Plenty of manuscripts can be rejected quickly, perhaps after reading only a few lines, but manuscripts that can be read all the way through and need to be thought about are the ones that take up a reader's time. And there are more of these.

The competition is tough, if you haven't picked up on that by now. Keep at it, and at the end of the process, after making contact with an editor and perhaps revising a manuscript several times, you might just have a contract. And then you are on your way to publication!

> **Can You Keep a Secret?**
>
> I once judged a contest for unpublished authors, in which I mostly read the first chapters of novels. Of more than 70 submissions, very few were easy to reject. Many, though perhaps after revision, could be published. In a competition this strong, sometimes it can be hard to get noticed.

The Least You Need to Know

- All publishers need fresh talent. You need to put your best foot forward when approaching them.

- Get to know publishers and editors at conventions and conferences.

- Be restrained when you first hear from an editor, at least in your response. Later you can celebrate all you want!

◆ Persistence is a key to success, but no guarantee.

◆ Publishers get swamped by manuscripts and often take months to respond. Be patient.

Part 5

Working With a Publisher

You've made it over the transom, and now you're working with a publisher—or at least you're about to be, because they've sent you a contract. So to start, Part 5 helps you understand the contract and explains how copyright law affects what you do.

Part 5 also introduces you to the revision process, as you work with an editor, and examines what happens when an illustrator gets to work. In the following chapters, I introduce you to some editors and an art director as well as some other folks who join the team.

Chapter 23

Oh Boy! A Contract!

In This Chapter

- What a publishing contract does
- How you'll be paid and what you'll have to do
- The mysteries of subsidiary rights
- Legal terms and other arcane knowledge
- Negotiating tactics

At some point, if you stick it out and develop your skills and have some luck, you'll hear from an editor who would like to offer you a contract. The excitement generated by this phone call, e-mail, or letter might lead you to unquestioningly hand over your first-born child, if requested—but negotiate the terms of a contract? You can't be bothered. You're going to be published!

Calm down and educate yourself about contracts first. In this chapter, you learn what a publishing contract involves, what to expect, and what to ask for. You might not be able actually to demand much, especially the first time around, but it's good to understand what you're signing. So read on and get ready to ask your editor questions.

Getting the Good News

The initial stages of the process vary. If an editor is interested in a manuscript—perhaps after corresponding with a writer about it, on first reading—she might have to obtain some kind of approval from the company to *acquire* it. At a minimum, this usually means getting several higher-ups to read it and to approve the *acquisition* during a publishing meeting or an acquisition meeting. Financial analysis of the expected costs and possible profits may also be required, perhaps in great detail, and perhaps just as rough estimates. If the book is a picture book, an illustrator's contract always comes after the author's contract, possibly a year or more later.

def•i•ni•tion

To **acquire** a manuscript, an editor receives approval from the company and then negotiates a contract with an author. Your manuscript is now (in a sense) the company's property. The editor has made an **acquisition**.

You might hear before or after the meeting. If the editor contacts you before the meeting, don't celebrate yet—the company might decide not to acquire your manuscript after all. Wait for the actual contract offer and *then* cut loose. To learn more about this process, read my article about it at www.underdown. org/acquisition-process.htm.

Contracts are complicated and full of terms most people just don't know. To help you assess where you should start in learning about contracts, take this short true or false quiz:

1. *Copyright* refers to the copy an author writes.

2. A *royalty* is an honorary payment you receive for winning a literary prize.

3. *Subsidiary rights* are the rights of subsidiaries, or divisions, of a publisher to publish your work.

4. *Joint accounting* is a clause you want in a contract—it means you and the publisher jointly track sales of a book.

5. An important negotiating tactic is to decide what you want before you start to talk and then walk away if you don't get it.

The answers? They're *false* for every one, but for different reasons:

1. *Copyright* is the right to make copies of an original work. Illustrations and text can be copyrighted.

2. A *royalty* is a percentage you're paid out of the money a publisher receives for the sale of a book.

3. *Subsidiary rights* are actually the rights a publisher sells to other companies to make a paperback edition, audio recording, or some other use of your work.

4. You *don't* want *joint accounting* in your contract. You'll find out why in the following section.

5. Walking if you don't get what you want can be counterproductive. Maybe you don't need what you thought you did, or a compromise will get you something you hadn't even thought about. Negotiating a contract involves give and take.

How did you do? If you got all of them right, you might not need to read this chapter. Otherwise, read on!

Tit for Tat

Publishing contracts exist for a very simple reason. You, as the writer or illustrator, are the creator of intellectual property. This property is not something physical like a house or a car; however, you can sell it, or sell the rights to make use of it. In short, you can sell the right to copy your work—that's your copyright. (Chapter 24 covers copyright in more detail.)

A publisher can do many different things with copyrighted work, from publishing it once in a magazine to publishing it in many different ways over a period of many years. But first, the publisher must get the right to use the property. It gets this right with a contract. The core of a publishing contract is the transfer of a creator's rights to his or her work to a company that (you hope) has the resources to use those rights in ways you could not. In return, you receive some form of compensation.

Class Rules

Don't hesitate to ask for an explanation of anything you don't understand in a contract. Many contracts are hard to understand, or are vague, and you need to know what the contract means. If you don't understand it, how can you truly agree to it?

What can you expect to see in a contract? Contracts may be only a few pages long or more than 20, but they all cover much the same ground. For the most part, author and illustrator contracts are very similar, but this chapter notes a few points that apply to illustrators only.

When you receive your first contract, the following information should help you navigate it. But if you run into something you don't understand, just ask. Your editor won't think you're stupid for doing so—he might not even understand what you're asking about and have to ask someone in his company's contract department. Don't sign your contract without understanding all of it first.

What You Gotta Do

Of course, you aren't just handing in your work and going on vacation. Publishers usually ask you to do more than that, and they'll spell out just what that is in the contract.

You'll be expected to revise your work to suit their standards. This can be sticky! What if they want you to make changes you don't want to make? The contract may allow them to make them without you. Most publishers want you to be happy with changes, but almost all publishers put language in their *standard contracts* that allows them to decide on their own when a manuscript or artwork is truly finished.

def•i•ni•tion

A publisher's **standard contract** covers all the items they think they need in a contract, which won't all just be to their benefit—some items will be there because everyone will expect them. The terms in this contract are sometimes referred to as *boilerplate*, implying they're just stamped on, like a plate on a boiler.

You'll also be expected to meet the publisher's deadlines. This may involve not only finishing the manuscript or illustrations on time, but also handling edits and other materials sent for checking at later stages.

The contract might even specify that you allow the publisher to use your likeness (a photo!), your name, and information about you to promote the book. Unless you're publicity-shy, you should have no objection to this. Publishers generally don't require that you actively promote your book, but they may encourage you to do so.

What Publishers Do

In return for your labor, and for the use of your creative efforts, you can expect certain things from publishers. Generally, a publisher …

- Pays you royalties on book sales, usually twice a year, and usually gives you some money up front (an advance). Sometimes, you get an upfront fee only.

- Pays you a share of any proceeds from selling the right to do something with it, such as make a book club edition or a film.

- Lets you see layouts, sketches, and the like while the book is being developed.

◆ Sends you free copies of the book on publication and allows you to buy more at a discount.

◆ Copyrights your words or your art in your name.

In practice, a publisher may do more than this, such as send copies of reviews and consult with you even when it's not required, but they'll try to keep their contractual obligations to a minimum. However, don't assume that a publisher will do something that isn't in the contract just because it's standard practice. If it's not in the contract, it might not happen.

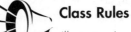

Class Rules _____

Illustrators' contracts should include a clause that covers care and return of art. Publishers typically return your art to you after they no longer need it for production purposes. Some actually agree to do so in the contract and may even specify its value to be able to compensate you if any of it is damaged or lost while it's under their control.

Your Allowance

You live on the income produced by your creative work. Well, most likely you still have your day job. But you certainly want to make a living from your creative work, so the payment you receive for a book may be the most important part of any publishing contract.

How you get paid depends on the publisher. Traditional trade publishers have long paid *royalties* based on a book's *list price*. Typically, the royalty is 8 to 10 percent for a hardcover book, and split between author and illustrator for a picture book. Newer publishers or publishers in other markets often pay royalties based on *net price*, which is the amount of money they actually receive when they sell the book; these are often 10 to 15 percent, again split if an illustrator is involved. The percentage may be higher, but keep in mind that a publisher may sell a book to bookstores and wholesalers at a discount as much as 50 percent off list price, so figure out what you earn per copy sold rather than focusing on the percentage.

def•i•ni•tion _____

A **royalty** is a certain percentage of the price of the book multiplied by the number of copies sold. It might be based on **list price** (or retail price), the price marked on the book, or **net price**, which is the amount of money the publisher receives for the book.

Contracts usually specify a paperback royalty, which is lower than the hardcover, and may go into other kinds of books as well, such as board books and big books.

Cash in Advance

If you're paid royalties, you'll also usually get an *advance*. This is money paid in anticipation of the money that will be earned from the book. For example, a writer might receive a $6,000 advance for a novel and a 10 percent list royalty. If the book sells for a list price of $16, the royalty is $1.60 per book. The first $6,000 counts against the advance, but after that, the advance has *earned out*. In this case, the writer receives more royalties after 3,750 copies are sold. Or imagine the case of a writer and illustrator splitting the royalties for a picture book. One of them might get a $4,000 advance and a 5 percent list royalty on a list price of $16. They will be paid 80¢ per book, and the book will earn out after 5,000 copies are sold. Until that point, the money earned is charged against the advance.

Sometimes, all you receive is your advance. Say a publisher pays an illustrator an $8,000 advance for work on a picture book, against a 5 percent *net* royalty. If the book retails for $16, and the publisher actually receives $8, 5 percent of $8 is 40¢ per book. The publisher would have to sell 20,000 copies of the book before it earns anything, and the book may never reach that level.

These two examples also illustrate a reality of picture-book contracts. Although the author and illustrator are generally paid the same royalties, the illustrator typically receives a larger advance. Writers find this annoying, but a picture-book illustrator usually has considerably more work still to do when the contract is signed than the writer does. Fair or not, it's a common practice.

Timing of advances is important, too, because you don't receive royalties until after the book comes out. Some publishers pay an advance on the signing of the contract, which isn't just good for you, it also helps them lock you in. If you want to get out of

def•i•ni•tion

So you won't have to wait until publication to be paid, a publisher usually pays an **advance** on the royalties, but you must wait for the advance to be recouped before seeing more income. An advance **earns out** when the amount earned in royalties reaches the amount paid out in the advance.

Can You Keep a Secret?

Most publishers pay royalties every six months. For January to June, for example, you might get paid in September. Why the delay? Publishers are waiting to be paid themselves, because booksellers can take months to pay, and they are waiting for returns (unsold books). Returns sometimes come back in such numbers that a book has negative sales in a selling period.

such a contract, you'll have to repay that money. Many publishers pay another chunk when they approve the manuscript or artwork, which might require considerable work on your part. And some publishers pay part of the advance on publication. This isn't as bad as it sounds, and it's still better than waiting to be paid royalties. Be sure you understand what you need to do to be paid your advance, or the different parts of your advance, and when it should happen.

Depending on the publisher and the type of book, advances for first-time authors usually range from $2,000 to perhaps $6,000, with illustrators receiving twice that, more or less. You may have heard of some higher figures for first books, but they're not typical; they're most likely for novels represented by agents and make up a small percentage of the total.

Work-for-Hire

Some publishers use contracts that put you in a *work-for-hire* position and pay you a fee instead of an advance and royalties. If the fee is a good one, this isn't necessarily a bad option. It's common for illustrators doing jackets or illustrations for textbooks. Mass-market publishers also use contracts that put writers in an employee role and allow them to copyright the book in the company's name.

Professional organizations such as the Author's Guild and Graphic Artist's Guild raise some red flags about work-for-hire contracts. Such contracts are fine if you're doing work like producing material about a TV character according to the publisher's detailed guidelines; they're not okay if you have created a truly original work. You want the world to know that *you* created that work, and you want to have the rights to your work when the book goes out of print. If your work is your own, not based on someone else's characters or a TV show or movie, try to keep the copyright in your name and resist the publisher getting the right to reuse your work in different editions or other media without paying you an additional fee.

def•i•ni•tion

Work-for-hire contracts are common in many businesses, not just book publishing. If you do this kind of work, you're signing over ownership of your creative output to the company that hired you. The company can use your work as it sees fit, although you might be able to negotiate some limits to that.

Subsidiary Rights

As I explain in more detail in Chapter 24, your creation of an original work means you have the right to dispose of a bundle of different ways in which your work can be used. The publisher will directly use the right to publish a book, but most publishers also want to acquire *subsidiary rights*—the "other things" you can do with your text or illustrations.

If you have an agent, the agent may retain some or all of the subsidiary rights. If you don't have an agent, publishers usually keep half of the subsidiary income and the illustrator and author share the rest. If the agreement is for your work only, you usually receive the entire half the publisher didn't receive.

Some subsidiary agreements are for other kinds of books. Until recently, many publishers sold the right to make a paperback of a book they published in hardcover. Now, most publish their own paperbacks. But books are also sold by book clubs, school book fairs, and publishers in other countries, perhaps in translation, perhaps in English. Publishers usually work pretty hard to sell rights in these areas.

Magazine rights are licensed under the names of first serial (before publication) and second serial (after publication). Many publishers are generous with the proceeds from the first serial rights, on the grounds that a magazine article based on your book that came out before publication would do a lot to publicize the book. They might pay an author 80 percent of the proceeds if a sale is made for first serial. That's not a given, but worth asking for.

The use of excerpts from your work, or even from the whole work in a larger collection, falls under the umbrella of permissions. With the interest in using trade books in the classroom well established, this is perhaps the most common area for a subsidiary rights sale because textbook publishers seek out material, sometimes years after publication of the original book.

A book's content can also be enhanced in various ways, ranging from videos to plays to maybe even television shows. Don't count on sales in this area, but if they come, they can be lucrative.

And then we get to the tricky area of electronic rights. The hype has died down, but publishers remain interested in obtaining the rights to publish or sell rights in this area, while preserving the usual

Class Rules

If you don't have an agent, don't make a fuss about "giving" the publisher the right to do something with your subsidiary rights. As an individual, in almost all cases you would find it almost impossible to do anything with any rights you did keep. Let the publisher sell them: 50 percent of something is more than 100 percent of nothing.

splits. The situation is still in flux, but don't expect to be able to insist on special terms. Publishers will drop a deal rather than give in on what they've set up as their standard in this area.

If you're just getting started, look at subsidiary rights as the icing on the cake. For your first few books, you can't expect much in the way of income in this area, so seeking changes to the standard language might not be a good use of your energy. Understand what this is all about, but don't make it a big issue.

Legal Language

Get past the things you must do and the payments and splits you can expect from a publisher, and you come to a tedious and sizable part of the contract: the legal language. Here you'll find a thicket of clauses, many designed to guard a publisher against some pretty unlikely bad outcomes.

Should you be concerned about these clauses? Well, are you concerned about being struck by lightning? No? That's about how concerned you should be about many of these, because that's about how likely some of these are to be activated—they may have gotten into the contract due to things that happened to the publisher's adult division (or even their TV or Internet division), or due to some contract manual reading someone in the contract department did on a quiet day.

What basic clauses should you expect? That really varies. Typical clauses include the following:

- ◆ A guarantee that you actually control the rights you're handing over—that you haven't already sold them.

- ◆ A warranty that you aren't infringing anyone else's copyright or saying anything libelous or otherwise illegal.

- ◆ What the publisher can do in the event of legal action against you and the publisher.

- ◆ How and under what circumstances the contract can be terminated or canceled.

> **Can You Keep a Secret?**
>
> Lawyers specializing in book contracts exist, but they are expensive. Instead of an agent or lawyer, published authors should consider joining the Author's Guild (see Appendix B). Members can get the services of the staff lawyers in deciphering a contract. Illustrators can join the Graphic Artist's Guild or consult their *Handbook*.

- What happens when the book goes out of print.

- What happens if the book isn't published in a timely manner.

Should you understand these clauses? Absolutely. Just don't expect to be able to change them, with the possible exception of the final two. Unlike some of the things discussed earlier, these clauses are usually not ones your editor has any authority to change.

Making Changes

So what can you change? How much you can change in the terms offered to you depends almost entirely on your leverage. If you're a first-time author, you have very little. If you have something of a track record or have been lucky enough to have acquired an agent, you might have more leverage. But there will still be a limit as to how far a publisher will go. A publisher also might not see a need to make any changes. They may already have offered you terms they believe to be reasonable, taking into account what their competitors do and what their own pay scale is from beginners to top-level authors. Sometimes, you just have to accept what's offered.

Regardless of just how much leverage you have, you won't get more by acting outraged or being inflexible. Start by offering a short list of changes you'd like. Discuss these with your editor. Be firm, yet polite and professional, and be ready to suggest or listen to alternatives. This approach, even in a negotiation in which you end up getting little of what you want, will earn you the publisher's respect and therefore increase the chances of improvements the next time around.

Persistence can pay off, too; in response to an initial "no" to a requested change, ask the publisher what they could offer you instead. Keep talking. The longer the negotiations go on, the more likely it is you'll be offered concessions in an effort to resolve them. But if you do negotiate for some time, be careful not to bring up previously resolved issues. As an editor who has been on the other side of such negotiations, I can tell you that will make it difficult to put together a package that will work for both sides.

If you want changes beyond the (usually small) ones you can get from a publisher when you aren't a big name, you need to be able to back them up with a reason. Tell them why they shouldn't be treating you as a run-of-the-mill author or illustrator. Be realistic. Having a family member who works for a movie studio, for example, does not justify withholding movie rights from the subsidiary rights section. Believing that your book could be a best-seller won't get you a six-figure advance. If a clause in their contract is completely out of line with what their competitors are offering, a publisher might change it. But they might not. I've heard very few arguments in this area that really hold up; most people do better by just asking for improvements.

Playground Stories _____

Literary agent Sandy Ferguson Fuller has this to say about negotiations: "Don't try to tinker too much with advance amounts, but do insist on reasonable royalty rates. With a standard trade book, definitely try to negotiate a royalty-based instead of a flat-fee agreement, even if you must waive any advance and agree to a substandard royalty. Be sure that the various deadlines are reasonable. Don't be unreasonable in your dealings with a publisher—but don't be intimidated either. If a contract isn't equitable or negotiations turn sour, turn away—believe in your work, take a risk, and persevere—you will find a better deal!"

Here are some goodies to ask for, beyond the obvious idea of a larger advance or more free copies of your book. In the long run, you may be able to get what's called an *escalator clause*, which increases the royalty after a certain number of books are sold. You can ask for a *flow-through clause*, which passes through your share of large subsidiary rights sales (if your advance has earned out) when the money is received so you don't have to wait for the next royalty statement. Ask for a higher royalty on "special sales," or deals made for large quantities of the book at a high discount, for which you usually receive less than your usual royalty. And ask again with the next contract.

As well as asking for goodies, watch out for no-no's:

◆ Object to your royalty being reduced on small printings of the book. (Losing an increase in royalty from an escalator clause isn't so bad as long as it doesn't go lower than it was to start with.)

◆ Avoid joint accounting, which ties together one book's advance with those of other books so all of them have to earn out their advances before you see royalties.

◆ Be sure the book is copyrighted in your name, not the publisher's name. You don't want to actually give up ownership of the copyright; you just want to let the publisher use it.

Your agent might have a somewhat different idea about what's important in a contract. So might you, and you should decide what that is. But no matter what you want, do not immediately walk away if you don't get it. Instead, try to do better. Even a publisher that won't make any changes at all to a contract may be worth working with for now, but go into all your negotiations with the attitude that the best contract is one with which both sides are happy. Be willing to compromise and to listen, and expect to be listened to and compromised with. If, time after time, you're unhappy with what you have when the negotiations are over, either you're working with the wrong publisher, or your expectations are too high. Find out by talking to other authors who are in a similar situation. Then, move on, or adjust.

The Least You Need to Know

◆ Contracts in publishing involve a creator (author or illustrator) handing over the right to publish a work in return for some kind of compensation.

◆ Publishers usually pay royalties to an author and make other commitments in a contract, such as providing free copies to the author.

◆ Publishers don't just hope to publish a work—they hope to sell its subsidiary rights, and a large part of a contract spells out just what's involved.

◆ Much of a contract is made up of legal language you probably can't change but should still try to understand.

◆ Ask for what you think you want in a contract, but be ready to compromise.

24

Copyright Basics

In This Chapter

- ◆ The what's and why's of copyright
- ◆ How unpublished works are protected
- ◆ Can you protect your ideas?
- ◆ Folktales and copyright
- ◆ Avoiding plagiarism—intentional or otherwise

Maybe you've worried about someone stealing your fabulous idea for a book. After all, few people have the genius necessary to come up with such a fine idea! But you don't have to worry because ideas themselves aren't worth much on their own, at least under copyright law. You have to *write* something to use the idea. Or maybe you wonder what you can take from someone else's work. In either case, you need to learn some copyright basics.

A Tale of Two Ideas

Do you feel a little shy about sharing your idea for a children's book with anyone because you fear that whomever you share your tale with will move with it and "steal" your idea? It happens to the best of us—especially when

Can You Keep a Secret?

Many writers believe that they must file with the copyright office before using the copyright symbol (©) on their work. In actuality, the use of a copyright notice *does not* require advance permission from or registration with the U.S. Copyright Office.

we're unpublished and wanting desperately to write a book. But there's a difference between an unpublished work and an "idea" for a book. Consider the following tale of two aspiring writers.

Both Writer A and Writer B knew that Jane Pen-Name had published several books and numerous magazine articles so they each approached Jane, seeking advice about writing a book. Jane, wanting to help, asked each of them to describe what they planned to do. Writer A candidly talked about his book series idea. Writer B, however, had a funny look on her face, paused, and said, "Well, I want to tell you, but I'm afraid you'll steal my idea!" After Jane reassured her that her "idea" was safe, Writer B relaxed and talked about her book concept.

Unfortunately, however, this "thievery" paranoia is common and can prevent you from receiving useful feedback by showing your manuscript to others. Some people even worry about showing a manuscript to publishers.

def•i•ni•tion

Your ideas become **original expression** and are thus protected by the copyright laws of the United States, and many other countries, when you take those ideas and actually create something original—a book, a story, a sculpture, a symphony, etc.

Ideas are not protected by copyright laws. An idea is an idea is an idea (with apologies to Gertrude Stein), and that's all it is. It's what you *do* with that idea that matters. In fact, one of the most frequent questions I receive on my website and at conferences where I speak is, "How do I stop someone from taking my really wonderful idea?" My response: "You can't!" But you can protect the *original expression* of your idea. Put it into finished form, and you can protect your own unique way of expressing your idea. The same applies to illustration. Copyright law protects original unpublished work of any kind as soon as it's created.

Let's look at an example: Gail Bigidea comes up with a great concept for a children's book about a girl and her horse. She tells her buddy, Claire Klepto, about her promising story line. Now that Gail has spilled the beans to Claire, Claire can use the idea and Gail has no recourse. But if Gail writes down her horsey tale—complete with the details of the singing ducks and talking trees and her own vocabulary and style—and then sees *that* story three years from now with "Claire Klepto" as the author, Gail can come after Claire with the full power of copyright law behind her.

Still not convinced that story ideas aren't important? Then think of any famous story, boil it down to its "core idea," and see if it still seems original. Take *Where the Wild Things Are* by Maurice Sendak. It's about a child and monsters. How many stories can you think of about children and imaginary monsters? About a child and his or her first pet? A first day at school? Dealing with a new sibling? Dozens for each type, right? And of course, people are constantly talking about the many sources for the *Harry Potter* stories; no, they aren't completely original, but J. K. Rowling did mix all those sources together in a completely original way. Does this mean that everyone is "stealing" from an original story? No, that's just part of the creative process.

What Copyright Is

This leads to the details of protecting your created work with a copyright. The forefathers of the United States put copyright into the Constitution (Article 1, Section 8). It says, "To promote the Progress of Science and Useful arts by securing for limited Times to Authors and Inventors the exclusive Right to their respective Writings and Discoveries." This part of the Constitution protects what's known as "intellectual property" and is put into effect through the laws of copyright, trademark, and patents. Most countries have similar laws. Today creators turn to the U.S. Copyright Office to ensure our artistic creations remain *our* artistic creations.

Copyright law matters most in publishing; trademark and patent laws are worlds of their own. From that basis in the Constitution, a series of laws have set up the rules and time limits for copyright. Title 17, U.S. Code, provides protection to the authors of "original works of authorship." Meanwhile, Section 106 of the Copyright Act provides the possessor of the copyright several inalienable rights with respect to the copyrighted work. Basically, the copyrighter holds the power over the reproduction, distribution, sale, and performance of the work. So anyone wanting to use your work must have your permission, and if you require it, must pay you for it. As mentioned in Chapter 23 on contracts, that's the basis of publishing as a business: you grant a publisher the right to use your copyrighted work in return for a payment.

> **Playground Stories**
>
> The copyright symbol informs everyone of the copyright protection. If the work carries proper notice and someone uses the material or steals it, they can't claim innocent infringement. Innocent infringement is when the party who used the creative property of another didn't realize the work was copyrighted. If the infringement isn't innocent, the infringer is liable for extra damages.

def•i•ni•tion

When a manufacturer or dealer distinguishes a product from competitors by a specific design, word, or letter, the registration that protects the company's representation is called a **trademark**. Trademark law most often affects publishing when trademarked names or characters appear in books.

Before I go any further, I want to point out that trade publishing is built on copyright—creative and individual expression. Much of mass-market publishing is built on another kind of intellectual property: *trademarks*. The stories in many mass-market books, although they may be copyrighted, don't sell because they're original. They sell because the consumer recognizes the trademark, either the publisher's own, like Golden Books, or something from another medium, such as Disney, Pokémon, or even Hershey's Kisses.

Safe ... So Far

Okay, so copyright laws protect your creation—not your mere idea—but what do you do about it? You don't need to register your work with the copyright office before sending it to a publisher. In fact, doing so marks you as an amateur. If the publisher selects your work for publication, the publisher will automatically file for the copyright for you. Just note on your manuscript the word *copyright* and your name and the date.

Can You Keep a Secret?

To find out more about copyright rules and regulations, hop online and navigate your way to www.copyright.gov, the official website of the U.S. Copyright Office.

Some have suggested that to prove the date when you did this, you can mail a copy of the manuscript to yourself and keep it unopened. The postmark establishes the date on which the manuscript took final form. This might not be accepted in a legal setting, however. It's best just to limit the distribution of the manuscript. Do send it to individual publishers. Don't post it online—that makes it too easy for someone to claim your work as their own.

But That's Not Fair!

You're relieved that your own work is protected, but what if you want to use someone else's work in some way? Should you just forget about it? No, copyright law doesn't protect everything: some creative works were never copyrighted, or their copyright has expired, and even those that are copyrighted can be used—so long as you follow *fair use* guidelines.

Keep in mind that facts can't be copyrighted. You don't have to acknowledge a source for widely known information, from addresses to dates from history to the way the elements in the periodic table are arranged. Ingredients in a recipe or materials for an activity also cannot be copyrighted—no "original expression" was needed to create such a list, although there may be some in the steps to follow in the recipe or activity. Most of us, though, aren't compiling mere lists of facts.

The Trouble with Folktales

What if you're creating a work that essentially retells an existing story such as a folktale? Your work differs in the details from the source but has more in common with it than the bare idea. Or you might want to tailor a folktale you heard as a child or came across in your travels or research. What can you do? After all, you know you didn't have the "original" idea.

The good news is that, in many cases, the story is in the *public domain*, meaning it's not protected by copyright law and may be used by other authors in any way they choose without permission. Copyright does not last forever (although the rules do change, and have as recently as 1998). Anything published before 1923 in the United States is almost certain to be in the U.S. public domain, and many other works may be as well.

def•i•ni•tion

Creative work that's not protected by copyright is in the **public domain**. The author of that work isn't entitled to any payment if someone else uses it and doesn't even have to be asked for permission.

Look at your source or sources. Was it published in a collection a long time ago? If so, you're in the clear. Keep in mind, though, that *unpublished* works get special protection, so steer clear of diaries and the like, unless you're ready to go on a search for heirs. Can you find multiple sources for a story, even if they're recent? That's okay, too. Cite all of them in your notes for the book, don't rely heavily on one of them, and go ahead and tell the story. Just like writers of historical fiction must check their sources, you—the reteller of a folktale—must check your sources, acknowledge them, and be sure you aren't relying on someone else's copyrighted work as your sole source.

Just because a story is in the public domain, or because you've been able to find several different versions of it, you should still do some careful work before using it. Do you know the culture from which it originates or in which you want to set it? If you

Class Rules

Using someone else's work as a source for your own telling of a folktale (or tall tale, biography, or work of history) is okay, provided you've used at least three sources and you explain how you used them in an acknowledgment or author's note.

don't, you might create an inauthentic story, with details or a plot turn or a moral that no member of that culture would create. Also, do you understand how folktales work? As Aaron Shepard, a successful folktale reteller, says, "If you want to retell folktales successfully, it's not enough to be familiar with just the tale you want to retell. You have to know folklore in general. Otherwise, there's not much chance you'll handle it right." In fact, Shepard continues, confirming, "Usually this means knowing folklore better than most editors."

Making Pictures from Other Pictures

If you're like most illustrators, you work from visual reference materials. For a picture-book story about a contemporary family, perhaps you shoot a series of color photos to use; for a historical setting, maybe you dig deeper and find references for the buildings, the clothing, the furniture, and even the style of glasses the main character wears. What's fair and what isn't?

The tough question you have to ask is, are you making use of someone else's original expression, and maybe even damaging their ability to profit from it? If you created some photos yourself, there's no problem. If you used visuals from many sources, there's no problem. If you used a historical public domain source, there's no problem. There *is* a problem if you base the composition of an entire illustration, from position of furniture to the postures of the people shown, on someone else's work. It doesn't matter if you've used different colors or a different medium. You've based your work too directly on theirs.

Can You Keep a Secret?

To learn more about copyright law and what it means to you, check out Stanford University's great resource site at fairuse.stanford.edu.

When in doubt, ask your publisher for guidance. And remember, you can use anything you create in any way you choose—although the scrupulous illustrator will obtain model releases from anyone who posed for them.

"It Was on the Internet" and Other Lame Excuses

Copyright law has a fairly simple core, but how it plays out in practice can get complicated. The situation isn't made any easier by the fact that there are some surprising misconceptions about copyright circulating in the general public.

One is the rather fuzzy idea that material on the Internet somehow isn't subject to the same rules as material in books. This just isn't true. You can't use a photo or a story from a website without the creator's permission any more than you can if they were in a book.

People also tend to have vague, and, let's face it, self-serving ideas about what *fair use* is. The common idea seems to be: "I'm using it, so that must be fair." The reality is more complicated. Yes, you can use material from copyrighted works, either in direct quotation or in paraphrase. What's fair depends not only on how much of another's work you use, but how you acknowledge it and make use of it. A properly attributed two-line quotation from a newspaper article is just fine. Use two lines from a short poem, however, and you've gone beyond fair use, even if you acknowledge it, because a poem is so short.

Copyright laws can get complicated, so the best thing to do is keep careful notes on any material you use that's not your own. Don't go ahead and seek permission to use that material, however. You might not need it, and you might end up paying a permission fee for something that falls under "fair use." Do get your notes out and discuss what you did with your publisher after you sign your contract. They may run it by their legal department, and at worst, you might have to make some revisions. That's far better than receiving a notice that you and your publisher have been sued for copyright infringement!

def•i•ni•tion

Copyright law allows an exception to the protection of copyrighted material. Under **fair use**, a modest quantity of a copyrighted work can be quoted in another work without permission or payment, provided that material is acknowledged.

Stealing Is Stupid

You might still have concerns about sending your manuscript to a publisher and having them put someone else's name on it. Or perhaps you're an illustrator and you're concerned that someone could use your carefully created sample illustrations without your permission. Stop worrying. That kind of stealing—by the publisher, by you, by anyone writing a book—is just plain stupid.

To start with, copyright laws do protect writers and illustrators. To steal your creation, the thief literally needs to take a recognizable chunk. In the form of a children's picture book, that might mean the entire story or some illustrations. Even taking extended passages from a book, or paraphrasing them in detail, is a copyright violation, and the victim, or his or her publisher, could go to court and win. Copyright "theft," in fact, is easier to detect and prove than theft of physical property.

Publishers in particular have very little if anything to gain from "stealing" people's creative work—and much to lose. Imagine you send a manuscript to a publisher. They advise you, "Sorry, not for us." Three years later, you see your story, word for word, on the shelves at the local bookstore. A nightmare, but it's not likely to happen. Why would a publisher do that? The gains for the publisher would be minimal—perhaps a savings of a few thousand dollars. But the loss to their reputation could be monumental if the story of what they did came out. The publisher would lose its good name—and that's enormously important to the company. Other authors, writers, illustrators, agents, and even people working for that publisher would no longer trust the company. If those people don't trust it, the publisher won't receive good submissions, staff will leave, and eventually the company could fall apart.

Such stealing is just not necessary. Publishers receive too many great stories from respected writers to need to connive to thwart the success of an unknown, previously unpublished writer by taking the writer's work and not pursuing a contract with that writer. Most publishing houses run on a schedule like a newsroom—harried and frantic. No one has time to steal your story. Of course, as we've all heard, stealing is said to happen in other parts of the media world, notably in the film industry. What's the difference? The big difference is that films often get go-aheads on the basis of an idea, with the screenplay worked and reworked to the point that no one author can claim it as his or her own (and because the studio owns the copyright, that's beside the point anyway). Thankfully, children's publishing—and most adult publishing—operate with more respect for the creator.

The Least You Need to Know

- Ideas cannot be copyrighted or protected, but work put into a final form can.

- You don't need to actually register your unpublished work with the U.S. Copyright Office to protect it.

- If you plan to retell folktales, check your sources. Be sure the story falls within public domain or has multiple sources before proceeding with a manuscript.

- Like authors, illustrators need to be careful in their use of reference materials.

- Unless you're a lawyer and understand fair use law, look to your publisher for guidance in using copyrighted material.

- Don't fret about a publisher stealing your story; publishers stand to lose more (their good reputation) than they stand to gain (a few bucks) from taking your work.

Chapter 25

Revising and Editing

In This Chapter

- Why revision is important
- How editing helps with revision
- Different kinds of editing
- Working productively with an editor

When your book is under contract, and sometimes before that, an editor is going to want to revise your manuscript. Don't be embarrassed—it's not because you're a novice or a bad writer. Editing and revising are central to producing quality books. Ironically, the writing that seems the most effortless is probably writing that's been sweated over the most!

In this chapter, I explain the different ways editors might work with you to make your writing better and give you some hints on how you can make that relationship more productive.

The Revision Process

Writing is *revising* and rewriting. Just about any writer will agree with that. The first words you put down on the page will not be the ones you end up with. Some writers revise well on their own and turn in manuscripts that need minimal editing. Others prefer to work with editors, often through multiple *drafts*. And others go through some of both, which if they like to keep printouts of their drafts, can result in box after box of revisions of a novel taking up space in their garages. (These do make for good visuals on school visits, though.)

def•i•ni•tion

To **revise** literally means to "re-see"; strive to see your writing afresh when you make changes. Each new version of a manuscript is called a **draft**. Your first draft is just that; a rough draft is one that needs polishing; and a final draft is the one you hope doesn't need to be revised again

Fun with Revision

Revision sounds like a lot of work, and it can be, but true writers savor the process. They know that getting something down on paper is the hard part and then you can play. The pressure's reduced, if not gone, as you revise. When you have something to work with, you can tinker and think and try different ideas. It can only get better (or so you need to tell yourself).

So revision is not only important—it's the best part of writing. But don't take my word for it. Jane Yolen, author of many picture books, novels, and books of poetry, points out that revision is what helps you actually recapture some semblance of that first, dazzling vision, which you then lost when you tried to get it down on paper.

Playground Stories

Jane Yolen says this about revision: "The words in my head were splendid, of course. Once on the page they needed enormous reshaping. Isaac Asimov is reputed to have said that he never revised anything. Then he must have done all that work in his head. I have never written a sentence that couldn't be improved. Even my book *Owl Moon*, which I once heard described by Bill Martin—the dean of children's literature—as 'the perfect picture book, not a word wrong,' could do with some reworking. When I read it to kids, I revise on-the-fly."

Author Larry Dane Brimner agrees, saying that in writing, "The real excitement comes from wordplay. I simply enjoy writing a sentence and then seeing if I can make it sharper or clearer or more beautifully expressed. For me, the enjoyment and art of writing is in rewriting."

Do-It-Yourself Revision

Much of your revision you'll handle on your own, and as you become a more experienced writer, you'll become increasingly able to polish your own work without help from others. Take this as far as you can, being sure to cover the different kinds of editing described later in this chapter, because the more finished your manuscript is when you submit it, the more likely an editor will be interested in it and the more rapidly it may go through the publication process. Manuscripts that need a lot of work won't be tackled until the editor has time to deal with them and will end up on a list far in the future.

Writer and teacher Barbara Seuling says she revises many times: "I revise a gazillion times, and I love the process because I seem to get better in layers. I really do 're-see' each time. I find it invaluable." You don't have to revise quite so many times, of course, but go as far as you can on your own.

Revising with Your Editor

Take advantage of working with an editor. Every writer, no matter how experienced, can use an editor's help when revising. An editor comes to your writing with a fresh perspective. It's not necessarily an objective perspective, just a different one, and perhaps one more akin to that of a reader reacting to your work the first time.

Editors do much more than correct your spelling. In some ways, an editor is a very experienced reader, someone who can be conscious of her own intuitive responses to your work. Editors notice gaps, incomplete characterizations, and vague or awkward statements. They point out problems and maybe even suggest solutions.

Can You Keep a Secret?

Good editing can make a huge difference to your work. An editor is a trained specialist—make use of her. As Barbara Seuling says in *How to Write a Children's Book and Get It Published:* "An editor is trained to observe and will see many things that you cannot see when you are so close to your material. It can be as simple as pointing out that your heroine behaves more like a teenager than a ten-year-old, or it can be more complex, like seeing that you tend to withdraw from potentially strong scenes rather than confront the emotional issues involved."

Ideally, when you and an editor are working on a revision, you'll form a partnership with the goal of producing the best possible finished piece.

The Writer's (and Reviser's) Reference Bookshelf

When you're revising, whether on your own or paired with an editor, you'll want to have certain books available for reference. Some are standard across the industry. Some are of greater use for writers of fiction or of nonfiction. As you develop as a writer, others will become your trusted companions, so modify the following list as you see fit (and see Appendix B offers more information about specific titles):

- *Webster's Third New International Dictionary*
- *The Chicago Manual of Style, 15th Edition*
- *Bartlett's Familiar Quotations*
- A compact print encyclopedia or CD-ROM encyclopedia
- *Dictionary of Modern American Usage*
- *Roget's International Thesaurus*

But It's *My* Story!

All writers fall into the same trap at some time or another: they fall in love with their own writing and believe it's *perfect*, that not one word should be added or taken away from this divine state. You've labored over the work; you've revised; you've listened to your writer's group. It can be tempting to believe that you can't possibly improve it anymore. This is almost certainly not true.

You don't need to take the editor's suggestions literally, on the other hand. It's possible that a problem he points out can be solved by making changes he hasn't actually suggested. For example, if an editor comments that a quiet character acts uncharacteristically noisy at one point in a story, the problem might not be with that incident. You intended that character to act that way, and you need him to. So you don't want to change that, but you've discovered that you need to make a different change. Even though you intended all along to create a character that gets rowdy in certain circumstances, you neglected to establish that earlier on in the story. So this editor's comment on one spot in the story, if you have listened to it carefully, could lead to changes in entirely different places.

It's Wonderful! Now, Let's Change This ... and This ...

When you get started with revision, don't expect an editor to exclaim over the perfection of your manuscript while making only minor spelling corrections. That's not what an editor does. Unless your manuscript is in unusually good shape, you can expect editing at three different levels:

- The overall structure of the manuscript

- The flow of the sentences and paragraphs

- The corrections of spelling, grammar, and the like

Hard work? Yes. But serious writers welcome it.

Playground Stories

Barbara Seuling notes that she much prefers editors who have something to say to her: "I've had editors who took my manuscripts and never touched a word, or gave me any feedback. I didn't trust them. I've heard other writers say the same thing. You feel like you can't trust that someone will be there to catch you if you fall. We all need editors. Then there's the other kind of editor that makes you just about fall in love—who takes every word and every line seriously, and gets into the mind and heart of what you have tried to do and helps you to achieve it."

Structural Editing

Some manuscripts require changes in the way they're put together. They may need to have characters dropped or added, they may need an additional chapter, or they may need to be reorganized. All these kinds of changes fall into the category of what we call *structural*, or *developmental*, *editing*. To do it, your editor may write you a letter, or she may just call you and ask questions, perhaps along the lines of these:

- "What happens to William in the second half of the book? He drops out of the narrative."

- "Have you considered dropping the first chapter and starting in the middle of things with the second?"

- "Could you go into more depth on how jet engines work?"

- "In the conflict between Sue and Naomi, do you need all four arguments?"

- "What if this were told in the first person?"

- "Could you show us in what ways Paul is dependent on his father, instead of just telling us he is?"

> ### Can You Keep a Secret?
>
> Write using active rather than passive constructions whenever you can. "Many soldiers were killed by the sudden freeze" should be "The sudden freeze killed many soldiers." "The kitten was being petted by Calla" should be "Calla was petting the kitten."

Think over these kinds of questions carefully, and if you make changes in response to them, think again. Have your changes affected the book in such a way that you need to make additional changes in response? If you think they do, don't be afraid to make them, or at least to discuss them with your editor.

Even short picture book–length manuscripts can need structural editing. I was working on the manuscript of Larry Pringle's *Bats: Strange and Wonderful* when I noticed that a few lines a couple of paragraphs into the manuscript would actually work better as the opening lines. I suggested this, Larry moved them and reworked them a bit to make them even better (the mark of a skilled writer), and now that book has an opening that has been singled out for praise by reviewers. Author and editor worked together well in this case. Try to do the same.

Work through this stage of revision as thoughtfully as you can. Editors respect writers who respond well to revision suggestions.

Line Editing

When the manuscript is in good shape, it still needs polishing. A careful editor will go through it line by line, with the aim of sharpening descriptions, getting rid of passive constructions, cutting out run-on sentences, and generally making it more of a pleasure to read.

def•i•ni•tion

> A **copy editor** reviews a manuscript for style, punctuation, spelling, and grammar and may also mark chapter titles, headers, and other design elements. After the manuscript is typeset, the **proofreader** reviews the resulting proofs to be sure they accurately follow the manuscript and the copy editor's annotations.

During this stage, your editor is likely to use some strange-looking marks and symbols in the margin of the manuscript and right on the text. Mostly these are the standard marks *copy editors* and *proofreaders* use. You'll see more of them later in the process, when the manuscript is copyedited. There aren't that many to learn. The following figure shows the most commonly used ones; you can find a guide to all the copyediting symbols in standard writing reference works like *The Chicago Manual of Style*.

What they'll write	What it means	The result
(cap) new york city	capitalize these	New York City
(lc) Please $TOP shouting	lowercase these	Please stop shouting
(lc) TOO MUCH NOISE	lowercase all of them	too much noise
It was dark ⌐ and stormy	run them together	It was dark and stormy
Up in the the air	delete this	Up in the air
A drink of water	insert something	A tall drink of water
dirty laundry	put in a space	dirty laundry
(break) Four score and seven	start a new line	Four score and seven
(tr) cats dogs and	transpose these	cats and dogs
The end⊙	insert a period	The end.
Planes, trains and	insert a comma	Planes, trains, and
To sleep perchance to	insert a semicolon	To sleep; perchance to
Bring to an end⊙	insert a colon	Bring to an end:
write off	insert a hyphen	write-off
(stet) Don't touch that!	ignore the mark	Don't touch that!

Take a moment to familiarize yourself with these common editing marks and what they mean.

Soon after this stage, you can expect your editor to declare herself finished with the manuscript. But you aren't yet. The copy editor still has to read it. And you'll then get another chance to learn copyediting symbols.

Just the Facts, Ma'am

For nonfiction manuscripts, and sometimes for historical fiction and folktales as well, many publishers will want to assure that the research you've done is sound. In classic *fact checking*, the fact checker works through your manuscript fact by identifiable fact, checking each in the sources you used and in others he or she locates.

Some manuscripts don't lend themselves well to fact checking. If you've written a historical fiction set in seventeenth-century England, the publisher will get a historian of the period to review your manuscript. If you've done a poetic piece describing the ebb and flow of life in a small salt marsh on the coast of Oregon, your editor might want to send it to a marine biologist with knowledge of that area. In either case, the fact checker will comment on his overall impressions but not necessarily check every fact.

Your editor will pass on comments to you, in some cases reviewing them first. This might seem like a burden to you, but it can also be a great opportunity, a final check that might well turn up a note-taking mistake or a distortion you meant to be a simplification.

Ask for What You Need

Working with an editor isn't all highfalutin' discussions about theme, plot, and turns of phrase, of course. Your editor, as you'll see in detail in the next chapter, is a busy person, probably juggling dozens of books and other responsibilities. Some editors are more active than others, too. So if you need something from him, you may need to ask for it—and you may need to ask for it repeatedly. Don't be bashful about this, but don't be obnoxious either. Just be politely persistent.

"Could You Take Another Look at This, Please?"

Because of the increased amount of work an individual editor is expected to do, some books don't get the editing they really need. The situation in children's books isn't as bad as in adult publishing—yet—where I've heard that at many publishers, manuscripts come in, get a quick copyedit, and go straight into production.

Editing, like writing, requires a kind of relaxed concentration and long stretches of time. Both of these are hard to find in a typical office. Some editors find they can only edit effectively if they take a day to work at home.

Class Rules

If you want to know what your editor thinks, ask her. If you need two more weeks to finish the manuscript, say so. If you don't understand what an editor wants you to do, ask her to clarify. Editors aren't telepathic, even though a good one may seem to understand what you're trying to do with a manuscript better than you do yourself.

What with the increasing workloads expected of editors, in some cases, if an editor thinks there isn't much wrong with a manuscript, and if he's got a lot of other things to do, he may be tempted to move it along without all the editing it needs. If you think that's happening with your manuscript, don't hesitate to express concern. If something's nagging you about your manuscript, tell your editor and ask him what he thinks. Don't accept reassurances—tell him that's not what you want. Tell him you want his expertise, and be as specific as you can be about what you think the problem is.

"Could I Have a Few More Days?"

Most likely you'll be working toward a deadline as you revise, or perhaps for the actual delivery of a manuscript that was signed up on the basis of a proposal. That deadline is there to help the publisher maintain a stable program of so many books per year, but also to help you finish. Deadlines are a useful spur. Are they absolute? No. We all miss deadlines, but we need them; very few books would get published without them. If you can't meet a deadline, ask for a new one. And try not to agree to a deadline you know you won't be able to meet.

 Class Rules

In all your dealings with your editor, be professional. Nothing turns editors off faster than a writer who complains constantly of overwork or tries to wheedle payment of an advance before it is due.

The Care and Feeding of an Editor

Your relationship with your editor will go far beyond the editing of an actual manuscript. Editors often hope that you'll have another manuscript in you they can work on. And you also want to work with them on other ones. So let a relationship develop. Discuss ideas with your editor. Let her know you're interested in hearing her suggestions for subjects for future books. Get to know her interests. You've probably got a lot in common. Make this a friendly relationship, and you'll find that it becomes a more productive one.

Every relationship you'll have with an editor will be different, as noted by Pam Muñoz Ryan, author of picture books and novels:

> Over the years I've had 15 different editors. And like any 15 different friends I might have, each relationship has been different. Some have been simple affiliations where both of us seem to play our author and editor roles rather specifically with formal direction letters and no friendly chit-chat. The books ended up being okay. Other relationships have been more personal, collaborative, and sometimes even fun. Those books were more successful. A few of my author-editor liaisons have been disasters and didn't work at all and I and my manuscript became the bridesmaid of another editor and sometimes another. When that happened, I rarely got bridal treatment, nor did the book. Those titles usually ended up in the mediocre category. But I have been lucky enough to have had a

Can You Keep a Secret?

When you start working with an editor he usually won't expect you to follow all the submission rules. Call him and discuss a story idea instead of formally querying him. Send him a few rough chapters and see what he thinks instead of waiting to finish your manuscript. Editors want to be involved in your work. Let them be.

few pairings that were epiphanies, where I had the opportunity to work with brilliant editors who were prophetic and inspiring. It is no surprise that those titles have won the most awards and are my best sellers.

Like Pam, if you stick with children's publishing you'll have a variety of experiences, but make the best of whatever situation you're in, pull what you can from an editor you might not really get along with, and make the book the best you can make it. And of course, enjoy the experience when you and the editor "click."

The Least You Need to Know

◆ Many writers think revision is the most enjoyable part of writing; it's certainly the most important.

◆ Be open to suggestions from your editor. Your manuscript *can* get better.

◆ Structural editing, line editing, and fact checking are three different kinds of editing your manuscript might go through.

◆ Be sure to ask for editing if you feel your manuscript is being rushed through.

◆ Feel free to build a personal relationship with your editor, and make the most of it if it's a good one.

My Editor Doesn't Understand Me!

In This Chapter

- ◆ Meet some editors
- ◆ A typical editor's background and interests
- ◆ Profiles of editors at different levels at different publishers

Writers typically don't get to know their editors very well at first, perhaps not meeting them in person until one or more books are out, so it's easy to have all kinds of notions about them. This chapter gives some sweeping generalizations about editors, but accurate ones, in my experience. And to help you get to know what your editor might be like even more, I also provide profiles of several editors, showing what they do and how they got where they are today.

What Are Editors Like?

While attending and speaking at conferences over the past several years, I've heard a lot of ideas about what children's book editors are like.

(Because I'm male and 90 percent of editors are women, I am an anomaly right from the start.) To some, editors seem to be book-loving, nurturing-mother archetypes, committed both to creating the very best for children and carefully grooming writers to be the best they can be. Others see editors as scary intellectual gods or goddesses who expect you to understand the difference between *metonymy* and *metaphor.* Still others see editors as skilled hacks dedicated to the smooth functioning of corporate machines.

There's some truth to all these imaginings, but it's a bit more complex than it might at first appear.

The New York Ivory Tower

Editors have some typical characteristics. One is that they are still mostly based in New York. Publishers exist all across North America, but because the large publishers are mostly in New York, the bulk of publishing professionals reside there, too. I've observed that editors are college-educated, with degrees from Ivy League colleges or similar small, liberal arts colleges. Editors generally come from the middle class or above, and they don't go into publishing to make money. In fact, as assistants, they may need some help from their families until they reach a level where they can actually live on their salaries. Children's book editors are mostly young, in their 20s and 30s, until they reach the senior level. This is a job in which people move up or out.

> **Can You Keep a Secret?**
>
> Children's book editors are mostly white. Although people of color are working their way up in the field, editing is still less integrated than many professions.

In short, editors don't "look like America," and may not look much like the writers they work with.

People Who Love Books

Why do people become children's book editors? For the most part, it's not because editors love children, or at least not in the way teachers or pediatric nurses do. Editors may not actually have children; some of the great editors in children's publishing such as Ursula Nordstrom and Margaret K. McElderry never did. Generally, however, editors loved books when they were children, and they still do.

Their love of books is a big part of why editors do what they do. They feel that they have a sense of what children will respond to in a book because the editors themselves still react in the same way. And they want to make more books like the ones they love. Editing is a great way to do this, because an editor's income is more regular than that of a writer or illustrator, and an editor can be involved in so many more books at once. Some editors write on the side, but many don't—their creative side is entirely fulfilled by editing. The opportunity to work with creative people like writers and artists is also part of the attraction.

Outside work, editors are a diverse group. Most read books other than the ones they're working on, and not just children's books. Some read serious adult literature, mysteries, and romance novels. But editors don't spend their entire lives reading. Like everyone else, editors may pursue outdoor sports, belong to a choir, quilt, or do woodworking. For the most part, editors don't dress in black turtlenecks and go to smoky bars to discuss Sartre. Their interests are as varied as anybody else's.

> **Can You Keep a Secret?**
>
> Nervous about holding up your end of the conversation if you meet an editor at a conference? Don't be. Just ask about the editor's favorite books as a child. She'll happily tell you, probably ask you about yours, and if the two of you somehow finish discussing those, just ask what she's enjoyed reading recently.

Cogs in a Machine

Editors love children's books and love to work with people like you. But let's face it, you don't pay their salaries, or at least not yet. The publishing company they work for does, and they wouldn't be doing a good job if they didn't put their company's interests first. That doesn't mean they'll always agree with their immediate boss. In some cases, they'll argue that something that seems to go against the publisher's interests, such as paying a writer a larger advance, might work in the publisher's favor in the long run by making that writer feel more loyal.

It's unrealistic, however, to expect editors to always side with you or champion difficult but exciting books. They know they have to produce books that make money for their publisher or lose their job (or, in the case of a smaller company, risk the publisher going out of business). They probably understand that side of the business all too well, and that means there will be times when they don't publish a manuscript they love because they know it will lose money.

> **Playground Stories**
>
> Increasingly, editors work from home. Melanie Kroupa publishes her books at New York City's Farrar, Straus and Giroux while working nearly 200 miles away outside Boston. Publishing follows the outsourcing trend used in other industries. The copy editor for a book may live in Arizona, and the designer might reside outside Chicago, for example. Core staff still come to the office, but others may not.

Sometimes they will take risks, and that will be more possible at some publishers than at others, but not at every opportunity. They can't.

We'd all like to believe that children's publishing is different from other businesses. Over the past decade, we all learned that it isn't, when every publisher of any size laid off staff, closed imprints, merged with another publisher, or did all of those. The business, at least in New York, is more corporate than it used to be, and editors must be able to navigate those new seas. Editors can no longer just be passionate advocates of books for children; they must also be corporate infighters. I hope you find an editor who balances those two characteristics creatively.

Who are those editors? Read on, and go online to www.underdown.org/cig-editor-profiles.htm for a new profile or two and any updates.

Mass-Market Success: Bernette Ford

I talked earlier in the book about the mass market. This segment of children's publishing doesn't get talked about much, so I'm starting with a look at an imprint that sells into the mass market, and the editor who started it.

Cartwheel Books is Scholastic's mass-market imprint with books for the very young. To get a mass-market presence, Scholastic hired Bernette Ford from Random House, where she had been working in their well-known mass-market division. She founded Cartwheel in the late 1980s and ran it successfully for many years.

At the time, Golden, Random House, and Grosset were the primary mass-market publishers for children. Now the big publishing houses all have their own mass-market divisions, and the market is more competitive. It's also become more dominated by books tied to TV, movie, or other licenses, and at the same time less distinct from the trade market. Now you'll find higher-quality mass-market books, and many mass-market books are versions of existing trade books—board books in particular are likely to be versions of hardcover picture books, rather than original creations.

def•i•ni•tion

A **novelty book** is any book with features added to it beyond the binding and pages: foldouts, die-cut holes, lift-the-flaps, pop-ups, or sound chips. Novelty books are similar to but different from *book plus* products, which are books packaged with something else such as a plush toy. Both are mainstays of mass-market publishers.

Cartwheel publishes 100 books or more per year, for babies up to 7-year-olds. A sizable number of these—40 or so—are original paperbacks for 3- to 6-year-olds, including books for the *Hello Reader!* program. About half are board books and *novelty books*.

Cartwheel sells to the big bookstore chains or to retailers such as Wal-Mart and Sears. Like other mass-market publishers, many of Cartwheel's books are produced on assignment, by writers whose work and resumés are kept on file, while others are created in-house or by packagers.

While she headed Cartwheel, Bernette enjoyed the challenges of this market and the shaping of each season's list from its beginnings to the point when she could look at it in the catalog and say, "That's a strong list." Fourteen full-time staffers worked with her to produce the list, along with a few regular freelance designers.

Bernette Ford now packages multicultural picture books for publishers such as Scholastic at her company Color-Bridge Books (www.color-bridge-books.com). Her work at Cartwheel Books shows just how much impact one individual can have in developing an imprint, even one publishing for the more price-driven mass market.

> **Class Rules** _____
>
> Mass-market publishers like Cartwheel are not a good place to send manuscripts, because they often don't want original work. Many of them develop texts in-house or hire writers to write them to their specifications. If you want to work with them, check their guidelines, which ask that you send them such materials as samples of your work and your resumé.

Change at a Smaller Publisher: Mary Cash

Holiday House is celebrated as a publisher of quality hardcovers, publishing a little more than 60 books a year—two thirds of them picture books, both fiction and non-fiction. The rest of the list consists of novels, mostly middle-grade level, and some older nonfiction. Their market is the reverse of Cartwheel's; they make 80 percent of their sales to the library and school market.

Holiday House is an independent company, owned and run since the 1960s by John and Kate Briggs. In many ways, Holiday House still does things the old-fashioned way, with no editorial meetings; the editor simply tells John about the books she wants to acquire. It was a bit of a shock when Regina Griffin, editorial director since 1996, announced in 2007 that she was leaving. But the company quickly moved Mary Cash up from the position as executive editor she had had with Regina, and Holiday House had only its third editorial director in more than three decades—Margery Cuyler had been in charge from 1974 to 1995.

As editorial director, Mary has a staff of only four and must do without the corporate structure of a larger publisher; corporations may add paperwork and meetings to an editor's time, but they also take care of some tasks. As a result, Mary has to wear more than one hat, so her responsibilities as subsidiary rights manager (she is the one who licenses its books to book clubs, audio and film companies, and the like) and managing editor cut into her editorial time. She gets much of her work done on the 30 titles or so she's personally responsible for during regular hours, but she has to take manuscripts home to read and edit in the evenings and on weekends.

> ### Can You Keep a Secret?
>
> Mary Cash has this to say about her work at Holiday House: "I have edited non-traditional picture books about math, history, language arts, and science. I'm always looking for new approaches to these subjects. I've also edited serious nonfiction and lighter fiction. I believe that humor in children's literature is undervalued. Humor can be essential for getting kids through tough, tedious, and even scary situations …. I hope that the books I edit will make school and learning more exciting, funnier, and maybe even fun."

Almost all the books Holiday House publishes come in as submissions, either from one of the regulars on their list or from someone just getting started. Holiday House is known for its loyalty to its authors and illustrators, so it might come as something of a surprise to learn that they make room for new talent, too. Perhaps a third of the titles on a list have a first- or second-time author or illustrator.

Mary's background prepared her well for her new responsibilities. She started out as an assistant at Farrar, Straus and Giroux (like Holiday House, a traditional and literary publisher), when such luminaries as Roger Straus, Robert Giroux, Michael de Capua, and Steven Roxburgh were all there to serve as role models. She moved on and moved up, and by 1993, was editorial director of both Doubleday picture books and Delacorte fiction at Bantam Doubleday Dell. She comments, "This was a company that knew how to sell books and I learned the indispensability of close working relationships with sales and marketing departments." She hankered for a return to an environment like the one at FSG and so moved over to Holiday House soon after Regina Griffin arrived there. When Regina herself moved on, Mary was ready.

Success at a Larger Publisher: Kate Morgan Jackson

As associate publisher and editor-in-chief of HarperCollins Children's Books, Kate Morgan Jackson oversees four imprints: HC Children's Books (hardcover books),

HarperFestival (novelty), HarperTeen (teen fiction), Katherine Tegen Books (a personal imprint), and HarperTrophy and the children's part of Avon (both paperbacks). The heads of the other personal imprints—Joanna Cotler Books, Laura Geringer Books, Brenda Bowen, and Virginia Duncan at Greenwillow—report directly to the publisher, Susan Katz. Together, these 10 imprints publish more than 600 titles annually, some of them paperbacks of previously published hardcovers. They publish more or less equal numbers of novels, picture books, and "others," which includes novelty books, CDs, boxed sets, and the like. This is a diverse program, with different imprints concentrating on different parts of the market, from bookstores to price clubs.

With such a large program to oversee, meetings make up a large part of Kate's day. These include acquisition, editorial, marketing, and business strategy planning meetings, as well as individual meetings with the editorial directors of the imprints. She does still make some time each day for editorial work and personally publishes two or three picture books per year. Although she does less hands-on work than she did when she worked as an editor, she still feels very much involved in shaping books—and the shape of HarperCollins's list.

Most of HarperCollins's titles come from authors and illustrators with whom they're already working or who have a track record elsewhere, or from authors with agents. They're also moving into the "brand" market, seeing brand names on books as a necessary way of getting booksellers' and children's attention.

Playground Stories

Although the higher you go in a publishing company, the more administrative work you do, people in managerial positions in children's publishing are still very much involved in creating books. As Kate Jackson says of her job: "I love the fundamental result of what I do—helping to create, and helping others to create, good books for kids. I feel strongly that what I do and what my team does makes a difference in the world. I love being around the creativity of the authors, the artists, the editors, the designers. I love being able to help shape and guide the direction of where this company and our list is going."

Some brands are of their own creation. HarperCollins has a rich and deep backlist, stretching back to the time of legendary editor Ursula Nordstrom, and recently supplemented by the acquisition of William Morrow's children's imprints, so they have less need than some publishers to create new programs from the ground up. Instead, they can mine their backlist; Kate was personally involved in developing one such initiative, the *Little House on the Prairie* program, an extensive line you might have seen in the bookstores, including picture books and paper dolls derived from the famous novels.

To reach her current position, Kate moved up within HarperCollins, where she arrived in 1991 after beginning her career at two college publishers. She feels very pleased to be where she is and comments that although the company has changed and expanded from the company it was when Ursula Nordstrom was the head of the children's department, "our heart and soul is still the unmatchable backlist of books, authors, and artists that she cultivated." HarperCollins might be a "corporate publisher," but such labels miss the day-to-day reality of a place where every new hire is assigned to read *Dear Genius*, the collected letters of Ursula Nordstrom, and where "her name is invoked on a regular basis in regard to what she did and what she would have thought and said." There's hope for children's publishing so long as such editors are remembered.

Moving Up at Clarion: Jennifer Greene

Although a lot has changed in children's publishing, I discovered when talking to Jennifer Greene, now a senior editor at Clarion Books, that at least at some companies, the traditional way still rules. Jennifer knew when she left college that she wanted to work in children's publishing, but her first two jobs were with companies publishing books for adults. Her break came when she took a course in children's book publishing at New York University with Virginia Duncan, who told her about an opening at Clarion. Jennifer has been with Clarion ever since.

When I wrote about Jennifer Greene in the first edition of this book, she told me about their mentoring program, which was very helpful to her as a junior editor. With the staff more senior, the mentoring program is dormant, but Clarion continues to support its editors in other ways, allowing Jennifer to work part-time while her children are small. The Clarion way of doing things also means a minimum number of meetings. Jennifer does have meetings, but only productive ones, such as working with the art director, a weekly session when the staff gets together and reads the slush, or meetings as needed with the sales and marketing staff. There's little paperwork, and Clarion doesn't even have publishing meetings. If Jennifer wants to acquire a title, she discusses it with other editors and then gets an okay from Dinah Stevenson, the head of the imprint.

> **Can You Keep a Secret?**
>
> I'm encouraged to have discovered that a number of publishers still work by having editors sign up the books in which they believe. That's how it works at Clarion and Margaret K. McElderry Books, and it's true in other places as well.

Jennifer works on a variety of books, as Clarion publishes a mix of picture books, fiction, and older nonfiction. They are particularly well known for their historical fiction and their biographies. Like Holiday House, their sales are primarily to the school and library market, although they are selling more to bookstores. Clarion's books regularly receive respected awards, and their authors stay with them. Their "traditional" system seems to work.

In this idyllic setting, Jennifer finds time to write thoughtful rejection letters. She loves finding new people and has pulled manuscripts right out of the slush. She also loves developing picture books, a deeply collaborative process involving her and the art director as well as the writer and illustrator, and working through the process that leads from the words to the pictures. Her only lament is that she wishes she could respond immediately to submissions, but she has too much to do. At least what she's doing is all satisfying. May there always be places like Clarion.

Passing the Torch: Margaret K. McElderry

When I wrote the first edition of this book, one of the greats of children's publishing, Margaret K. McElderry, was beginning to pass the torch at her personal imprint. Now fully retired, Margaret may have been the last of the generation of editors with a background as a librarian, having started her publishing career as editor of children's books at Harcourt, Brace in 1945. Today, Margaret K. McElderry Books continues as a small imprint within a large company, publishing 35 or so books per year, under the direction of Emma Dryden, who also heads Atheneum BFYR. The list is about half picture books, some of them imported, and almost half middle-grade and young adult fiction, with a few poetry and nonfiction titles. Like Holiday House, the imprint publishes primarily for the school and library market and for the independent bookstores.

As an editor, Margaret K. McElderry did a lot to bring in books from foreign publishers, starting with German, Swiss, and Scandinavian authors in translation—such works as Margot Benary-Isbert's *The Ark*. She brought in authors from Britain and Australia, including Mary Norton, Margaret Mahy, Lucy Boston, and Patricia Wrightson. She worked with and developed writers and illustrators such as Irene Haas, Carol Fenner, Sarah Ellis, Eloise McGraw, Louise Borden, and X. J. Kennedy. Books she edited have won just about every award there is to win, from Caldecotts and Newberys on down.

> **Playground Stories**
>
> Margaret K. McElderry's tip for writers is a simple but powerful one: "Read, read, read."

How is it that Margaret was able to publish what she wanted to? Perhaps it's because what she wanted to publish so often seemed to be what children wanted to read and librarians wanted to buy. Or as she commented to me wryly, "It doesn't hurt to have a book that sells awfully well every once in a while." And so she continued to do what she had always done, handing over the administrative work to Emma Dryden, who worked with her from 1990, to work from home for a few years, before retiring completely.

Emma is head of both Atheneum and McElderry Books, and like every other editor at a corporate publisher I talked to, spends a good bit of her workday in meetings. She finds time to edit picture books, fiction, and poetry while overseeing a staff of nine.

I find it heartening that imprints still exist with such a direct link to the early years of children's publishing. Atheneum and McElderry aren't the only ones, either. As long as there's such a connection to the roots of children's publishing, and to the children of today, I'm hopeful about the future of our field.

So there you are, a peek into the lives of some editors from trade and mass-market publishing. I hope you'll agree that as long as such people are involved in children's books, there's hope that books children will love will still find a place at publishing companies, and that these portraits gave you a better sense of the person behind the name in the market guide.

The Least You Need to Know

◆ Children's book editors typically come from white, middle-class, college-educated backgrounds.

◆ Editors share a love of books, regardless of the level at which they work.

◆ Administrative duties at larger publishers can take up much of an editor's time, but editors still find time to edit.

◆ Editors at independent publishers and smaller imprints get to spend more of their time editing.

◆ Margaret K. McElderry was one of the great editors of our time.

Chapter 27

Making the Pictures

In This Chapter

- ◆ How a publisher chooses an illustrator
- ◆ The steps in the illustration process
- ◆ What an art director does
- ◆ The limited role of a writer in the illustration process
- ◆ What an illustrator should keep in mind

The manuscript is done, and now it's time for the book to be designed and illustrated. In this chapter, I tell you how a publisher chooses an illustrator, the stages of the illustration process, and the role of the writer (or lack of it) in all this. I also point out some pitfalls before reminding you of the magic that illustration brings to a book.

It's Not Done Yet!

When the manuscript is written and edited, the book is only *half* finished. If it's a picture book, it now needs to be illustrated. If it's a novel, it needs an illustration for the jacket and perhaps some illustrations inside, scattered throughout the book or opening each chapter. Other books get illustrations, too—you'll see a hen's tooth before you see a children's book without an illustration, even if it's only on the cover.

At this point, the writer's role suddenly diminishes, which can be hard for some authors to take. They might feel that because the story belongs to them, they should have a hand in visualizing it, too. Typically, though, the publisher not only picks the illustrator but gives her the freedom to illustrate as she sees fit, subject only to the art director's supervision. And if you think about it, that makes sense: with the publisher responsible for so much of the time and expense of creating a book, it's no wonder they want to be the one deciding who illustrates a book. And after all, they've probably got more experience than writers in making that kind of decision.

If you're an illustrator, this probably sounds good to you. If you're a writer and it doesn't; remember that your skill is with words and an illustrator may well be able to take your story places you never imagined. As picture-book author Tony Johnston comments, "You have to trust whoever's at the other end."

Creating a book is a team effort, with different people playing different roles, bringing different abilities to the challenge of producing the best possible book. Whether you're the author or illustrator, your job is to do the best you can in your role, and let the publisher manage the team.

> **Playground Stories**
>
> Experienced illustrator Megan Halsey says this about the manuscripts she likes the best: "Most good manuscripts have crisp, clear visuals that I see in my mind's eye while I read. I look for an element of fun, a good story, and tantalizing visuals to illustrate." Illustrators build on what's already there but often go beyond it.

Finding a Good Match

How does the publisher—either the editor or the art director—choose an illustrator? That depends on many factors; here are some of the most important ones:

- Finding a style that suits a book's intended audience
- Finding a good match for the "feel" of the book—cheerful art for a cheerful book, edgy art for an edgy book, and so on
- Availability of an artist—popular illustrators are booked years in advance
- Preferring an illustrator already associated with that company
- Matching a "known" illustrator with an unknown author, or vice versa

Writers might be involved in the decision, depending on the publisher's policies and the writer's relationship with the editor. If an editor does show a writer samples, she will listen to the writer's preferences, within limits. If as a writer you have very specific preferences, try to express them in a way that leaves your editor some room to move. Maybe you've imagined your story all along with Allen Say's dignified oil paintings. You can suggest that style to your editor or comment that you've always liked his work. You might not know about them, but dozens of artists work in a style more or less like Say's. Your editor can find them, if he agrees with your suggestion.

Playground Stories

I did take an author's suggestion once—because it was so obviously an exciting match for an unusual manuscript. I was finding an illustrator for Evelyn Coleman's *The Foot Warmer and the Crow*, a powerful folktale-like story about a man escaping from slavery. I showed Evelyn samples of the experienced picture-book illustrator I felt was the best choice. Evelyn asked me to consider Daniel Minter, an unknown artist. I reluctantly let him send me a package of samples. When I opened it, I knew that the strong forms on Daniel's brightly painted carved panels were just right for the book.

If you're an illustrator and know you're being considered for a book, be cooperative and hopeful, but don't count your chickens before they turn into a contract. Many, perhaps most, illustration assignments are made quickly, without a lot of agonizing over choices. If a publisher asks for more samples (or, rarely, a sample done "on spec"), they may be looking only at you and want to see more of your work to confirm that preference. Or they may have a stack of possible candidates and are trying to winnow them down.

Illustration is an act of interpretation, and there are many ways to interpret even the simplest of statements. If you'd like to see this in action, get your hands on *Mary Had a Little Lamb* as illustrated in three different ways: by Tomie dePaola in simple, bold paintings; by Bruce McMillan in bright color photographs; and by Salley Mavor in three-dimensional fabric art. If you can't find these books, ask a children's librarian if she can show you a folktale for which they have different picture-book versions. Examine the different versions. You may well prefer one, but can you really say that one is right and one is wrong?

Playground Stories

"In most cases, [writers] have little or no say on the art, even if you are shown samples as a courtesy. In general, this makes good sense, since most authors think they know more about art than they do. Picture-book writers must keep in mind that a picture book is a collaboration between writer and illustrator." So says Aaron Shepard, picture-book author and folktale reteller, in *The Business of Writing for Children.*

The Role of the Art Director

When illustrations are called for, an art director (or A.D.) steps in. At some companies, this person works with an illustrator independently of an editor. At others, the A.D. and the editor work closely together. But just what is an art director, and how is this person different from a designer? Some basics follow, along with a profile of Susan Sherman, art director at Charlesbridge Publishing.

Designer vs. Art Director

Art staffs at publishing companies consist of one art director and some designers. But although the titles are different, both kinds of staff may do very much the same job. How can that be?

def•i•ni•tion

Art direction involves working with an illustrator on just about every aspect of the work they're doing, including deciding what to illustrate, the sequence and pacing of illustrations, composition of individual illustrations, and color palette.

The term *art director* doesn't just mean that this person is the director of the art department. An art director is someone who provides *art direction*, much as an editor is someone who edits. The designer, on the other hand, deals with the other aspects of the book, such as the typeface used, the size and shape of the pages, and where the illustrations actually go. The two roles overlap, of course, and someone with the title of designer often does art direction, and vice versa.

Introducing Susan Sherman

To learn more about what an art director does and what people like about such work, I'd like you to meet Susan Sherman, A.D. at Charlesbridge Publishing. Long based in Boston, Susan previously worked at Little Brown when it was privately owned, at Houghton Mifflin, and then at Little Brown again after it had become part of a larger corporation.

Susan loves doing what she does and says that in some ways she's like a teacher. She wants to help make the book, and specifically the art in it, be the best it can be. To accomplish that, she has to find the best way to encourage, push, or redirect people with very different personalities. When I discussed this with her, I was struck by how similarly she as art director and I as editor describe our roles. There are key differences—she might use sketches to get across an idea, while I would use words—but the roles of art director and editor are in many ways complementary, and their contributions are key parts of the intensely collaborative process that creates a picture book.

She comments that the role of the art director has not changed, although the job has at many companies. Just like the editors I profiled in the previous chapters, meetings are now a big part of the A.D.'s day at larger companies. For this reason, Susan's glad to be working at a smaller, independent publisher again, where the staff work more collaboratively and it's possible to be experimental and take a few risks.

Another big change was brought by computers. Computer design gives a publisher more control over design and a greater ability to make changes. Type, for example, is now generated by the computer. In the past, design staff had to send out to have type set, and changing a typeface or even the size of type cost time and money. The other side of this, of course, is that more work is now done by (usually) the same number of staff. The publisher has more control but must do more in-house.

Regardless of the technology used, every book brings a new challenge. For Chris Van Allsberg's *Polar Express*, the challenge was dealing with dark art on dark paper. The Houghton Mifflin production staff had to find a company that could reproduce that accurately. David Macaulay's *Black and White* was one of the first books the company designed on the computer, which made it much easier to set the four different typefaces used in that unusual book.

A Look at the Illustration Process

The illustration process varies greatly from one publisher to the next, and even from one book to the next. When the illustrator is signed up for a book, some art directors give very specific instructions and then carefully oversee each subsequent stage. This is more likely with mass-market and educational publishers, who have to keep the very specific needs of their markets in mind. Others let the illustrators develop their own ideas. During the process, the art director steps in to provide feedback when needed and generally does what he can to help the illustrator do the best possible work and ensure that the final art will be suitable for production needs.

The Illustrator's First Steps

Creating a picture book is the most demanding project for an illustrator, so I'll concentrate on this. As an illustrator, your first step is to break up the text and plan the sequence of illustrations. To do this, you should create a *storyboard*. A storyboard shows all the pages of a book, laid out in miniature, starting with the single page 1, continuing through all the double-page spreads (such as 2/3, 4/5, and so on), and ending with another single page, probably page 32. This allows you to plan out the book and be sure you haven't left out a title page, a copyright page, or any other essential elements. Do a preliminary breakdown of the text and use your storyboard to plan the visual flow of the story.

At this point, you might want to explore alternatives for a particular illustration. You might toss off 20 or 30 versions, in the form of *thumbnails*, or small, very loose *sketches*, to help you explore possibilities. As Jeff Hopkins, an up-and-coming illustrator, puts it, "It's like brainstorming on a page." When Jeff has more or less settled on one, he roughs out what he's doing with each page of the book and may submit this preliminary work to the publisher, again in the form of thumbnails.

def•i•ni•tion

All the pages of a book are planned out in a **storyboard,** which shows each page and two-page spread in miniature. Editors or art directors often ask an artist to send them **thumbnails.** Artists use these rough thumbnail-size sketches to try out ideas and develop the layout and pacing of a book before moving on to full-size **sketches.** See examples of both kinds of sketches online at www.underdown.org/cigthumbnails.htm.

Thumbnails are done mainly to look at different compositions or to see how the book will work as a whole, and so they can be very crude. Should a character appear in a particular pose? What are the scenes to show so the book has a good pacing and illustration and text appear in balance on the pages? Visual pacing and page turns at the right moments in the story come in at this stage (although of course they may be rethought later on).

Creating a picture book means thinking about the book as a whole, not as a series of individual illustrations. Some illustrators start telling the story visually on the title page or cover, for example. Pat Hutchins, in *Rosie's Walk*, uses the turning of a page to set up a series of predictable but enjoyable surprises: a fox attempts to pounce on a hen, but (page turn) suffers one setback after another. Or consider the farmer's hat in Nancy Tafuri's *Silly Little Goose*. Early in this simple story of a goose looking for a place to build her nest, the hat blows off the farmer's head and is seen in the background of most of the pages, until, after discovering that various other potential nesting sites are already occupied by other animals, the goose finds the hat and uses it. When my daughter was two, she was very excited when she noticed and followed this purely visual story. She'd enjoyed the main story, but this added to it. Or reread *Where the Wild Things Are* by Maurice Sendak, and see what he does with the size and shape of the illustrations at different points in the story. There are many ways to put a picture book together—perhaps you can create a new one.

> **Playground Stories**
>
> For the details of the composition process, there's no better place to look than Uri Shulevitz's *Writing with Pictures*, which goes into more depth than I possibly could here. You'll find dozens of visual examples of the different stages in creating a picture book, accompanied by the wisdom of a master of the picture-book form.

Getting Closer: Sketches

Next come the actual sketches. (Some illustrators go straight to them anyway.) These might look very finished, or they might look very rough; different illustrators use this stage differently, so do what works best for you. Some illustrators spend time sketching their characters in many different poses, while others go straight to rough versions of what they envision for a particular page.

When the book is roughed out, the illustrator usually does a final set of full-size sketches. These show the complete book as the illustrator intends it to look and may be put together into book dummy form. At this stage, the writer may get a look at the sketches. If so, writers are expected to comment on such problems as a visual detail that contradicts something in their text; this kind of thing is easily overlooked during the process of working on the art. Writers are not expected to comment on the art itself, and even if they do, their comments won't be passed along to the illustrator. With some publishers, mass-market publishers in particular, the writers may see nothing from the time they deliver their manuscript until they get copies of the finished book.

The editor and art director typically review the final sketches together. A copy editor often goes over them, too, checking to be sure there are no discrepancies with the text.

The Finishing Touches

After any changes have been made and the sketches have been approved, the illustrator has to get to work on the final art. For some, this is the least enjoyable part of the process. Creating characters and imagining the illustration sequence is fun, but now the task is to follow what's been approved and create finished art that also retains the energy of the sketches.

Other Kinds of Books, Other Kinds of Illustrations

Many books only have an illustration on the cover, or perhaps the cover and some small illustrations scattered throughout the book. These kinds of books are more typically handled by designers and may be completely designed before an illustrator comes into the process.

When an illustrator is brought in, generally, he or she will be given instructions as to what's needed on the cover and what scenes the publisher wants illustrated for any interior illustrations.

Some companies see jackets as part of the marketing of the book, so they'll be more concerned with making an attractive cover than with making it accurately reflect what's in the book. The illustrator might not even read the entire book—or even be given it. Sometimes the illustrator gets detailed instructions from the art director and a summary of the book's contents.

Illustrating Nonfiction

Nonfiction may be done a little differently from fiction. If a book is being illustrated with "stock" photographs, or photos gathered from different sources, the author sometimes does the gathering. (If not, the publisher's photo researcher handles this.)

Nonfiction may also be illustrated with art and then the writer may be asked to help out—or even be required to do so. There's a logic to this: while doing research, the writer probably came across good sources for the illustrator to use, whether they're pictures of animals or period costumes. Why make the illustrator find them all over again? And if the writer hasn't found good visual references for specific scenes, maybe they don't exist. The publisher needs to know this, and the writer may need to rewrite the text so it doesn't depend on illustrations that can't be done.

The writer may also have personal knowledge or experience on which the book is based, and this can help with the illustrations, too. Sneed Collard, the author of *Forest in the Clouds*, didn't read other books to write this picture book about a visit to a high-altitude "cloud forest" in the mountains of Costa Rica. He went there. And he took pictures. When the illustrator, Michael Rothman, was ready to get to work, Sneed passed on several dozen slides to him. Michael also did his own research in published sources, but those slides were a useful part of his visual references.

It's Not an Exact Science

The computer has transformed book design in general, and picture-book design in particular, but even if you're now able to revise a book layout 17 times instead of twice, you still end up with a book that looks good and that fits within a multiple of 8 pages. If you're new to picture-book illustration, be aware that there are still technical limits to what you can do, and be sure to discuss them with your art director before you put pen, brush, or digital stylus to paper, canvas, or pad.

If you are planning to do full-page art that "bleeds" off the edges of a page, meaning it's not confined by a frame or set margins, be sure to ask your A.D. for page templates. These will give you accurate dimensions to work within, taking into account the exact trim size for the book, gutters, and bleed. The A.D. will also be able to tell you how much larger or smaller than the final size of the book you can do your art. You can go "up" or "down" a certain amount, but art that's reduced too much gets dense and dark, and art that's blown up gets less sharp and can become washed out.

> **Class Rules**
>
> Colors shift to some extent when art is scanned and converted into digital files using the four-color CMYK (cyan, magenta, yellow, and key or black) system. Mostly they stay in sync with each other—most people think the full range of color is there and it only becomes obvious that it's not when you compare a printed book to the original art. Certain colors, though, just don't pick up well—anything "neon," bright green, or orange—so avoid them in art being used for illustration. Ask for a test scan of your art if in doubt.

For the most part, you have much more freedom now than you used to. Once upon a time, art had to be on flexible paper, of no more than a certain size so it could fit on a scanner's drum. Now, if you want to do your art on inflexible wood panels or create three-dimensional illustrations, your publisher can most likely find a way to deal with it. But if you plan to do something out of the ordinary, be sure to discuss it with your publisher or A.D. first. Working with unconventional media does cost more, and some publishers might not be willing to accommodate your creative urges.

Letting the Magic Happen

The illustrator makes a picture book what it is and is important to other kinds of books as well. Once the author has done her best with the manuscript, it's time to let the illustrator do his thing.

Playground Stories _____

Illustrators might bring not only their interpretation of a manuscript; they might add purely visual elements to the story. Tony Johnston's *The Quilt Story* includes a family that goes west in the nineteenth century. Tomie dePaola, the illustrator, put a cat in every picture until the point in the story when the family actually left. He knew from his own research that families heading west didn't take their pets. A reader may or may not notice that detail, but it's there, adding another level to the story.

Let the magic of illustration happen. Time after time, I hear from authors, when a book is done, how pleased and surprised they are by the illustrations, and by what they've added to the book. The authors might have had something in mind for the illustrations; they've ended up with more than that. The illustration process does not always go well, but most times, it does. Play your part in it the best you can, and watch the magic happen.

The Least You Need to Know

- Editors may or may not involve the writer in choosing an illustrator. If they do, as the writer, be sure you're professional and reasonable.

- Illustrators usually do thumbnails and sketches before moving on to do finished art.

- If writers see sketches, they can comment on how they match up with the text.

- Writers may be asked to provide reference materials for an illustrator of a non-fiction book.

- Illustration can be magic! Let it happen to your book.

Chapter 28

The Rest of the Process

In This Chapter

- ◆ Who does what after the manuscript is done
- ◆ From manuscript to a finished, sellable masterpiece
- ◆ Why it takes so long—book production, step by step

When a writer hands over a manuscript, a team of individuals all geared toward producing the best book possible takes over. The illustrator isn't the only person to step in. In the next months, many others are involved in designing, manufacturing, marketing, and producing your book. You might not work directly with any of them, but they play a valuable part in the success of your book.

Your Editor ... and Beyond

In other kinds of publishing, often two editors are involved with a book. One, the acquisitions editor, acquires the manuscript, and the other, the development editor, does most of the actual editing. This division does not exist in most branches of children's publishing. Instead, one editor handles both (as well as other) functions. Most likely the writer works with this same person until the manuscript goes to the copy editor. Edits could be substantial or minimal, depending on many variables (as described in Chapter 25).

Then others start to get involved. After the substantial editing is done, the copy editor steps in. After or at the same time as the copyedit, design and illustration begin, as I discussed in the previous chapter. All the while, a managing editor keeps track of the schedule and the materials for the book. Finally, a production manager gets involved in planning work with a printer. Then *galleys* or final *page proofs*, which you might or might not see, arrive. The final checks on the book are *blues* (for novels and such) or *color proofs* (for picture books), which you probably won't see. And lastly, the printer prints and binds the book. Voilà! That's the cycle of production on your book, in broad outline.

def•i•ni•tion

Galleys are long pages of type, not set up into the actual book pages. **Page proofs** are set up like a book. **Blues** or *bluelines* are used to check the final film of the book. **Color proofs** are a check on color for picture books.

What's Your Copy (Editor)?

When the manuscript needs no further editing, according to your editor, it moves to the copy editor. You might be thinking, *Yuck, another person messing with my words.* But don't think like that. The copy editor gives your book polish—and makes you look even better as an author. The copy editor may seem picky and overbearing, asking a whole lot of questions and making changes to your sentence structure, spelling, use of capitalization, grammar, and other details. The copy editor might even question your choice of words. She asks all the questions and fixes any errors for your benefit, however.

The copy editor also makes sure your manuscript conforms to your publisher's house style, which may address such matters as when numbers should be spelled out and when they should be written as numerals. The copy editor makes sure you've spelled or capitalized a name the same way throughout, double-checks the front and back matter, confirms the accuracy of names, and generally focuses on all the little things that are easy to forget or overlook.

So although you need to check your manuscript thoroughly and turn in the best book possible, rejoice in the meticulous, keen eyes of a copy editor, which provide a further, objective check. Not many people in this world possess the patience or mind-set to accomplish this task. Bow down before the copy editor and praise her! She might just prove your best buddy on the team!

In the end, if the copy editor suggests a change you don't like, you don't have to go along with it. Provided you have a reason for wanting to do it your way and your editor agrees, you can overrule the copy editor.

Some publishing houses keep a staff of copy editors; others hire freelance copy editors. Sometimes, picture books are copyedited in-house, while longer nonfiction and novels go to freelancers. Either way, your book receives very focused scrutiny. Your copy editor is an important member of the team working on your book, although you'll almost certainly have no direct contact with her. Instead, your editor will send you the copyedited manuscript, perhaps with handwritten notes and Post-it tags, perhaps with annotated electronic files. You address the comments and questions and return the manuscript with revisions—also written on the manuscript or on Post-it tags (or notes in the files)—to your editor.

If you have questions or concerns about the copy editor's suggestions, discuss them with your editor. Ultimately, it's your editor who has the final say and must be satisfied, though he will defer to the copy editor on many issues.

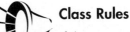

Class Rules _____

If the copy editor makes changes you don't agree with, you can say so—but you better have a reason. Needing to have your characters use slang so you can capture the flavor of their speech is a good reason. Thinking it "looks better" to spell out all numbers below 100 when the publisher prefers to stop at 10 is not.

High-Fashion Time: Designers

The "look" of a book comes from the conceptualization of the designer and, if there is one, the illustrator. The designer brings the text of the book alive with the cover design, the width of the margins, the regular typeface, the display type (the type used for titles and headers)—everything.

Especially in children's books, a designer's tasks vary greatly. There's a huge difference between designing, say, a novel and a picture book. But in a nutshell, the art director, who oversees the designer, and the designer or designers of the publishing house, create the actual design. They decide how all the various elements of a book (the ones reviewed in Chapter 10) will look on the printed page.

Usually the designer suggests several design possibilities. The editor, illustrator, and sometimes you sit down and choose the actual design. Today, designers work in a computer program such as InDesign when creating and assembling a book's design. In the past, he would take the typeset pages or galleys from the printer and paste them onto thin cardboard, often called *mechanicals*, to show how the pages would look.

If there are illustrations, they are incorporated into the design. Some publishers have high-tech scanning equipment in-house the designer can use to generate electronic images from the original illustrations. Other publishers outsource this task to companies that specialize in fine-resolution scanning. When this is the case, the designer prepares the original art for scanning. When the scanned images come back, the designer incorporates them into the layout.

Playground Stories

Tired of reading about all the stages in the creation of a book in the abstract? Then jump on the web to see a wonderful display of the various stages in the creation of Ellen Raskin's novel *The Westing Game*, which won the Newbery Medal in 1979, at www.education.wisc.edu/ccbc/authors/raskin/intro.htm. This web exhibit concentrates on the writing and revision of the manuscript, but Raskin was also an artist and designer. On the "Book Design" page, you'll find fascinating examples of the work that went into page layouts and jacket design.

Just the Facts, Ma'am

The fact checker—like the copy editor—looks closely at the text, possibly the illustrations as well, to detect any discrepancies that may exist, so this happens later in the process. Unlike the copy editor, the fact checker isn't concerned about grammar. She focuses specifically on factual information.

Fact checkers play a role in nonfiction but may also be called in on historical fiction. Are the names, dates, and places accurate? Are there any anachronisms? Are there any contradictions? Did this person really say that? Is the information up to date? So many questions, so little time. The fact checker then tracks down the answers to ensure your book does not carry any mistakes or omissions!

100 Proof

Haven't enough people looked closely at the book? Well, no. The proofreader takes the typeset pages and checks to be sure the typeset book actually follows your manuscript and all the little changes made to it in the copyediting stage. He also looks— another pair of eyes—for obvious or glaring mistakes before the book is shipped off to the printer for manufacturing.

Look upon your proofreader as the last person in the line to be sure all is well. Sometimes everyone from you to the editor to the copy editor can miss something, and the proofreader's fresh set of eyes catches it.

Lights! Camera! Action! The Production Manager

While the proofreaders, designers, fact checkers, and editors are working their magic, the production manager is scrambling to put the book into tangible form and keep costs within budget. The production manager decides what printer will print the book and when. The production manager literally finds and buys the paper on which the book is printed, too.

Children's books oftentimes incorporate interesting design elements—like the sparkles on the rainbow fish in *The Rainbow Fish*. A production manager was the person who found the paper, the sparkles, and the printer to produce that book—all while keeping the costs within budget.

Class Rules

Don't complain to your editor if the grade of paper or type of binding for your book isn't what you envisioned. Paper and binding costs are a major part of the cost of a book. A production manager may search far and wide to find the grade of paper necessary for a high-quality, glossy picture book, but not be able to get it at the right price. Cost and quality always have to be juggled.

When the book is all done—with a complete design, all elements in place, from the art on the front of the jacket to the bar code on the back—the editor or designer hands it to the production manager. She sends it to the printer and then coordinates the rest of the process.

Final Steps: Printing, Binding, and Shipping

The printer takes the files from the production manager and makes film from them, following the design and making sure the illustrations appear where they should.

But checking that isn't just up to the printer. The publisher may have already produced proofs for checking, but the printer will do it again. First come blues, a blue-colored printing from the film, which are checked by the publisher. If the book has color art, the printer may also produce color proofs, showing what the art will really look like. Usually there isn't time for either author or illustrator to see these, so just your editor and the designer review them

And then the book is printed, and bound, and shipped. It will probably take a few weeks (if printed in North America) or a couple of months (if printed abroad) to make it to the publisher's warehouse, but it's on its way!

Can You Keep a Secret?

Publishers send books overseas to be printed for one reason: cost. Printing a full-color book isn't cheap, but it's less expensive in Hong Kong and other parts of the Far East. When perhaps 20¢ per copy can make the difference between making or losing money on a picture book, the opportunity to save that much or more by printing overseas is hard to pass up.

So That's Why It Takes So Long!

Considering the process, no wonder it can take up to three years from the time an editor buys a manuscript until the book hits shelves! Especially with picture books, where illustration can easily add a year to the schedule (and that's only if the illustrator started work right away), don't expect a book to make it into stores with any great speed. Your editors will give you timelines for the production of your book. Be patient—the wait is worth it. When a book follows the correct process thoroughly and meticulously, the end result will be better. Better to take three years for a beautifully produced, strong-selling picture book than a year for a slipshod, weak, unattractive book that no one wants to buy, right?

Electronic workflows have saved time for some publishers, and so your book may get done more rapidly. Here's what you can expect, time-wise:

- Several months in the editing stage, once your editor gets to the book

- A couple months for copyediting

- A year or more for illustration and design

- A few more months for proofreading and fact checking (if it's needed)

- Several months for layout (composition), printing, and shipping (distribution to the sellers)

That's a long time, although it can be considerably shorter if your book isn't illustrated—and it can be even longer if the publisher's schedule is full.

But at least when your book is completed you can go find it in the stores, right? Not exactly. The publisher first wants to get it to reviewers and show it to booksellers, as explained in the following chapters. So it's a few months more waiting while that happens. And *then* your book will be on the market. Woo-hoo!

The Least You Need to Know

- Where your writing was a solo process, you now belong to a team of individuals all working toward a common goal: the production of your book.

- Although the people working on your book may make changes, try not to take the changes personally. The editors are there to make your book the best it can be.

- Several people—the copy editor, fact checker, and proofreader—check and recheck everything in your book. Get used to the constant queries.

- The designer and the production manager are the people who create the final look and feel of a book.

- Understand that producing a children's book may take up to three years from start to finish (beyond the time you took to write it). Be patient.

Part 6

My Book Is Published! Now What?

On that happy day when your children's book is published, you might think your work is over. Well, not quite, because it still has to be marketed and publicized. In Part 6, you learn what your publisher does, what she might do, and what she almost certainly won't do where these areas are concerned. If you want to play a role, this part gives you tips for how to do that productively, from doing your own publicity to putting on bookstore events and school visits.

Although they might not come with your first book, you learn about some of the awards and other forms of recognition you can expect in Part 6. I also give you some guidance on building your writing career. If you want to publish additional books, you might want to know what you can do to bring in an income between royalty checks.

Chapter 29

Selling Your Book

In This Chapter

- How sales, marketing, and publicity all fit together
- The scoop on publishers' catalogs
- Why reviews matter
- You're in the bookstores!
- Freebies, giveaways, and other marketing tricks

After all the work you and your publisher put into your book, what comes next? You might hope the publisher will launch a major publicity campaign and dole out the big bucks to get the word out about your book. Don't hold your breath.

In this chapter, you learn what you realistically can expect the publisher to do to publicize and market your book. This chapter also gets into how ads are used in publishing and what it *doesn't* take to make a best-seller.

Marketing and Sales People

So far in this book, you've met the publishing people who help you turn manuscript and artwork into a finished book. If that's all that a publisher did, your wonderful book would sit on the shelves of their warehouse, unseen. To get a book out into the world, the publisher has staff dedicated to selling, marketing, and publicizing. Their roles are different, but hopefully dovetail together.

Take This Book, Please

Months before a book is due to go on sale, salespeople fan out across the country to persuade bookstore buyers, library buyers, and others to order it. If you're a famous author or illustrator with a track record, their job is easy because the bookstore or library will want the book. The only issue is how many copies they'll take.

If author and illustrator aren't well known, the salesperson has a more difficult job. Maybe they can persuade the buyer that the book is so wonderful the staff will want to show it to customers and talk them into buying or reading it. Or maybe the buyer will want to know what the publisher is doing to help get the book off the shelves and out the door. This is known as "supporting" the book. So the salesperson will talk about the publisher's marketing efforts and upcoming publicity.

Paying for Attention

Very broadly speaking, everything a publisher does to promote a book that costs money falls under the heading of marketing. This ranges from putting the book in a catalog to making give-away items to paying for a window display in a bookstore to buying national advertising.

Being in the catalog is basic—people have to know the book exists. But beyond that, a book's marketing budget can range from nothing (in which case the publisher is hoping great reviews will help it to sell) to hundreds of thousands of dollars.

Free Attention

Reviews may be free in a way, but someone still has to handle the publisher's publicity efforts. Some publicity work, such as sending out review copies, is fairly routine. A publicity campaign may be far more elaborate, however, and involve getting an author on talk shows and into magazine features, as well as the more usual newspaper reviews.

Good publicity and marketing support the sales efforts of the publisher, although the best sales and marketing and publicity work still don't guarantee that it will sell—a sobering thought.

I'm in the Catalog!

The first and most basic marketing of a book is its appearance in a publisher's catalog. Savor that first recognition you have that, *My goodness! I'm actually published. That's my book!*

For their part, publishers produce catalogs to showcase all their new offerings each season as well as their strong backlist titles. You should expect your publisher to list your book in the catalog that covers the time period in which its publication date is scheduled. For example, say your book has a *pub. date* of March 2009. The publisher may include it in its fall/winter 2008–2009 catalog, if it releases three catalogs per year. If it does two, your book will be in the spring 2009 catalog (the other season being the fall).

A variety of people use catalogs. Sales representatives within the publishing house use them when they go on sales calls to promote new books at bookstores, at libraries, and to wholesalers. They're given away at conferences and other venues to librarians, booksellers, and teachers. The publicity department may send catalogs to contacts at magazines or to book reviewers. And if a person just calls the company and asks for a catalog, more than likely the publishing house will send one out. The publisher's catalog is the first step in getting the news out that your book is available.

def•i•ni•tion

A book's **pub. date** is the official (and somewhat arbitrary) date when a publisher says the book will be available in stores. Reviews of the book are often timed to come out before the pub. date—but the book itself may have already left the publisher's warehouse weeks earlier, or may have been delayed.

Can You Keep a Secret?

Typically, the catalog entry for your book includes your book's cover, title, author's and illustrator's names and biographies, a brief description, pub. date, ISBN, price, trim size (the size of the book's pages), and recommended age level. Elsewhere, the catalog offers information on ordering or licensing rights.

Not on the Shelf, but in the Store

Publishers sometimes send special advance copies of books to select bookstores. These glitzy—and costly—versions of bound galleys are known as *advance reader copies* or

ARCs. Why do publishers do this? The publisher hopes that someone in the store will get excited about it, order more copies, and talk about it with their customers, thereby generating sales. For this reason, in children's publishing, an edgy, hip young adult ARC is more likely to reach a bookseller than a picture-book *f&g* is. The bookstore will still see the picture book when the salesperson calls on it, of course.

def•i•ni•tion

An **ARC** or **advance reader copy** is an advance paperback version of a book, often created from the final version or close to it, with a full-color cover that duplicates the illustration and design of the actual book jacket. **F&g's** are pages that have been folded and gathered, but not bound.

The Big Mouths

Most publishers send out advance copies (if it's a picture book) or *bound galleys* (if it's a novel or longer nonfiction) of your book to major reviewers as a standard publicity effort. Major reviewers? Like who?

def•i•ni•tion

Publishers may produce a rough version of novels and similar longer books, called **bound galleys** (from the old term for the long pages created when a book was typeset, before it was laid out in pages). This allows reviewers to write about the book before its arrival in stores.

Certain publications always receive lists and advance copies of books. These reviewers and publications are the driving force in many ways for the sales of books, especially to libraries, who wait to see reviews before making purchase decisions. Some of the places your publisher will send notification and a copy of your book are …

Publishers Weekly   More booksellers read this than the other magazines.

Booklist   The publication of the American Library Association produces thoughtful, respected reviews.

School Library Journal   *SLJ* reviews the most books per year, although the quality of the reviews varies.

Kirkus Reviews   *Kirkus* is slightly more selective than *SLJ* and more literary in approach.

The Horn Book Magazine and *The Horn Book Guide*   The more selective, *The Horn Book Magazine* reviews a limited number of titles every other month. The *Guide* comes out twice a year with more reviews.

These trade publications exist to report on the upcoming titles and the publishing industry, so booksellers as well as librarians read them. Sometimes, Hollywood producers and directors read them, too, to learn about books they think will make good films.

The publisher wants the trade journals to review and write about your book, thereby generating sales. Book people read *Publishers Weekly* (*PW* for those in the know), *Booklist, Library Journal, Kirkus Reviews,* and *The Horn Book.* Good reviews encourage libraries to try books by unknown authors and may spur a bookstore to take a book. In some cases, these magazines put a star or a pointer before reviews of particularly recommended books—if you get stars from more than one magazine, your book will do well.

The Other Mouths: Local and Special

There are, of course, many other mouths, some louder than others. A publisher won't send copies of your book to every newspaper and magazine in the country. Most of them, unfortunately, don't review children's books. So don't feel slighted if you don't see your book reviewed in the magazines and newspapers you read. That's just a reality of the business.

Local publications look for the local hook to any story. You have a better chance of getting publicity from the *Sacramento Bee* if you live in Sacramento than if you don't. Your publisher may want to grab this natural publicity opportunity and send your book to the local reviewers of children's books. Be sure to give your publisher a list of all the local outlets—television stations, radio stations, newspaper columnists, and regional magazines—with a contact name, the address, and a phone number. The more organized publishers will request this information from you. Provide it whether you're asked or not.

Class Rules _____

Don't depend on your publisher to send review copies of your book to the papers and magazines you think they should. Check first with your publicist to find out if they do plan to hit your hometown newspapers or the specialty publications you suggested in your author questionnaire. If not, send a news release and a copy of the book yourself. Try to find a newsy "hook" for your story so you're not ignored by publications that usually don't cover children's books.

Sometimes a publisher will target specialty publications. For example, let's say you write a nonfiction book about gardening for children. Your publisher might want to send copies of the book to women's magazines that include sections on activities with children—such as *Ladies' Home Journal* or *McCall's*. Many parenting magazines might like to focus on the book or include the title in a roundup of gardening books for kids in a spring issue of the magazine. And don't forget the gardening magazines. As with local publications, if you see a way to hook into the interests of national special-interest magazines, make a list with all the contact information for the marketing or publicity representative.

def•i•ni•tion

A **press release** alerts the media to the publication of a title. After an overview of the title, a release may tie in to an event or a news angle—depending on the book—to garner further media interest. Press releases also note a contact person and details about the book.

In a slightly different approach, a publisher may have a list of people and publications—sometimes hundreds of them—to which only a *press release* or a catalog and request for review copies goes out. If a reviewer's interest in a book is piqued by the press release, he or she can fill out a review copy request and receive a review copy. Many times, the publisher keeps reviewers from smaller media markets on this list. Although *The New York Times* may receive the f&g's of your cool picture book, *The Seattle Times* may receive only the press release and request form.

Going Long and Deep

What author or illustrator doesn't think of it—sitting on *Oprah* chatting with the queen of talk about a book? I'm sorry to shatter your *Oprah* or other talk-show dreams, but

Can You Keep a Secret?

To increase your chances of having a producer for a national talk show choose your book as a focus for the show, provide your publicist with suggested show topics and suggested interview questions. This saves the publicist time and makes the producer's job easier.

publishers rarely send review copies of a title to a major talk show unless the book has some kind of universal appeal (to adults) or news hook. Publicists know that the producers of these shows rarely handpick a book—especially a children's book—for discussion on a show. It's the author or the author's story that does it. So if you're Jamie Lee Curtis hawking your children's tale, you have an edge.

Nevertheless, sometimes your publisher will find a reason or hook to send Oprah your book. And sometimes you can help them out with suggestions. If you feel strongly about it, and provided that you keep your publisher informed, you might even launch your own campaign. Lori Mitchell, author/illustrator of *Different Just Like Me*, got her book onto *Oprah* and *Maury Povich*, as well as local television. For more information about her book, and to learn what helped it get on TV, visit www.differentjustlikeme.cc. This won't work for everyone, and it's a long shot at the best of times, but efforts in this area do pay off.

Publicity efforts are labor-intensive. You can count on some basics from your publisher, but if you want something unusual to happen, you may have to do it yourself.

Free! Take One!

On top of publicity efforts, there could be many ways to market your book. *Freebies*, given out to generate interest in your book, are one way. Here are three of the most common types of freebies:

◆ *Bookmarks* are given to bookstores to be put in bags or tucked into books. You can also hand them out on a school visit.

◆ *Posters* are expensive and are usually produced for established authors and illustrators only. They're given away at conventions; bookstores put them in windows, libraries on the walls, and schools in classrooms.

◆ *Postcards* are great for mailings about events you're doing; your publisher might also send them out to generate buzz.

def•i•ni•tion

Freebies are one of many promotional items given away for free to promote your book.

First, the bad news: publishers rarely go deep into their pockets for this sort of free stuff—free for the customer, that is—because the cost often outweighs the benefits of added sales. But for the good news: sometimes a publisher does produce such giveaways to help market your book. In fact, when a publisher creates and produces a freebie, it does so to generate name recognition instead of sales.

Creative Genius

Publishers don't limit their marketing ideas to postcards and posters. In fact, marketing departments brainstorm interesting ways to promote your book—as inexpensively as possible. For example, to promote a book called *Bugs for Lunch*, Charlesbridge sent out lunch bags to elementary school teachers with cartoon bugs and the title of the book printed on them. The paper bags proved inexpensive to produce and, thus, worthwhile for the publisher to manufacture.

Some publishers create complete party kits for the booksellers to use to run story hours or displays to showcase the book at the checkout stands of the stores. These are called dumps.

For Teacher's Eyes Only

Children's book publishing often has an educational focus, so publishers may strive to gain the attention of teachers. Just as helping a talk show's producer with story ideas linked to your title may provide you with a publicity hit, creating materials aligned with a title that will help the teacher in lesson planning will get you sales.

Consider the teacher who needs to deliver a unit about rain forests and comes across a kit for your book about rain forests. The kit includes a taped conversation with the author (you!), suggested review questions, handouts, and project ideas—all based on rain forests and the book. That teacher is not only more likely to buy the book, but might also talk it up with other teachers.

> **Class Rules** _____
>
> Before devoting yourself to postcard production and bookmark creation, consider how long it will take to complete whatever publicity feat you're choosing to accomplish. Then, factor in how much money you stand to make to help you decide whether your project is worthwhile.

Do It Yourself

If you find that your publisher doesn't plan to produce any of these marketing materials, you might want to produce some yourself. Bear in mind that endeavors like event kits and postcards require time and money—and the efforts might not yield desired results. Discuss your plans with someone at your publisher first, as they may be able to give you some guidance, or even cover some of the cost.

Your Ad Here

Publishers think carefully before investing in advertisements because they usually know about more cost-effective marketing ideas than buying an ad. When they do buy ads, they buy them for their own reasons, so don't try to lobby for them. Still, ads sometimes work.

Targeting Bookstores

Bookstore managers, owners, and large chain buyers read *Publishers Weekly* (*PW*) religiously. A marketing manager will first think of an ad in this magazine because it reaches such large numbers of the right kinds of readers.

A children's book publisher does not buy an ad for a single juvenile title as a standard procedure, though. Special issues tend to get the ads. *Publishers Weekly* has a children's book focus twice a year, when the new season's books are highlighted. These are the issues in which the publishing house may highlight some strong, upcoming titles in an ad, or more typically list all their new titles in one comprehensive ad.

Another approach children's book publishers commonly use is purchasing an advertisement featuring several books. If a publisher decides to promote several Christmas, Kwanzaa, and Hanukkah books, the house may place an ad for all the titles within the pages of *Publishers Weekly*. Now buying an ad in *PW* becomes a more targeted—and cost-effective—way to reach numerous booksellers simultaneously.

Publishers hope that these strategically placed ads bring increased revenue and sales.

> **Can You Keep a Secret?**
>
> Two issues every year of *Publishers Weekly* are known as the Children's Announcement issues. The magazine publishes lists of forthcoming titles from every established publisher, and publishers typically buy ads in it to showcase their newest offerings.

Targeting Libraries

Libraries buy books. If your book appears to be a title that librarians might buy— perhaps an exciting nonfiction title—your publisher might place an ad in *Booklist* or *School Library Journal* to draw attention to the book amid all the other titles out there and get it noticed. These ads are most likely after publication, if a book gets a starred review or gets named to an award list. A publisher may then take out an ad to highlight these achievements to that audience.

Targeting Consumers

You've seen the ads for adult novels in the margins of magazines, but what about children's books or young adult literature? That's less common. But if a publishing house acquired the rights to all novels based on a popular teen television series, to piggyback on the success of the show, the publisher might place an ad in a magazine such as *Seventeen*, a consumer publication, to target the youth who actually read the novels. Or a publisher might buy an ad in a consumer publication such as *USA Today* or a national magazine if a celebrity is associated with the title.

A publisher probably won't buy an ad in *The New York Times* or some other newspaper your friends read because the cost is so high, and also because the ad will not reach enough people who might actually buy the book. Don't feel bad if you don't get an ad in such a newspaper. An ad is an investment, and it has to have a good return.

Targeting Teachers

Many teachers use books as resources or tools in their classroom, so children's book publishers may focus an ad campaign on teacher's journals and trade publications. Let's say you just wrote a great easy-reader book—it's imaginative, fun to read, and everyone at the publishing house seems to think it's the coolest book with built-in teacher appeal to hit the shelves in a decade. Well, then, an ad for your book might find its way into a teacher's magazine or journal.

Advertisements are rarely placed, but when they are, the marketing department thinks about the most appropriate venue to target with an ad.

Ground-Level Marketing

You've now read about some pretty big ways to market—ads, freebies, teacher's kits— but other smaller ways exist to get your book out there, too.

def•i•ni•tion

Publishers reimburse bookstores for the costs of ads, events, or displays through **co-op money.** The bookseller's usually limited to a percentage of their actual sales of the publisher's books; if they sold $2,000 worth of books the previous month, they may be able to spend $100 in co-op money.

Co-Op Money

Let's say you book yourself to read your latest picture book at Barnes & Noble during story time the following month. Wouldn't it be nice to place an ad in the local paper advising the public of your reading? Yes, it would, and it may be possible for the bookstore to place that ad through the use of *co-op money*. In this situation, the bookstore and the publisher cooperatively share the cost of an ad.

Publishers may also have to provide co-op money just to get good placement for a book in a chain. Have you noticed the special tables or little shelves at the ends of bookcases (called end caps)? Publishers must pay for their books to be placed there.

Bookstore Giveaways

Sometimes a publisher initiates contests on a smaller scale to generate interest in a particular title or titles. The contest may focus on either the consumer or the bookseller. A bookstore may compete, for instance, in a "Best Window Display Showcasing *If You Give a Moose a Muffin*" contest. The publisher appoints a winner who receives a prize, like a trip or a certificate. Consumer-oriented contests may include drawings for books during story time or discounts on certain titles.

Internet Marketing

With people, and especially teens and children, spending more and more time online, publishers' marketing efforts have moved online, too. Publishers create websites to promote a book or series, do podcasts, try "viral marketing" (e-mails they hope will be forwarded), and even create MySpace pages for the characters in a book. As Diane McNaughton, vice president of marketing for Houghton Mifflin, said in *Publishers Weekly:* "the online world is where the kids are."

You can do this, too. As always, coordinate with your publisher, but if you see a way to generate interest on the Internet that your publisher doesn't want to pursue, don't be afraid to pursue it yourself.

Making a Best-Seller

Good results in marketing aren't always a result of hard work. You might think that if your book is good enough, and if your publisher will just buy that ad in *PW,* your book will make it to *The New York Times* bestseller list. Unfortunately, what makes a best-seller is often name recognition, a tie-in to some sort of entertainment, or just the fact that it's another book in a successful series. Check out *PW*'s list of top-selling children's books for the previous year, and you'll see what I mean.

I'm not saying your book will never sit among these best-sellers—it may—but that takes time and also a certain amount of luck. But on the flip side, if your children's book never sees *The New York Times* book review or best-seller lists, don't despair. You can be a successful children's book author or illustrator without any of your friends and family realizing it and without seeing your name next to J. K. Rowling's or Maurice Sendak's. In fact, many children's book authors forge a highly successful career without ever seeing their titles on even a specialized children's books best-seller list. Getting there requires hard work and longevity in the business. Don't settle for one book. Work on building a career.

Playground Stories _____

I looked at *Publishers Weekly's* list of the top 20 best-selling new hardcover books in 2006. None of them were by unknown authors or illustrators. Outside a couple on a hot topic (pirates), they split more or less evenly into three groups. Some were by names such as Jamie Lee Curtis or children's book names such as Eric Carle or Kate DiCamillo. Some were parts of series (*Lemony Snicket* and *The Magic Tree House*, for example). And some were tied to movies or TV series, such as *Dora the Explorer* and *Cars*.

The Least You Need to Know

◆ You can expect a basic publicity effort from your publisher to promote you and your book.

◆ Nearly all publishers send prepublication review copies of books to key review magazines and may also send them to second-tier, local, or specialty publications.

◆ Many great marketing ideas exist—such as bookstore party kits and bookmarks—but it's questionable whether they actually increase sales.

◆ Advertisements can be expensive, so publishers target particular publications for optimal exposure, or group several titles into one ad.

◆ Although most everyone maintains aspirations of having a best-selling book, when it comes to children's books, best-sellers are typically connected to celebrities, TV shows, or movies.

Chapter 30

Do-It-Yourself Publicity

In This Chapter

- Preparing your publicity campaign
- Helping your publisher help you
- Creating an angle to generate interest in your book
- Tips for approaching and targeting media outlets
- The why's and how's of bookstore events

As an author or illustrator, you might want to go above and beyond what the publisher offers in terms of publicity. Or you might not have a clue how to generate a buzz about your book. You also might be wondering about your local bookstore. (Hint: don't do signings if you can avoid them.)

In this chapter, you learn how to nudge the publisher into doing the little extras, how to do your own publicity, and how to promote your book in bookstores.

Nudge, Don't Push

There's a fine line between contributing constructively to the marketing and publicity of your book and harassing the publisher with your ideas.

If you do have ideas, approach the publisher in a professional manner. The publicist for your book *will* want to know of any ideas you have regarding the publicity for your book, and many publicists ask authors to prepare a list of their publicity ideas. (Marketing departments may also send a detailed questionnaire. If you get one, fill it out thoroughly. Your publisher needs that information.)

After you offer your ideas, let go! Publicists, like your editors, live a harried and hectic workday. Your publicist does not want to hear your voice three times a day. Instead, politely extend your list of publicity ideas and wait to hear from the publicist. A follow-up call about two weeks after submitting your ideas, however, is okay.

I remember a story from an author at a conference who thought that planetariums might be really great places to publicize her children's book about stars and constellations. The author went down to her local library and researched all the planetariums and natural history museums in the nation—about 2,000 in all. She took the list to her publisher, who put together a pamphlet about her book (and a few others) and sent out a mailing to the entire list. The mailing was a big success for the publisher and the sales of the book.

This author simply provided the publishing house with the tools necessary to act on an idea. Although the author put in hours of work—researching all the addresses and locations of planetariums and natural history museums—the work paid off.

Now let's pretend that the author suggested sending a pamphlet to planetariums but didn't do anything more. Would the publicist have had time to sit down and research the mailing list? No—he had his hands full getting information about this season's 50 books out to the standard media sources. By going that extra mile for the publicist, the author helped that publicity idea come to fruition.

Or let's say the author had told the publicist the great idea, did not create the list, and then called the publicist every day to see if a pamphlet had been designed and sent out. How would you react if someone did this to you? More than likely, the publicist would have erased the messages on voicemail as soon as she recognized the author's voice. Don't let this happen to you! Nudge, don't push, and be ready to roll up your sleeves and help.

Class Rules

Publicists know that the best resource in a book's publicity campaign is the author or illustrator. Oftentimes, the author taps into a creative tie to the book that yields a huge public response. It behooves you and the publicist to work in unison. Get to know your publicist and give him your ideas—just don't bother him with a million phone calls to share trivial ideas.

Lend a Helping Pen

Want to know a great way to move along a productive publicity campaign? Offer to write the press materials for the publicist. A publicist doesn't have unlimited time to devote to your book and may only be able to send it to a standard review list. If you want a wider campaign, offer to help. If you create the materials for the *press kit*, the time the publicist didn't have to spend on the kit can instead be used on your campaign.

Follow these steps when approaching your publicist or marketing manager about your ideas. Make an initial phone call and politely say, "Hi, I'm _____, the author of _____. I'd like to help you in any way I can and actually have some publicity ideas. Where might I send them?" If you feel comfortable offering to write the press materials, do it. Put together a packet of *clips*, your ideas, and any press materials you've written and mail them to the publicist. Keep in mind that you can use the materials if the publicist doesn't. Wait a few weeks before calling. Give the publicist a chance to look over the materials. Don't bug the publicist. I said that before, didn't I? Let me say it again: don't bug the publicist. If it appears that your ideas won't be implemented, start using them yourself.

def•i•ni•tion

A **press kit** is a folder of materials about your book sent to the media—newspapers, radio and television stations, journalists, magazines—to alert them to your book's release. The best press kits link the book to a newsworthy item or a hook. A **clip** is a copy of an article you've written or that has been written about you or your book.

Here are several possible items to include in your press kit:

A *press release* or *new book release* announces the publication of your book, briefly describes it, and contains contact information. If something about the book connects to some current event or hot issue, the release can touch on the newsworthy aspect of your book.

Author and illustrator biographies, typically one page, detail your life and publishing career. Who better to write this than you?

The press kit may contain *clippings* from previous articles written about your book or you in a magazine such as *Booklist* or *Publishers Weekly*—especially if your book received an outstanding review.

> ### Can You Keep a Secret?
>
> If you prepare elements for a press kit, save everything on your computer and send the files to the publicist. That way, your publicist will be able to quickly make corrections or edit the documents.

Written like an article, a *mini-feature* actually contains much of the same information as the press release, just in a different format. Because it's actually an article, publications may publish it directly.

If your book can spawn a demonstration that might prove of interest to a talk show, say what you could do with *suggested show or event ideas.* If your book shows kids how to care for pets, for example, outline what you could do in a short segment on a show.

If a journalist becomes intrigued by your book, the more work you can have ready for the journalist, the better chance the writer will do the story. *Suggested interview questions* can be a great help to get you interviewed.

"I Did It My Way"

Frank Sinatra crooned it in his tune "My Way." Once you learn where your publicist's efforts end, you then need to decide how much of "your way" needs to be implemented. Essentially, how much time and energy do you want to devote to publicizing and fueling sales of your book? If you want to self-publicize, take a look at what you need to do.

In the end, you might decide to let the marketing department handle everything. They know their business, and even if they don't do everything you wish they would, they'll do what in their professional judgment is likely to pay off. So self-publicize by all means, but don't feel that what you do will make or break your book.

> ### Playground Stories
>
> Don't spend too much time on your campaign. Bruce Balan offers this comment: "I spent many years becoming quite well-versed in self-promotion. I've been interviewed by scores of magazines, radio programs, and newspapers. I've created brochures, flyers, and review sheets. I've sent mailings to bookstores. I've spent money to hire a publicist. I've thrown publication parties. I've traveled to, and spoken at, conferences, trade shows, schools, and seminars. And I've come to a few conclusions:
>
> ◆ If your publisher is not supportive of your book, it probably doesn't matter what you do.
>
> ◆ Even if your publisher is supportive of your book, there are no guarantees of success.
>
> ◆ The authors I most admire are those who write well. Not those who promote well."

You Gotta Have an Angle

To publicize a book, even a children's book, you need an angle. You need to make your book stand out in a crowd of hundreds of titles—both in the stores and for the media. Remember, the media offers information to readers and viewers. In the case of television, the reporters also need to show something. Conversations with authors are just okay, but it's better if you can "do" something. For a news program to generate a story, they need a news angle—or at least a human interest angle. So your first step in publicizing your title is conceptualizing a hook or an angle.

What's a hook? Let's look at some examples. Say you've written a how-to garden and plant book for kids. A huge storm sweeps through your town, destroying gardens and felling trees. Your angle could be the rebuilding of gardens, teaching kids how to help in the recovery process. Nonfiction can be easier than fiction, but say your picture book details the story of a little boy moving from the neighborhood he's lived in from birth to a new neighborhood and new school, a classic theme, and yet you can find a hook. Find out the statistics on children changing schools and the psychological impact. Offer tips in your press packet for acclimating to a new school. Hook adults into buying the book to help their children; the media will want to offer this "good" information to parents.

Be creative! How can you hook people and get them interested in your book?

Roll the Presses

So you've got a press kit and a press release. What are you going to do with them? Your first stop on the self-publicizing train is your local media. Because you live some-place and wrote a book, you're news. Whether you live in a town or out in the country, try the local papers, radio stations, and TV stations. If you live in a big city, don't expect the major newspapers to be interested (although it certainly doesn't hurt to try *The New York Times*, the *Chicago Tribune*, or the *San Francisco Chronicle*). Go for the neighborhood papers, the free monthlies for parents, the local cable TV show, and so on. Where do you get your local news? Go there! Fire off those releases you've written to the local media.

> **Can You Keep a Secret?**
>
> Susan Raab, children's books marketing consultant, has a fantastic archive of her "To Market" column at www.raabassociates.com/tomarket/tomarket.htm. Elsewhere on her site, you'll find information on her book *An Author's Guide to Children's Book Promotion* (which illustrators will find useful, too).

After you've sent your releases and kits to the local media, concentrate on bigger media outlets—but in many cases only if you can accommodate an interview or plan on traveling in the area. Let's look a little more closely at your publicity options.

Any *newspaper* outside your area will want one of two things—a news link or an appearance in their town. Contact the feature editor if the angle you have involves a trend or a news item. Contact the children's book review editor if you plan on a signing or an appearance someplace.

Class Rules _____

Author tours are expensive, and children's publishers don't pay for them. Unless you have money to burn, don't put yourself on a six-city tour across the nation. Certainly, if business takes you to Boston for a week and time permits, contact the media about appearances. Otherwise, save the travel for a vacation someplace fun!

Radio programs can call you and conduct live or taped interviews over the phone. Find a media directory in your local library or online and go through the listing of shows by content. If your children's book focuses on sports fitness for children, pitch yourself as an interview on the morning sports show. Producers of talk radio continually scramble to fill their airtime with interesting and informational interviews. Don't limit yourself to approaching only the book shows. Generally, these shows deal with weighty adult books anyway.

For *television*, look locally and anywhere you might be traveling. Television programs need to show their viewers something—why not you? You'll still need an informational or newsworthy hook for the appearance. I've given examples of hooks tied to specific book subjects, but you can make yourself the hook. For example, until he got to be known as an illustrator, David Wisniewski got more attention from having gone to clown school than from having created a beautiful book.

Self-publicizing can be a full-time job, or you might decide to skip it completely. Consider your options. Whatever you decide to do, connect your efforts to any bookstore events you do—a way to get attention for your book on its own, but also a way to support your publicity efforts. Keep your publisher informed, too.

A Tale of Two (or More) Bookstores

Ask just about any author or illustrator, and you'll hear their story about doing a reading from their book and then sitting at a table and signing books … for all of 17 people. I'm telling you: *don't do signings*. If you go to work with a bookstore, make an event out of it. Bookstores want events because they bring more people to the store.

Once upon a time, the little bookstore up the street ruled the roost. People came from all over the neighborhood to buy the latest fiction title or charming picture book. But today, more and more independent bookstores are giving way to *superstores* stocked with more than 100,000 titles across many departments. You know the big companies: Barnes & Noble, Borders, Tower, Crown. Almost anywhere you go, you'll find a Borders and a Barnes & Noble going head-to-head. Now factor in the smaller bookstore chains and the independents stores; with so many choices, competition to draw in and retain customers rages.

One of the ways these bookstores contribute to the community and bring in a loyal buying base is through the efforts of community relations departments. Some chains have a public relations person in each store. The PR manager of a bookstore chain may address the media over a controversial title, but more common duties include planning events around books and author book signings. He or she creates a monthly calendar of events, everything from weekly story times to monthly book club meetings to author signings and informational seminars. By hosting these free and open-to-the-public events, the stores draw in more customers, thereby selling more books— more of your book! The best events, those that bring in the customers, are the parties and seminars. And nowhere are the book parties happier, bigger, or more fun than in the children's departments.

Kids love books and love socializing at events that deal with their favorite book. Can you remember your own fascination with the *Little House on the Prairie* series or the *Hardy Boys* books? Wouldn't you have loved to spend an evening once a month dressing up like Laura Ingalls, reading passages from *Little House in the Big Woods*, and learning how to make a treat Laura probably made more than 100 years ago? Little girls today can enjoy activities like these by participating in *American Girls* Clubs run out of bookstore chains. Bookstores also offer budding consumers and their parents other opportunities to love (and buy) books.

def•i•ni•tion

In the book business, a **superstore** is a large store typically stocking more than 100,000 titles. Some superstores even sell other products besides books, such as CDs, DVDs, stationery, and toys. Two superstore chains are Barnes & Noble and Borders.

Class Rules

Unadorned book signings can be brutal, both for authors and bookstore personnel. Unless the author is a celebrity, the public won't show up. The author is left to sit at a table as people nervously walk by.

From story time hours to character costume parties to parent/child book clubs, bookstores are clamoring for ways to excite children to read and their parents to purchase.

Thus, a great opportunity arises for you to self-publicize your book. And the best part? You can hit only the local stores or travel as far and wide as you please. But having an event surrounding your book at one or several bookstores isn't necessarily easy. More likely than not, calling and asking a befuddled floor salesclerk about a book signing won't result in an event. You need a plan, and you need to talk to the store manager and/or community relations coordinator/manager.

Making Contact

Let's say your book, *Giggles and Grins*, a pop-up book of funny faces and jokes, just shipped to bookstores everywhere. And in your hometown, three bookstores exist as possible event targets. The first thing you must do—before pitching a giggly good event—is find out if the bookstore even offers customers a *calendar of events*. The smaller mall stores, for instance, don't have the room or staff to host events. Call the store first and ask an employee whether or not the store hosts book-related events. If they don't, don't bother the staffer anymore. Move on. If they say yes, ask to talk to the events planner.

def•i•ni•tion

Bookstores that showcase author signings, story times for children, book clubs, and other author-related events out of the store typically print a monthly calendar that details each event, including the date and time. A paragraph description gives customers a clear idea of what to expect. These flyers are usually called **calendar of events** or the **event calendar**.

As mentioned earlier, many bookstores now employ a person to handle all book-related events and community interaction, often called a community relations coordinator (CRC) or a community relations manager (CRM). They can help you publicize your book in a bookstore. The CRC in a typical store looks actively, if not desperately, for authors and illustrators like you to do events and fill the dates on their calendars. If the store you're hoping to book an event in doesn't employ a special community relations representative, you'll want to speak directly to the store manager. In some cases, the person you need to reach isn't even in the store; Borders, for example, handles events through "area marketing managers," each of whom is responsible for several stores. So be sure you find out whom you need to contact.

Leave a Message at the Tone

Chances are pretty good that you'll get a direct number for the community relations coordinator. Chances are equally as good that you'll need to leave a message. Because of the sheer number of calls this employee receives—everyone from schools asking for donations to authors wanting to book an event—the CRC may be on another line or out in the community working.

Because these employees receive an inordinate number of calls in which the caller rambles on and on about his or her business, you will endear yourself and retain a greater chance of store support for your event if you leave a short, clear message. Begin your message or call with your name, preferably spelled, and your phone number. Repeat the number. Give the title of your book and the ISBN. State the time frame in which you'd like an event to occur. Tell the CRM that you'll send a press release about the book and any media clippings (if you have them) and a letter detailing the event you envision. Send the letter, and wait patiently to hear. Follow up if you don't hear back in a reasonable time.

If you can include a review copy of your book, do it. If the CRC or CRM decides to schedule an event with you, he or she will need to scan the cover of the book for posters that may be displayed in the store before the reading.

And don't wait to call and attempt to book an event with a bookstore just weeks before your arrival in town. Calendars of events fill up three months or more in advance. The CRC or CRM actually writes the copy for the calendar a month in advance and then the copy must go to the designer and the printer. Think ahead—at least three months into the future. If you don't, you're likely to hear, "I'm sorry, but my calendar is already full!"

Party Plans

Once you've made contact, you'll likely find that whoever it is you've contacted wants to see your ideas on paper. It's up to you to sell the store on the event idea. The CRC wants to throw well-attended events that bring in customers. If an event such as a straightforward reading and signing by an unknown author seems unimaginative and certain to fail, the CRC won't book it. Or if the CRC does book it, you may end up wishing he hadn't.

So put on your creative cap and come up with a plan—several ideas to pitch the store's way for fun events. Your options are only limited by your ingenuity, but you'll need to work with what's possible in the store. Some standard event categories occur in the children's departments of bookstores for which you can design your event:

Class Rules

Don't book a party or gathering in two competitive bookstores around the same time. You glut the market of interest in your book and the event. Give your favorite store first priority. Then, later on down the road, book another event at the competition. There will be less confusion and more trust in you as an author.

Preschool/school-age story times   Most stores offer story times twice a week or more. Oftentimes, the children's department supervisor or another employee picks picture books at random and reads them during the story hour. Really great story time facilitators incorporate themes into the hour and sometimes even include finger-play games and singing.

Series club event   Kind of like a book club for kids, groups of devotees to a particular series gather at the store to meet and talk about their favorite books in the cycle. The *American Girls* Clubs are good examples of this kind of event. Often, the facilitator of the club brings in other works of children's literature. For instance, if the *American Girls* Club focuses on the character living in the 1940s, the leader may showcase a display of old radios from the era and share other books the girls might like to read to further explore the role of women during World War II.

Character parties   At these events, your children's beloved storybook characters make an appearance—like Clifford the Big Red Dog, or the Mouse from *If You Give a Mouse a Cookie.* Then several of the stories from that character's repertoire or from the author who created the character are read to the kids. If your book features a lively character, you might want to make your own costume or create puppets of the characters. You can read your book in costume or put on a puppet show!

Author readings and presentations   The author of the book reads the book. But don't stop there! Sometimes, as in the case of David Carter, the famed author of those fabulous pop-up bug books, the author or illustrator treats the kids to a chalk talk, showing the audience how the ideas become a book. Puppets or props (with practice first!) can also enhance a reading.

Activity event   In this type of event, an activity focuses on a book. If you're an illustrator or author/illustrator, this kind of event could be for you. Show your audience how you made your book, and turn them loose to make their own.

You Gotta Have a Gimmick

Back to your plan. The CRC or CRM will help you more if you help him more. Meaning: give him every possible idea you have for an event and offer to help publicize the event, too. Just as when you attempt to garner media coverage, you'll need to go the extra mile here, too. Send the CRC a press kit if you have one. With the press kit, include a cover letter with the following information:

◆ Your name, your book's title, ISBN, and publisher

◆ Where the publisher can get copies of the book if not distributed through standard means or self-published

◆ The event you envision

◆ The dates and times you're available to accommodate an event (Remember, think three months or more in advance.)

◆ How you plan to publicize the event and draw in book-buying crowds

◆ A template for a press release/event announcement to send to calendar editors and various local publications

Check with the store shortly before the event to confirm that they've sent out the press kits and that they're expecting you. Even the best-laid plans can go wrong! On the day, come early, introduce yourself to the staff, and introduce yourself to customers. They won't all know about your event, but they might be happy to stay for it.

Do all of this, and you're well on your way to having a real *event*, not just a book signing or reading. Almost all the people coming to one of those will be loyal friends and family. You want to get people who don't know you to come, too. Plan and publicize an event, working closely with the bookstore personnel, and you will draw people.

Can You Keep a Secret?

Keep copies of event calendars that list your presentation. Moreover, keep copies of the event proposal letter and press kit you sent to the CRM. The next time you're looking to self-promote your book through a bookstore, you can reuse your ideas and also provide the new CRM a glimpse into the success of your last event. The calendars also typically list phone numbers for the stores, so the CRM can easily call the store that already hosted an event with you and either find out what worked fabulously or refrain from repeating any mistakes.

And afterward, don't forget to write a thank you note to the CRM. With any luck, they'll remember you warmly, and that can only help when your next book comes out.

The Least You Need to Know

◆ Offer your publicity ideas to your publisher's marketing and publicity departments—but do it gently.

◆ Don't just make suggestions, make materials. You can use them for self-publicizing, too.

◆ Don't devote all your time to the success of your book through diligent marketing and publicity—write more books!

◆ Conceptualize "hooks" for your book to generate interest in different media outlets and make your book stand out over all the others on the market.

◆ Bookstores, eager to draw in a loyal customer base in the midst of fierce competition, host book signings and author events regularly. You can fuel sales of your book by booking an author event in bookstores.

Chapter 31

Back to School

In This Chapter

- ◆ What a "school visit" is and what you must do to set one up
- ◆ What to expect in payment and fees
- ◆ Some of the many possible kinds of visits
- ◆ Benefits that go beyond promoting your book

So far, you may be getting the idea that you can play only a limited role in the marketing and publicizing of your book. True—except for one key area. Going back to school, by which I mean doing school visits, can do lots for the sales of your book over the long term, and at the same time serve as a useful source of income for you.

School Visit Basics

School visits happen all over the country, at every level of school, and they work. Subject-area teachers want to generate excitement about science or math or American history, and English teachers, reading teachers, and librarians are always looking for ways to ignite a love of reading and writing in students. Author visits will do this, or so they hope. Illustrators do school visits, too, although you might have to work a little harder to persuade a school that you can make your visit curriculum-relevant.

A school visit does not necessarily mean you address a school assembly or launch into a monologue in a fourth-grade classroom. A teacher or a school will most want you to visit if you produce some sort of learning activity or program. These can take place in individual classrooms or in larger groups. As you'll find later in the chapter, there are many possible kinds of visits.

Before going any further, ask yourself if you're cut out for school visits. Are you comfortable with speaking to a room full of children? Note that you shouldn't have to be keeping them in order—the teacher or librarian *should* do that—but can you keep them engaged? If you're not sure, start small with just a few children at your child's school or your neighborhood library. Schools want dynamic speakers who will get children excited about reading or a particular subject, so don't go out into schools if that's not you. You can promote your books in other ways.

If you can do school visits—many authors and illustrators enjoy them—you'll find that they're a great way to promote your books. But note that they work best over a period of time. As you do more and more visits, you build up an audience for new books, and you inform people about your backlist. School visits, in fact, may be the single most effective thing you can do to keep your books in print.

The basic things you need to do for an actual visit are simple: work out a plan in writing with your contact person. Then visit the school and get the students excited about books in general and your books in particular. And you get paid for this.

Yes, you can and should charge a fee for most kinds of school visits. Many schools have budgets for author visits and might not take you as seriously if you *don't* charge a fee. Considering the time involved to prepare and travel, even as a beginner you should charge $250 to $400 for a one-hour presentation and several hundred dollars for a full day at a school; experienced authors charge considerably more. Schools in rural areas or the inner cities may have less money at their disposal, so do waive fees when necessary.

> **Can You Keep a Secret?**
>
> Remember that doing a school visit well is hard work, and that the number of books you sell is unlikely to compensate you for your time. You deserve a fee, negotiated in advance and paid on the day of your visit, and reimbursement of your travel costs.

As you get ready to embark into the world of school visiting, don't set off without *Terrific Connections with Authors, Illustrators, and Storytellers* by Toni Buzzeo and Jane Kurtz. If you take a cursory look at it, it seems to be for librarians and schools who want to have authors and illustrators visit them. But it's also the best (indeed, so far as I know, the only) guide for the authors and illustrators themselves. You just have to read it the other way around. If any resource is indispensable, this one is—I drew on it heavily while writing this chapter.

Making Contact

If you want to make school visits and have ideas for some workshops or other learning experiences, your next step is to set up some. How do you do that? There are many ways. Whichever way you use, keep in mind that you may need to plan several months to a year ahead—if you contact a school in March, for example, the earliest you'll actually visit is likely to be September.

When you're just getting started, contacting schools in your area and letting them know you're available is a good first step. If you're calling a school "cold," you can start at the top and talk to the principal. Explain what you want to do and ask who you should speak to. Some people find that it may be best to just ask to speak to a reading teacher or librarian—or to ask the school secretary who she thinks would be most interested in bringing an author or illustrator to the school. If someone is interested, follow up with him: get him copies of your book(s), or a proposal for your visit, as soon as possible.

Publishers also get requests from schools for popular authors and illustrators. Typically, the well-known ones get many more requests than they could possibly fulfill, and in such cases the person in the marketing department who handles school visits will suggest someone else. Let this person know that you're eager to visit schools, and you're on your way.

Pursue school visits through as many avenues as possible. Contact local arts councils to see if they have lists of recommended writers and artists. If they do, get on the list. Join local and national organizations that work in children's books and literacy. Send out a mailing—but be sure to follow up with phone calls. And of course, talk to everyone you know, ask other authors and illustrators for referrals, volunteer in your local school or library, and generally get involved in your community.

> **Can You Keep a Secret?**
>
> In many states, the state arts commission sponsors grant-based programs to help school districts pay artists such as writers and illustrators to come do programs of varying lengths. Typically the artist registers with the arts commission, which then produces a list for school districts to draw from.

If you develop a good program, and if you have a steady flow of books coming out, soon you'll have more requests than you can handle.

"Well, No One Told *Me* You Were Coming"

Talk to any veteran of a school visit, and you'll hear stories ranging from the horrific to the totally wonderful. One horror is to go to the school office and be met with a blank stare from the school secretary when you attempt to explain why you're there: "Well, no one told *me* you were coming." Another is to discover that none of the students in the classrooms you're visiting has read even one of your books.

On the other hand, people also tell stories of arriving at a school that has been decorated to reflect the content of one of their books; of the excitement of being in a room full of children who have read every single one of their books; and of being dazzled with wonderful artwork, plays, and student-crafted books, all done in preparation for a visit.

As Toni and Jane emphasize in their *Terrific Connections*, preparation is important. They went so far as to craft a two-page "wish list" to use with schools. You might want to create your own, because you've got to try to be sure the school is as prepared as you are. This could become the basis for the written agreement that details what you'll do and when. If you've carefully crafted a lively presentation for fifth graders that shows the stages your manuscript and book went through, you would have a hard time adjusting it on the fly for a first-grade class you weren't told about.

Be polite and professional in manner, but be sure to ask questions about what the school is doing and what they expect of you. You should even be sure you have breaks and lunch time in your schedule. Cover the practical issues: if you're going to do a book signing, be sure the books have been ordered well in advance. Don't let the school assume that you'll bring them. Get this all down in writing and have someone at the school sign off on that document before your visit.

With the practical side nailed down, get to work making sure that you will have the best possible experience with the children, and that what you will do in the school won't just be a fun break from routine, but a learning experience that will feed into the regular curriculum. When planning a school visit, Toni starts by creating "extensive, standards-based curriculum guides" about her books and sends them to all the schools she visits, with tips on how to use them. She wants to be sure all the children she meets have read at least one of her books before she visits. Strive to do the same, and make suggestions for follow-up activities, too.

You're in the Spotlight—Now What?

So after all this talk of planning, what should you do in a school visit? First of all, keep in mind the age level of the students you're facing as you plan your approach: second graders appreciate lots of visuals and a chance to interact with you, while older students may respond well to a short presentation followed by a group discussion. For either group, take "stuff"—books, proofs, marked-up manuscripts, the contents of your idea file—concrete materials that will help them connect to the somewhat abstract notion of creative process.

Adjust to the setting in which you are working. You may visit one classroom for 45 minutes, speak to an assembly, or spend a week or more as an artist-in-residence. You may be the only book person visiting or be part of a month-long children's literature festival.

The Assembly

In an assembly, you typically address the whole school. This is not an ideal situation! When a school asks for you to address an assembly, answer their question with a question of your own: could the assembly be limited to one grade, or a limited number of grades? If you have to face the whole school, your book and your presentation must appeal to all grade levels of the school—such as from kindergarten to sixth, or from ninth through twelfth. This will be a challenge. In assemblies, in particular, you can't stick to your identity as an author or an illustrator. You must be a performance artist engaging a diverse array of kids.

Story Times and Reading

You may be asked to go into a classroom and read your picture book to the kids. Or if you've written a young reader or young adult novel, to read a passage from it. Don't settle for this if you can avoid it. Talk to the teacher and find out how you can tie into the curriculum she's teaching, and develop pre- and post-visit activities. At the very least, try to see to it that the children read some of your books before you arrive, and build an activity around them, with your actual reading time kept to a minimum.

Class Workshops

Sometimes, focusing on your book is enough. Classes involved in making their own books as part of learning the writing process, for example, may invite you to talk about how your book came about. Children are fascinated by the multiple drafts you go through, intrigued by a copy editor's marks (so similar to their teacher's comments), and especially interested in materials like color proofs, which you sometimes can get from a publisher after the book has been printed.

For teenagers or middle graders, writing workshops can feed especially well into a school's curriculum. If you're a mystery writer, for example, you might create mystery stories with ninth graders, starting with some exploration of the elements of a mystery. Or build a subject-area workshop, if your book or books are suitable for that.

Workshops don't have to be tied to school time. You might want to offer a weekend or Saturday workshop for students throughout the district. Perhaps your book deals with horseshoeing. Why not give a seminar or workshop on the "Lost Art of Shoeing a Horse" to all the 4-H students? Or if you've written a novel, you could turn your experience into a writing workshop and critique seminar for students. The ideas are limitless; brainstorm a few right now.

Storytelling

This category applies especially to folktale tellers, but novelists or nonfiction writers might also find ways to dramatize their work. *Storytelling* requires a dramatic retelling. Your voice, gestures, accent, mannerisms, some props, and so on are all employed to enhance the story. If you have a flair for the dramatic and are good at memorizing stories, this is a great option for you. And don't ignore older students. High school students relish a really well-told story, too.

Carnivals and Other Fund-Raisers

Many schools hold carnivals as fund-raisers during the year. Always looking for interesting booths, the school might let you set up a reading–book sale booth at the carnival, for a fee or otherwise. Here's a case where the school doesn't pay you; in fact, the school might require you to donate a percentage of the sales.

Or you might work with a school that's planning a book fair and offer to do readings to make the event more than just a book sale. Of course, you'll want them to carry your books and provide some signing time.

Beyond Schools

Everything in this chapter focuses on schools, but you can apply this approach to other related venues. Libraries welcome authors, both for individual sessions and as part of larger events such as "Read Across America," sponsored by the National Education Association and described as "the nation's largest reading event." You can find a place at local book festivals, young author conferences, and the like, too.

The contacts you gain by being active in schools may ultimately lead to invitations to regional conferences and national conventions of educational organizations. You can even do virtual visits by having an online chat with a classroom of children on the other side of the country, or extend a visit by working with some students on a project to be posted on their school's website. Your imagination may be the only limit to the possibilities. Stay active, talk to people, and sooner or later you'll find yourself exploring some of these other options.

On the Road

How busy do you want to be? You'll have to figure that out for yourself. If your books are the kind that work in the schools, you can be very busy with school visits, and doing so will not only sell an existing book but also create an audience for future ones. Imagine you've successfully visited 100 schools over a three-year period. When a new book comes out, teachers at all the schools you've visited will be interested in hearing about it, and many of the students will remember you, too. So be sure all those schools know about your new book and then go on the road with a new program.

Being on the road is not a wholly positive experience, as Jane Kurtz says: "Travel can be draining—longer than ever waits in airports, for instance, and the occasional 'conference center' that is suspiciously like a dorm. But I do think we are lucky. We have this opportunity to connect directly with our audience, to get our books into the hands of readers who had never heard of us or our books before we visited their school or town." Generally speaking, school visits are a great way to gain recognition of your book, but most authors probably won't make an income able to support them on school visits alone. So take advantage of the benefits of school visits, but not to the detriment of your writing. Continue to write. Ultimately, more books will result in more income.

Finally, keep in mind that, as Jane notes, school visits are a way to connect directly to your audience. It can be immensely satisfying—if not overwhelming—to be in a roomful of children, all of whom have read your book, love it, and are excited to be meeting, perhaps for the first time, a real live author or illustrator. Memories of such experience, or letter(s) from children received months afterward, will help keep you inspired. You owe it to yourself to have these experiences.

The Least You Need to Know

◆ You can promote your book at a school visit in many ways, including reading the story, giving a presentation, or selling your books as a fund-raiser.

◆ It's important to identify and work through the right channel when planning school visits. It might be a teacher, but it might be the library media specialist.

◆ School visits can pay very well, but you may need to charge less when getting started or waive your fees with schools that lack the funding.

◆ School visits can add significantly to the sales of an existing book and can also help you gain recognition and an audience for future books.

Chapter 32

I Won a Prize!

In This Chapter

- ◆ The really big awards in children's literature
- ◆ National awards you might hope to win
- ◆ Lists that make a difference in your reputation
- ◆ Why state awards mean something

Right now, you might just want to get your book out into the world and aren't thinking ahead to the response it may get, but listen up! Many opportunities exist within the children's publishing world for authors to achieve recognition and awards. Not that winning a blue ribbon always gains you everything, but it can help provide longevity for your career and aspirations. After all, if you win one of the major children's book awards, consider your book a classic with almost guaranteed sales for future generations. Also, publishers will be a good bit more eager to sign you up for another book if one of your books gets an award.

In this chapter, you learn about the many ways you can achieve recognition and the admiration of your colleagues.

The Big Ones—Newbery and Caldecott

Walk into any big bookstore (and smaller ones, too), and you'll likely find an entire bookcase showcasing the Newbery and Caldecott Award–winning books. These two awards remain the Academy Awards of the children's book industry. Unlike other children's book awards, which may have little immediate impact on sales, these two also drive publishers back to the printers for tens of thousands of copies. Why? The public recognizes them, and the winners are going to sell. Let's take a close look at each.

The Newbery Medal

Each year, the Association for Library Service to Children (ALSC) of the American Library Association (ALA) awards the Newbery Medal to "the most distinguished American children's book" published the previous year. Just a little history: on June 21, 1921, Frederic G. Melcher proposed the award to a meeting of the Children's Librarians' Section of the ALA and suggested that it be named for the eighteenth-century English bookseller John Newbery.

> **Can You Keep a Secret?**
>
> For a complete listing of all Newbery and Caldecott medalists and honor books, consult *The Newbery and Caldecott Awards: A Guide to the Medal and Honor Books,* published by the American Library Association. Or online, visit www.ala.org/alsc/newbery.html and www.ala.org/alsc/caldecott.html.

The Newbery holds special significance among all children's book awards because it was the first children's book award in the world. Although only one book receives the actual medal each year, several more books, referred to as "honor books," are also named.

Past Newbery titles include *The Higher Power of Lucky* by Susan Patron, *The Tale of Despereaux* by Kate DiCamillo, and *Sarah Plain and Tall* by Patricia MacLachlan.

The Caldecott Medal

The Newbery Medal certainly paved the way for more recognition of outstanding children's writers. However, the illustrators of children's books found no kudos thrown their way. So in 1937, to give illustrators the honor and encouragement they deserved for bringing tales to life in picture books, a second medal was created. The result was the Caldecott Medal, named in honor of nineteenth-century English illustrator

Randolph Caldecott, awarded annually by the ALSC to the artist of the most distinguished American picture book for children. (Of course, the author deserves some credit, too, for creating the text that inspired the illustrations, but the illustrator receives the Caldecott.)

Recent winners include Emily Arnold McCully's *Mirette on the High Wire*, Eric Rohmann's *My Friend Rabbit*, and Chris Raschka's illustrations for *The Hello, Goodbye Window*. And just like the Newbery Medal, those books not chosen but deemed wonderful anyway earn the title "honor book."

Class Rules

The terms and criteria for the Caldecott Medal include this note: "The committee should keep in mind that the award is for distinguished illustrations in a picture book and for excellence of pictorial presentation for children. The award is not for didactic intent or for popularity." Just because a book sells well doesn't necessarily make it a winner among the experts.

Other National Awards

Just because you don't win a Newbery or Caldecott doesn't mean you'll never receive any recognition for your hard work. A variety of other awards exist to provide credit where credit is due—and offer an additional list of noteworthy books beyond the Newbery or Caldecott.

The National Book Awards

In 1950, a consortium of book publishing groups sponsored the first annual National Book Awards Ceremony and Dinner in New York City. The goal of the consortium was to enhance the public's awareness of exceptional books written by Americans and increase literacy and the joy of reading. For more than 50 years, the National Book Awards have conferred the preeminent literary prizes each year within four different genres. The winners earn a cash award along with a crystal sculpture. The "young people's literature" tends to go to a middle-grade or YA novel. Recent winners include Pete Hautmann's *Godless* and Jeanne Birdsall's *The Penderwicks*.

I Have a Dream: The Coretta Scott King Award

The Coretta Scott King Award honors African American authors and illustrators for outstanding contributions to children's and young adult literature that promote understanding and appreciation of the culture and contribution of all races. Named after

Can You Keep a Secret?

For a complete listing of all the Coretta Scott King awards since 1970, surf online to www.ala. org/csk. Check out titles of past winners and peruse them to gain an understanding about the focus on multicultural literature and the world.

the wife of slain civil rights leader Dr. Martin Luther King Jr., the award, beyond honoring Mrs. King's courage and determination to continue her husband's work for peace, also honors the late leader.

In 1999, the Coretta Scott King Award celebrated its thirtieth anniversary. The 2007 winners of this award were *Copper Sun* by Sharon Draper, and for illustrations, *Moses: When Harriet Tubman Led Her People to Freedom*, illustrated by Kadir Nelson with text by Carole Boston Weatherford.

Big Award from *Little House* Lady

Few children don't know who Laura Ingalls Wilder was. Her series of books beginning with *The Little House in the Big Woods* provides pertinent historical information, as well as entertainment. Every two years, the ALSC confers the Laura Ingalls Wilder Award on either an author or illustrator whose books, published in the United States, have made, over a period of years, a substantial and lasting contribution to literature for children. Call this a lifetime achievement award.

Past recipients of this award include Russell Freedman, Virginia Hamilton, Marcia Brown, Maurice Sendak, and Ruth Sawyer. James Marshall was named the winner in 2007.

Teen Angst Awards

Angst, rebellion, rock and roll, and entertainment—these are hallmarks of the teenage years. With the powerful emotions rumbling around within adolescents, it's no wonder this group embraces books that speak to them. And for those writers who really speak clearly to the teen audience, two awards stand out: the Margaret A. Edwards Award and the Michael L. Printz Award.

The Margaret A. Edwards Award

Established in 1988 and run by the Young Adult Library Services Association (YALSA), this $2,000 award recognizes an author whose work or works provides young adults with a window through which they can view their world and helps them grow and understand themselves and their role in society. Past recipients of the award include S. E. Hinton for *The Outsiders* and *Rumble Fish* and Robert Cormier for *The Chocolate War*.

The Michael L. Printz Award

With the new millennium came a new award that distinguishes the best of the best of young adult literature—with edge. The Michael L. Printz Award honors the highest literary achievement in young adult books for a novel published the preceding year. In 2007, *American Born Chinese* by Gene Luen Yang became one of the first (if not the first) graphic novels to be recognized by a major award. Look for the latest Michael L. Printz Awards. The winners are certain to be creating the best YA literature.

Are these the only national awards? Of course not. As you spend more time in this field, you'll learn about others, from the Scott O'Dell Award for the best historical fiction, to the Golden Kite Award given by the Society of Children's Book Writers and Illustrators to a member, to the Orbis Pictus Award given by the National Council of Teachers of English to the best nonfiction for children. None of them have as much of an impact as the two biggies do, but they'll all help your reputation and may help backlist sales—continued sales over time.

Get on These Lists!

Earning an award such as the ones discussed so far probably takes as much luck as skill. Dozens of authors and illustrators may have a serious chance in any year, but only one or a few are chosen. Needless to say, you might not ever receive a Newbery or Caldecott. But that doesn't mean you can't see your book on some noteworthy lists—lists that might not have an immediate impact on sales but do add luster to your name and possibly longevity to your book.

ALA Notables

To recognize the best children's books of the year, the ALA doesn't just pick a few select titles for its awards. A committee also compiles the list called "ALA Notable Books for Children," made up of 60 or 70—or perhaps a few more—children's books the committee considers to be the best of the year. Unlike the procedure with many other awards, the committee discusses the books it is considering in a public meeting at the ALA's semiannual conventions. Getting on this list almost certainly means your book will sell better to libraries.

> **Class Rules** _____
>
> It's up to you and your publisher to help your book get on lists and be considered for awards. Each award, medal, and notable list requires a process. An editor or committee needs to see your book to know it exists. Check that your publisher is actively submitting your books to the awards. If not, research the awards yourself and make your own submissions.

Children's Choices

Do you want to get past the gatekeepers and be recognized by your true audience—children? Then being named to the "Children's Choices" list, an annual publication sponsored by the Children's Book Council (CBC) and the International Reading Association (the organization for reading teachers), may be your highest aspiration. Children all over the country vote on books submitted by publishers, eventually creating a list of about 100 titles. Every year, you can find the latest list online at the CBC's website, www.cbcbooks.org.

Outstanding Science

Every year, science teachers across the United States recognize the best trade books on science for children in a list chosen by a panel named by the National Science Teachers Association (NSTA) and published with the help of the CBC. The list, with more than 100 books on a variety of subjects, is published every year in *Science for Children*. Copies are available online at the NSTA website, www.nsta.org, or you can order them from the CBC.

Notable Social Studies

The National Council for the Social Studies creates a list similar to the science teachers' list, but this time with a focus on social studies. About 150 books come from such areas as biography, contemporary issues, history, and world culture. Published every year in *Social Education*, the list is available online at www.socialstudies.org/resources/notable or by mail from the CBC.

Parents' Choice Awards

The Parent's Choice Foundation is a nonprofit organization dedicated to evaluating and recommending books, among other things. Learn more at www.parents-choice.org. Receiving a Parent's Choice Award helps you sell more books to parents and teachers.

End-of-Year Lists

I'm probably not alone in liking to package things up and box them together at the end of the year. It's closure, I guess. Regardless of the reason, your book might place nicely on an end-of-the-year list. The most influential of the annual lists of children's books are the *Publishers Weekly* roundup, the *Booklist* "Editor's Picks," and *The Boston Globe/Horn Book* "Best Books of the Year."

Can You Keep a Secret?

Starting to feel overwhelmed by all these awards? If you want one handy place to start, just go to the Children's Book Awards page on my website, www. underdown.org/childrens-book-awards.htm. On the other hand, if you want to know a lot more, get *Children's Books: Awards and Prizes*, published by the Children's Book Council, from your local library, or access the online version at the CBC website, www. cbcbooks.org.

Wowing Them All Over the Country

In response to literacy problems and to place an emphasis on the benefits of reading, many states now pass out their own awards for outstanding literature for young people. They may be sponsored by local branches of national organizations, by state education departments, or by state organizations. These outstanding books may be evaluated by teachers, librarians, or children. Authors from all over the country may be eligible or only state residents.

Getting named to one of the lists may not do much for your book. Being on a number of them, however, will because it makes it more likely that school libraries will purchase it. Some, like the Texas Bluebonnet Award, give a boost in sales just to books nominated because children all over the state read and vote on the books and so their schools must have copies on hand. Your publisher should take care of sending your book to the relevant committees. Be pleased if you hear you've been named.

I've mentioned just a few of the organizations and magazines that give awards or that create lists of recommended children's books every year. Some will get you more recognition than others. Some will help you reach a specialized audience, while others speak to a national audience. Right now, making sense of them all may be difficult, so keep your eyes open, ask questions if you get an award or are named to a list you've never heard of, and check the resources listed here and in Appendix B.

The Least You Need to Know

◆ Many awards exist in the publishing world to recognize children's book authors and illustrators.

◆ The original and most esteemed award in the United States for a writer is the Newbery Medal.

◆ The original and most esteemed award in the United States for an illustrator is the Caldecott Medal.

◆ Beyond awards, lists of notable books abound; these lists remain a good way for you to receive recognition.

◆ In many cases, to be considered for all these awards and lists, the publisher must submit information or applications; if your publisher doesn't act, sometimes you can.

Chapter 33

Building a Career

In This Chapter

- ◆ Challenges for the published author
- ◆ Dealing with books going out of print
- ◆ Ways to make money
- ◆ The importance of continuing to learn and grow

With your first book published, you might think your struggles are over. You have a grip on the ear of an editor or art director, and your books will now flow from your desk to publisher and out into the world.

The reality is a bit more complicated than that. This chapter reveals some of the challenges that still lie ahead and points out some possible solutions. It's a big world out there, and I want to give you a few more tools so you can succeed in it.

Becoming a Pro

By the time your first book is published, unless you're very lucky, you'll have already spent several years working toward becoming a children's writer or illustrator. Inevitably, you've learned a lot and have absorbed and built upon the advice and information in this book. You are a professional. As a professional, you need to think strategically about what you do.

Your overall challenge now is to balance writing and illustrating with the other things you must do to keep your career going. You can't spend all your time promoting your already published books or bringing in income from other sources. Earlier, I covered promoting your book, and later in this chapter, you'll see some examples of what you can do to add to your income. Don't get carried away with either of these! You need to be sure to set aside time to work on what you most want to do so your other activities don't take over your life.

You need new projects because you want to have new books coming out regularly. Each new one helps remind readers of your earlier ones and get them hoping for the next. Ideally, when one book is about to be published, you'll already have others under contract and be starting to think about still others. Just like a publisher, you need to have a pipeline.

Can You Keep a Secret?

Some authors work with more than one publisher to ensure a steady stream of new books. It's best not to do this unless each is publishing a different kind of book, such as picture books at one and chapter books at another. Illustrators might find it easier to work with a few publishers at once, but don't get too scattered. And try not to hop from one publisher to another. Building up a backlist at a single publisher ensures that your books get more support.

Obstacles You'll Face

Don't get carried away by what I'm describing! Many people only dream of having the "problem" of having to balance different demands on their time. After your first book comes out, the next ones aren't necessarily any easier.

The First One's Easy

Everyone is excited by something new and possibly different. Publishers with a book by a first-time author or illustrator are excited to have discovered fresh talent, reviewers are intrigued, and readers are curious to see if something totally new has come along. Your book is the new kid on the block everyone wants to meet.

After that first book, reality sets in. If it doesn't do well, by which I mean meet expectations for sales and reviews, the next one will actually be harder. You're already a has-been, even if there was nothing at all wrong with your effort. The publisher might have expected too much. One reviewer might have had a bad day. Or the combination of text and art that everyone at the publisher loved didn't appeal to your readers. And bad luck with a second or third book can have a worse effect. Your publisher can decide not to do another book with you.

What to do? First, don't blame yourself if something like this happens. Someone liked your first book enough to invest in publishing it, after all. Work to make your next book even better. If your first book isn't out yet, hope that your first few books all do reasonably well. After that, your reputation can stand an off day.

Dealing with Censorship

It may seem hard to believe, but censorship is an issue in children's books. It's probably more of a constant pressure for textbook publishers, who must produce work that won't offend anyone, but because children's books are sold to schools and libraries, their presence on the shelf or in the classroom can be and is challenged.

Most often, fantasy novels are challenged for their magic and witches, and realistic young adult novels are challenged for their language or handling of sex. But just about any book that contains any content one particular parent doesn't want his or her child exposed to can be challenged. It might even be taken off the shelves, especially in classrooms or school libraries.

Should you be concerned that your career will be damaged by censorship? Probably not, because most trade publishers aren't bothered by a few incidents of this type. But your career can be damaged by self-censorship. Don't anticipate the objections and try to head them off. Children can understand and deal with almost any subject, if it's presented in an appropriate manner for their level of understanding and maturity. So if you want to write about a tricky subject, create a scary and sophisticated illustration, or even just use realistic

Class Rules

What do Captain Underpants, Tiger Eyes, and Harry Potter have in common? They're all characters in books that have been targeted for removal from libraries—books by Dav Pilkey, Judy Blume, and J. K. Rowling, respectively. Censorship can affect you. Find out about the extent of the problem and how to deal with it at National Coalition Against Censorship's website, www.ncac.org.

dialogue in a family argument, follow your own sense of what's right. If you've gone too far, your publisher will tell you.

Dealing with Self-Doubt

Perhaps the most difficult challenge to overcome is that posed by your own doubts. You might wonder, *Am I really cut out to be a professional? Did I just have one good book, and that's it?* If you're a writer, you may have lots of new ideas but not know which to pursue. Or you may feel that you can't generate new ones. Illustrators can have similar doubts: you might freeze up when confronted by a new manuscript and wonder how you'll ever complete it. You may end up feeling that you aren't very good after all—that your editor or art director turned your work into what it was. Don't listen to these self-doubts!

Remember that after your first inspiration, it took you a long period of revision and polishing before your first book was finished. Why should your next books be any different? Don't be embarrassed to go back to the writing ideas in Chapter 2. If you're an illustrator, look again at those picture books that inspired you. And be sure to allow yourself time to write or sketch, even if it's only a few minutes to use your journal or note down a few observations. Keep going back to the well, and sooner or later, the bucket will come up full, and you'll be off again.

Books and Their Untimely Deaths

One of the sad facts of the publishing world is that books don't stay in print. You want all your books to be available forever, so this can come as a rude shock, especially if it happens only a few years after a book was published.

Today, sadly, books are going out of print even faster, often within a year or two of their original publication. Don't take it personally—you might even find some comfort in knowing that you've made it to this point. After all, one definition of an established author or illustrator is that they've got more books out of print than yet to be published. Remember, too, that there are some actions you can take to keep your book available or get it back in print.

Going OP

Publishers keep books "in print," meaning they're available even if you don't see them in every bookstore, only so long. At a point when the cost of keeping books in a warehouse and in the catalog is greater than the income a publisher makes from selling them, or when the cost of reprinting a supply that would take no more than three years to sell is too high, publishers declare a book *out of print* (*OP* or *OOP*). Recently, many publishers require higher sales levels to keep books in print, so more books go out of print sooner.

As an author, this can be very frustrating, when you suddenly can't get copies of a book for a school visit or when you see backlist sales cut off before the list has a chance to develop. But out of print does not mean gone forever, so be ready to take action.

def•i•ni•tion

A book is **out of print** (OP or OOP) when it can no longer be ordered from the publisher and the publisher has decided not to print more. If a publisher wants to leave its options open, it may declare a book *out of stock indefinitely* (*OSI*), meaning that although it has no copies left, it might still decide to print a fresh supply.

Get Your Books and Your Rights

If you get some warning that a book is about to be declared OP, don't try to keep it in print, either by frantically promoting it or by lobbying your editor. You probably can't do enough to generate sales to make a difference, and your editor most likely is not involved in OP decisions. In fact, at the larger companies, an inventory manager, who may not even be in the same building, makes the decision in consultation with the marketing department (can they increase sales?) and the production department (can the book be printed cost-effectively?). Your editor may not know that your book is out of print until after the decision has been made and books have been *remaindered*, or sold off at a discount.

def•i•ni•tion

A publisher may **remainder** a book and sell off all its stock when putting it out of print, or it may sell only some of its copies to reduce its stock. In either case, the books usually end up on sale for less than half the regular retail price.

You can let your editor know ahead of time that you want to hear as soon as possible about any decision to declare your book OP. You need to know so you can buy as many copies of the book as possible before they're all gone. Publishers sell off what's in the warehouse at a greatly reduced price, perhaps not much more than the $2 or so it cost to manufacture it. You may be able to get hundreds of copies this way. Buy as many as you can afford and then worry about finding space for them. This is a better dilemma to be in than not hearing until after the books are all gone, as happens all too often.

Get your rights back, too. Once the book is out of print, ask the publisher for a letter formally returning your copyright to you. Even if you're not entitled to this by your contract, ask. If you are entitled to it by your contract, press your case as far as you must. Sometimes, a polite letter from your lawyer will shake this letter loose. Don't accept an OSI status for your book, either. This can be a legitimate designation for a few months while a publisher waits for orders to come in, but don't let it become a substitute for out of print.

Back from the Dead?

When you've got your books and your rights, what do you do? You can sell your books on school visits and make them available through online booksellers.

Putting the book back in print is more difficult. Publishers don't jump at the chance to republish a book another publisher let go. They assume they won't be any better able to reach other customers than the first publisher was. Although a few publishers do republish books, the numbers of books that come back to life in this way are small compared to the many hundreds of books that go out of print each year.

Another option, which I mentioned in Chapter 21, is to reprint the book yourself. This can take a lot of time and money, so explore your options carefully before deciding what to do.

What to Do Until You Can Live on Your Royalties

Many children's book authors and illustrators dream of the time they're able to live on the royalty income from their books. In reality, few writers end up being able to quit their day job or to stop relying on a spouse with a steady income and a health plan. Illustrators may be able to find a steadier income from their own work, especially if they like doing educational work. But writers can find jobs that are both flexible and relevant to what they want to do, which is write. As you know from Chapter 31, school visits, while promoting your book, also can be a handy source of income, especially once you have several books on the market. (And illustrators don't forget that you can do this, too, although schools may not know what to make of you at first!)

In the following sections, I give examples of other kinds of work you might be able to do on a flexible schedule and at home. You'll undoubtedly find out about other kinds of work just by comparing notes with other writers at conferences.

Packagers

I mentioned packagers in Chapter 18 as a possible home for some kinds of series. They're also a potential source of writing work, perhaps closely related to the work you do.

Companies such as Alloy Entertainment and Parachute Publishing produce many paperback series for publishers, hiring writers to create the individual books from an outline and a guide to the series often called a "bible." To get this work, you need to have samples to show and be prepared not to be credited on the cover for your work.

Some packagers also produce nonfiction, sometimes by one-person operations. Often known as "work-for-hire," you may not get to keep the underlying copyright in such work, but in at least some cases you do get your name on the cover.

> **Can You Keep a Secret?**
>
> If you do your research in the writer's guides, you're likely to find a few packagers who specialize in just about any type of children's book except the high-end literary titles.

Writing and Editing

Over the years, as you've gone over manuscripts in critique groups and corrected your writer friends' grammar (while they corrected yours), you will have picked up some general writing and editing skills, which you can use either inside or outside children's publishing. Start by looking locally. Many businesses need help with manuals and press releases and newsletters. Local free papers may expect you to work for free, too, but you can gain some writing credits and move on. Magazine and book publishers all need proofreaders and fact checkers, and if you're local, you've got a leg up; you can be a face instead of a voice on the phone and even come in and work in their offices or pick up and drop off materials.

> **Can You Keep a Secret?**
>
> Helping freelance writers and editors make sense of the job market is the Editorial Freelancers Association (EFA). Based in New York but with national membership, the EFA has a job line, an annual pricing survey, an educational program, and other resources. Find out about them online at www.the-efa.org.

But there's no reason why you can't look outside your local area. If you're willing to take some time researching writer's sites on the web that have job listings, you can tap into a national market. Have writing samples and a resumé ready, and if you're looking at specialized jobs such as proofreading be prepared to take a test (so learn the proofreading marks; some are listed in Chapter 25).

Textbooks and Supplemental Materials

Chapter 20 pointed out that some educational publishers acquire manuscripts, either by submission or on commission. These companies also need workbooks and activity books, from straightforward drills to more creative mixes of experiments, arts and crafts projects, and other hands-on activity books. They need passages and stories to be read in tests and test preparation books. They need stories and activities written to fit a particular theme and format in a textbook, so they work with writers, often as packagers do, on a work-for-hire basis.

In the market guides, you'll find companies such as Cottonwood Press, Evan-Moor Educational Publishers, Mitchell Lane Publishers, Perfection Learning, Prufrock Press, and Teacher Created Materials. Look for others, too. Some accept submissions, so you must always check their guidelines.

Teach! You've Learned a Thing or Two

By now, you've learned a good bit about writing or illustrating from the time you've spent on your own manuscripts. Perhaps you've taken some courses or workshops and felt you could have done better at leading the group. Consider doing just that!

Contact local colleges with active adult education departments to find out if they offer children's writing courses. If you're an illustrator, look into teaching illustration at local art schools. If they don't have such courses, suggest that you could offer one and find out what you would need to do to set one up. You can also set up classes online or offer advice and manuscript consulting by mail. You'll need to find ways to let people know about yourself.

Keep Learning

As if you didn't have enough to balance already, I have one more pressing item for your agenda: don't ever stop learning and growing. Many published writers and illustrators have told me that although they reach a good level of ability and confidence in what they want to do, they never feel that they can say they have nothing more to learn.

You've got to stay excited by what you're doing if you're going to pass excitement on to your readers. You've got to keep an open mind about everything. Your readers do. So don't stop reading the latest books for children, don't stop debating them with your friends, don't stop trying new challenges, don't stop going to conferences. If you're going to sustain a career, you can't coast along.

Take Yourself Seriously

As you move forward, believe in yourself and don't let yourself be intimidated, either by an unfamiliar challenge, by a dry spell, or by a publisher. Keep moving, and you'll reach your happy ending. I think a story that Deborah Kogan Ray told me illustrates this point well.

Today, Deborah is an established, well-known illustrator with something like 100 books to her credit. In the 1960s, she was a novice illustrator, taking her portfolio to two publishers on her first trip to New York. Something about her art caught the attention of the legendary Ursula Nordstrom, head of what was then Harper & Row.

In short order, Deborah had a contract … and a problem. She didn't know how to produce pre-separated art, the then-standard for picture books. With the help of some very patient design staff, she learned, and she was working away on the finished art for the book when her contract was canceled, with no explanation. She sued for the remaining $500 of her $1,000 advance, and Harper settled before the case went to trial. Deborah picks up the story:

> I found lots of work with other publishers, but remained *persona non grata* at Harper & Row for eight years.
>
> One day, I received a letter and manuscript from an editor named Elizabeth Gordon [at Harper], who was not on their staff when my troubles occurred. She wanted to take me to lunch and asked if I would consider illustrating *I Have a Sister, My Sister Is Deaf.* My immediate question was, "Don't you know that I sued Harper & Row?" She wasn't concerned.
>
> I illustrated the book. It is still in print. The question of what caused Harper to break my first contract has never been answered.

Suing a publishing company is not to be undertaken lightly, of course, but the principle applies in other situations. If you need more space to write in your home, find a way to create it. If you are asked to make substantial revisions and you don't understand why, ask for clarification. If you haven't seen any reviews of your book, even though it's been out for six months, ask why. Take yourself seriously and work to be a partner with your editor and publisher.

That's what Deborah did. She not only won her case, she ended up working with Harper again, and she got something else from the experience: "As to the great settlement from my lawsuit: I took my $500 check and bought my first drawing table. It had a side table, a straight edge, a paper drawer, and big drafting board with a crank to move it up and down. It was the biggest, fanciest drawing table that I could find."

Out into the Big World

Publishing companies can seem like enormous and powerful entities to writers and illustrators. Taking one on like Deborah did seems like a David and Goliath story. But widen the focus a little more. Children's publishing, itself a large and complicated world, is just one part of the publishing industry, which in turn is a pretty small part of any country's economy. I hope you've come to understand it better, but I know that our beloved industry is at the mercy of forces beyond our control. As you travel on in your career, I hope you'll remember a lesson to be learned from a small boy, oddly enough named Harold.

I refer to Harold in *Harold and the Purple Crayon* by Crockett Johnson (published by Harper & Row, now HarperCollins, in 1955). Harold has a purple crayon with which he draws what he wants, conjuring up problems at the same time, which he then proceeds to solve. He draws a mountain so he can see where he is, but falls off the other side, and quickly draws a balloon, and on he goes. In the end, he gets to the place he most wants to be. You can read this just as an imaginative adventure, or as a story about dreaming, but I think it also has something to say about how to live in the world.

Harold doesn't settle for what's in front of him. He creates the world he wants to live in. When some aspect of it doesn't work out the way he had hoped, he finds a way to fix it. I often point out at conferences that we can be like this small boy. Like Harold, we can work to make our world be the way we want it to be.

> **Can You Keep a Secret?**
>
> Harold of *Harold and the Purple Crayon* isn't the only children's book character from whom to draw inspiration. Consider Charlotte in *Charlotte's Web,* saving Wilbur's life with words. Or Max, in *Where the Wild Things Are,* who stops monsters with one very powerful word. What can you learn from your favorite character?

In fact, this is what those of us who care about children's books *must* do. We are a sizable community—illustrators, writers, editors, librarians, teachers, and, potentially, millions of parents. We all vote. We can lobby our local, state, and national elected officials for better library funding. We can support the use of trade books as well as textbooks in classrooms when the subject is debated at local school committee meetings. We can create books with our purple crayons. But we can do much more. We can and should work to make this a world in which the kinds of books we care about continue to have a place—a larger place than they do now.

This may take a bigger crayon, but it's important not to lose sight of this bigger world and the impact we can have on it. Use your purple crayon, not only to create your own worlds between the covers of a book, but to make the world we live in a more hospitable place for the books we love and the children who need them.

The Least You Need to Know

◆ Now that you're published, your next challenge is to build yourself a career.

◆ Books go out of print more quickly nowadays, but there are actions you can take to keep them available.

◆ Working with packagers and educational publishers, doing other freelance editing and writing, and teaching writing might be some jobs you can fit in around your writing.

◆ Keep learning, take yourself seriously, and never forget that you can have an impact on the world.

Appendix

Glossary

An expanded version of this glossary, featuring additional publishing terms, is maintained at www.underdown.org/cigglossary.htm.

acquire To make an agreement with an author to publish a book. Once the contract is signed by the author, the editor has made an *acquisition*.

acquisitions editor The editor involved in signing authors to write books. The acquisitions editor generally manages the manuscript as it comes into the publishing house and then passes it on to a development editor. These roles are typically combined at children's publishing companies.

advance Money paid by a publisher to an author or illustrator before the book goes on the market, in anticipation of sales. The advance is charged against royalties and must "earn out" before any royalties are paid.

advance reader copy (ARC) A higher-class bound galley, fully designed, given a color cover, and usually done to generate interest in a novel.

agent A well-connected professional who places your work with publishers, keeps track of your royalties, and perhaps provides career guidance in return for a percentage of your earnings.

art director (A.D.) A publishing staff person who works with illustrators, providing art direction—guidance to the illustrator as he or she works. This person might be the head of the art staff.

artist's representative An agent for illustrators.

assignment *See* commission.

audience   The people for whom you are writing. In children's books, this can mean a specific age level.

author's representative   *See* agent.

back matter   Supplementary material in the back of a book, such as a glossary, a recommended reading list, an index, or information about the book.

backlist   Previously published books. A publisher's backlist is an important source of revenue, because backlist sales are more predictable and dependable than *frontlist* sales.

binding   What holds a book together. A trade hardcover binding is usually sewn and glued. A library binding is more durable, with cloth reinforcement and often a different sewing method. Paperbacks are usually bound with glue only.

bleed   Not what publishers do to artists and writers, bleed is a technical term referring to illustrations that extend off the edges of pages.

blues or **bluelines**   A printing, in blue only, from the final plates for a book. Usually only editors see these as a final check. If changes are needed, they have to be made to the film, which is expensive. Some publishers no longer use blues.

board book   A type of picture book, printed on paperboard, usually intended for infants and toddlers.

body   The main part of the text of a work, not including elements such as the table of contents or index.

boilerplate   Standard language in a contract.

book plus   A book packaged with something else, such as a plush toy.

bound galley   An advance copy of a novel or nonfiction book, typeset but not proofread, and usually without the final form of the illustrations. It's usually bound as a paperback.

chains   Companies that own many individual bookstores. The two biggest in bookselling are Barnes & Noble and Borders. They contrast with the *independents*.

chapter book   A short book with chapters, a bridge between easy reader and true novel.

clips   Samples of articles an author has written.

colophon   An item in a book's frontmatter that gives information about how the book was produced, from typefaces to the kind of paint an artist used.

color proof   A proof used as a final check on the illustrations in a book before it goes to press.

commission   When doing work "on commission," the publisher hires you, tells you what to do, and usually pays a fee instead of royalties.

concept book   A picture book that explores a concept instead of, or perhaps in addition to, telling a story.

co-op money   Money a bookseller spends to promote a publisher's books, which is then reimbursed by the publisher.

copy editor   The person who reviews a manuscript for style, punctuation, spelling, and grammar.

copyright   Literally, the right to create and distribute copies of a creative work. Under copyright law, you hold a work's copyright from the moment you create it.

cover letter   The letter that accompanies your manuscript or art samples.

critique   A thoughtful, usually written evaluation of a manuscript, concentrating on problems of structure, tone, characterization, and the like.

designer   The person choosing type, doing layout, and otherwise settling the design of a book. Some illustrators do their own design work.

development editor   The editor who actually edits a book. *See also* acquisitions editor.

development house   *See* packager.

draft   A version of a manuscript. The *first* draft is the first one written; the *rough* draft is an unpolished version; the *final* draft is the last one.

dummy   A manuscript laid out in book form, with sketches of all the illustrations and sample finished pieces.

e-book   A book that must be read in an electronic format, either on a personal computer or a handheld reader, instead of on paper.

early or **easy reader**   A book written with a controlled vocabulary for children who are learning to read.

earns out   To reach the point when the royalties on a book have paid back the advance paid to the author.

endpapers   The sheets of paper in a hardcover book that attach the cover to the pages; these can be plain colored paper or have a design or illustration.

exclusive submission   A manuscript sent to only one publisher.

fair use   A limited exception to copyright law, allowing others to draw on or use excerpts from a copyrighted work without formal permission.

fairy tale   Like a folktale in form, but told specifically for children and with a more literary style.

fantasy   A type of fiction in which the rules of the world are different; animals talk, magic works, and strange creatures exist.

fiction   Writing from the imagination, or writing containing elements of imagination, fable, or tale. Also known as "lies," or "something you've made up."

film   What most books today are printed from.

flat fee   A payment made as the only compensation; the opposite of an advance against royalties.

flow-through clause   A nice clause to have in a contract, this clause obliges the publisher to pass on subsidiary rights payments when they are received, not when the next royalty statement happens.

folded and gathered (f&g's)   A sheet or sheets from a print run, folded, cut, and generally made ready for binding but not bound. F&g's are often used as *review copies* for picture books.

folktale   A story, usually with an underlying message, that's been passed down orally and may appeal to both adults and children.

form rejection letter   A letter turning down a manuscript. If it is an unsigned photocopy, you've received a standard response. If personalized in any way, assume this is a good sign.

freelancer   An independent contract worker who is employed by the publisher. This person doesn't work on salary or as a full-time employee for the publisher. Many writers find extra income by freelancing; children's book publishers may send out design and copyediting work to freelancers.

frontlist   The books a publisher is releasing this year or season; the new books.

frontmatter   The material placed before the body of a book, including such elements as the title and copyright pages, a table of contents, or an introduction.

galleys   Long pages of typeset text, not yet broken out into book pages, not much used today because of computerized typesetting and page layout.

genre   A specific category of story, such as fantasy or mystery.

glossary   You are reading one.

graphic novel   A novel published in comic-book format, laid out with text panels integrated into illustrations.

hardcover   A book produced with a hard, stiff outer cover, usually covered by a jacket. The covers are usually made of cardboard, over which is stretched cloth, treated paper, vinyl, or some other plastic.

historical fiction   Fiction in a historical setting, in which the main character, and often many others, are invented, while the setting and other details are based on careful research.

imprint   A part of a publisher with a distinct identity, name, and staff.

independents   Bookstores not owned by large companies, usually free-standing or having only a few branches. The term can also apply to publishers not part of larger corporations.

index   An alphabetic list of topics and key words to be found in a book, with their page number locations.

informational book   *See* nonfiction.

institutional   One of the markets in children's publishing, named for the institutions the books are sold to—schools and libraries.

ISBN (International Standard Book Number)   This number gives the book a unique ID, like your Social Security number, for orders and distribution. Recently expanded from 10 digits to 13, an ISBN also identifies the publisher and language of publication.

jacket   Short for *dust jacket*, this is the paper cover on a book. Originally intended to keep it clean, it's now used to catch the eye of the reader via dramatic art and type.

journal   A blank book to write in whenever you can; not just for recording events, but for exploring ideas and jotting observations.

layout   The arrangement of all the elements of a book's design, from text paragraphs and illustrations to chapter titles and page numbers.

license   The right to do something. In publishing, the right to publish a book or books, or to use something from one book in another product. An "audio license," for example, gives a company the right to produce an audio tape of a book.

line editing   Close, line-by-line editing of a book, concentrating on tone, style, flow, sequencing, clarity, and such matters.

list price   The price a publisher gives a book in their catalog and once the price at which it would be sold by bookstores; now used to calculate royalties based on list, even if the book is sold for less.

lists   Semi-annual (or more frequent) groups of books produced by a publisher, announced and placed in a catalog together. A publisher's list is simply the books it produces.

literary agent   *See* agent.

manuscript   A writer's work before it's typeset and printed; originally "hand written," as the word implies, now it's likely to be produced on a word processing program.

mass market   The kind of publisher who sells books through general retail outlets, usually with wide appeal and low prices.

middle grade   An age category roughly corresponding to the middle grades of school, perhaps the fourth through eighth grades, to which many of the classic children's novels belong.

ms./mss.   Short for *manuscript* or *manuscripts*.

multiple submission   Correctly used to mean sending more than one manuscript in one submission, but often used to mean a manuscript sent to two or more publishers at the same time.

net price   The price a publisher actually receives for a book.

niche publisher   A publisher who specializes in a subject of interest to a small group of people and sells its books nationally, but only in specialized outlets.

nonfiction   Also known as an "informational book," writing in which the author retells historical events, crafts a biography, passes on knowledge, or presents activities or experiments.

novelty book   Any book with features added to it beyond the binding and pages; for example, foldout pages, die-cut holes, lift-the-flaps, pop-ups, or sound chips.

one-time use   In a contract, allows for only one form of publication.

original expression   What copyright law protects: your own unique way of expressing an idea, telling a story, or creating a work of art.

OSI (out of stock indefinitely)   This means the publisher has no copies of a book on hand but might choose to reprint it in the future, so the publisher is not calling it out of print. If it did, it might be obligated to return the rights to the book to the author.

out of print (**OP** or **OOP**)   The publisher has no copies of a book on hand and does not intend to reprint it.

packager   A company specializing in creating books up to the printing stage or the distribution stage; marketing and distributing the book is handled by the publisher. The packager's name may appear on the copyright page, but the publisher's appears on the spine.

page proofs   *Proofs* laid out in page form; a later stage than *galleys*.

paperback   A binding with a soft cover, usually a light cardboard. A *trade* paperback is usually the same size as a hardcover book and printed to the same standards. A *mass-market* paperback is usually smaller, designed to fit in a rack, and printed on cheaper paper.

pedantic   Describes a story in which the moral or message the author wants to teach overwhelms the plot.

permissions   Agreements from copyright holders granting the right to reproduce their work.

picture book   A book for younger children, which has pictures on every page and tells a story through words and pictures.

press kit   A folder of materials about a book sent to the media to alert them to a book's release.

prewriting   The all-important work a writer does before actually starting to write. This can be as simple as jotting down ideas, as methodical as creating an outline, or as complex as doing character studies.

print on demand (POD)   A printing technology that allows 1, 10, or 50 copies of a book to be printed at a time, instead of a print run of thousands.

proofreader   The person who reviews the proofs for errors before a book goes to press.

proofs   The typeset pages of a book before it's printed.

pub. date   The publication date; the date when a publisher says a new book will be available.

public domain   Not copyrighted, either because it never was or because the copyright has expired or lapsed; public domain material can be used without attribution or permission, although good writing practice means making a note of sources.

query letter   A letter you send to a publisher to ask, or query, to see if the publisher is interested in seeing your manuscript.

reading fee   A fee charged to read and comment on a manuscript. If this is charged by an agent to determine if he will represent you, it is not a legitimate fee.

regional publisher   A publisher who specializes in subjects relevant to a particular part of the country and sells its books mostly or entirely in that area.

remainders   Surplus books sold at a steep discount. A publisher may "remainder" a book and sell off all its stock when putting it out of print, or it may sell only some of its copies to reduce its stock.

response sheet   A feedback device, on which a writer lists certain ideas, devices, or grammatical points for the audience or an editor to consider.

response time   The time it takes a publisher to reply to a submission, usually measured in months.

returns Unsold books sent back to a publisher by booksellers or wholesalers. Unlike many other businesses, retailers can usually return books for a full refund. Returns often come back several months after a book is published.

review copies Copies of a book sent to reviewers, usually before publication, and often in the form of bound galleys or f&g's.

revise Literally to "re-see"; to rewrite, perhaps making extensive changes. Often, when a new edition of a book comes out, the author has revised the previous edition.

rights The many different ways a book can be *licensed,* ranging from book club rights to movie rights and even theme park rights. Also called *subsidiary rights.*

royalties Money paid to an author by a publisher on the basis of books sold. It may be a percentage of the list price, or the price for which the book supposedly will be sold to a consumer, or of the net price, or what the publisher actually receives (often 40 to 50 percent less than the retail price).

sales rep Short for sales representative. An individual who represents a publisher to a potential customer, such as a bookstore or wholesaler. The sales rep can be a house rep, hired by the publisher; or a commissioned rep, independent, and paid a commission for every book sold.

SASE A self-addressed, stamped envelope, included with all submissions and query letters for the return of the manuscript or a response from the publisher. When soliciting publishers to publish your work, you should include a SASE.

self-publish An individual doing everything a publisher does, from editing to printing and distribution.

series A number of books that are related to each other in theme, purpose, characters, style, or content, or all of these things. Series often have an overarching title; for example, *The Complete Idiot's Guide* is a series of books. These books are geared toward a specific audience (not idiots, of course).

signature A group of pages, based on the smallest number of pages a particular printing machine can print on a sheet of paper; many books are printed on sheets that take 8 or 16 or some other number of pages. When folded and cut, each sheet forms a signature.

simultaneous submission Sending the same manuscript to more than one publisher at the same time.

slush pile The unsolicited manuscripts that a publisher receives from writers who aren't represented by agents.

softcover *See* paperback.

special sales Sales of a book to nontraditional outlets, such as gift stores, or for use as premiums. For example, a publisher might sell 10,000 units (books) to a corporation that wants to distribute the books to employees of the corporation.

spine The center panel of the binding of a book, which connects the front and back cover to the pages and faces out when the book is shelved.

storyboard An illustrator's plan for a book, showing every page at much reduced size, ideally all on one sheet of paper.

structural editing Editing involving the structure of a manuscript, usually done at an early stage.

submissions Manuscripts sent to a publisher by an author or agent. Submissions can be exclusive, multiple, or simultaneous.

subsidiary rights *See* rights.

subsidy publisher *See* vanity press.

superstore Regarding bookstores, a large store with 100,000 or more titles, a coffee shop, and other amenities.

tear sheet Originally a sample of an illustrator's work, torn out of a magazine or other source. Now can also be a photocopy of such a sample.

teen A label for books for teenagers, typically published in paperback, often in series, and bought by them in bookstores.

thumbnails Small, rough sketches done by an artist before full-size sketches, which may be literally not much bigger than thumbnail size.

trade The kind of publisher who sells books to bookstores, and also to some extent to libraries.

trim size The horizontal and vertical dimensions of a book's pages. A book with an 8×10-inch trim size is 8 inches across and 10 inches high. A hardcover book has covers that extend beyond the pages, so book size and trim size aren't always the same.

tween A recently coined term for books for pre-teens, roughly equal to middle grade, applied to books children buy for themselves.

unsolicited submission/manuscript A manuscript that a publisher did not solicit, or ask for, from an author.

vanity press A company the author pays to publish a book, rather than the other way around. The name comes from the fact that such publishers rely on the vanity of people who want to see their words in print and are willing to pay for this service.

work-for-hire   Work done for a publisher or other company to their specifications, usually paid for with a fee and with copyright signed over to the company.

young adult (YA)   The upper end of the age range covered by children's publishers, possibly starting at age 12. Often used to designate a section in a library or bookstore.

Appendix B

Resources

I could almost fill a book with the books, magazines, organizations, and websites I've come across while researching this book. Unfortunately, I can't fit all the good ones here, so I've included a list of some of the best. An expanded and updated version of this list, with short reviews, is available on my website, The Purple Crayon, at www.underdown.org/ciglinks.htm. I've included a list of resource websites at www.underdown.org/more-resources.htm.

Essentials

These are the basic books you'll want to acquire:

- ◆ *Children's Writer's and Illustrator's Market*
- ◆ *Essential Guide to Children's Books and Their Creators*
- ◆ For writers: Your favorite writing guide (see Chapter 11)
- ◆ For illustrators: *Writing with Pictures*

Books on Writing

Aiken, Joan. *The Way to Write for Children*. St. Martin's Press, 1999.

Cross, James. *The Giblin Guide to Writing Children's Books, Fourth Edition*. Writer's Institute Publications, 2006.

Frey, James N. *How to Write a Damn Good Novel, How to Write a Damn Good Novel II: Advanced Techniques,* and *The Key: How to Write Damn Good Fiction Using the Power of Myth.* St. Martin's Press, 1987, 1994, and 2000.

Heffron, Jack. *The Writer's Idea Book.* Writer's Digest Books, 2000.

Patterson, Katherine. *The Invisible Child: On Reading and Writing Books for Children.* Dutton, 2001.

Peck, Richard. *Love and Death at the Mall: Teaching and Writing for the Literate Young.* Delacorte, 1994.

Rosenthal, Lisa, ed. *The Writing Group Book: Creating and Sustaining a Successful Writing Group.* Chicago Review Press, 2003.

Seuling, Barbra. *How to Write a Children's Book and Get It Published, Third Edition.* John Wiley and Sons, 2004.

Shepard, Aaron. *The Business of Writing for Children: An Award-Winning Author's Tips on How to Write, Sell, and Promote Your Children's Books.* Shepard Publications, 2000.

Suen, Anastasia. *Picture Writing.* Writer's Digest Books, 2002.

Yolen, Jane. *Take Joy: A Book for Writers.* Writer, 2003.

Books on Illustrating

Bang, Molly. *Picture This! How Pictures Work.* Seastar, 2000.

Bossert, Jill. *Children's Book Illustration: Step by Step Techniques: A Unique Guide from the Masters.* Watson Guptill, 1998.

The Graphic Artists Guild Handbook: Pricing and Ethical Guidelines. Graphic Artists Guild, 2007.

Hand, Nancy S. *Illustrating Children's Books: A Guide to Drawing, Printing, and Publishing.* Prentice Hall, 1986.

Howard, Rob. *The Illustrator's Bible: The Complete Sourcebook of Tips, Tricks, and Time-Saving Techniques in Oil, Alkalyd, Acrylic, Gouache, Casein, Watercolor, Dyes, etc.* Watson-Guptill, 1993.

Lee, Marshall. *Bookmaking: Editing, Design, Production, Third Edition.* W.W. Norton, 2004.

Salisbury, Martin. *Illustrating Children's Books: Creating Pictures for Publication.* Barron's, 2004.

Shulevitz, Uri. *Writing with Pictures: How to Write and Illustrate Children's Books.* Watson-Guptill, 1985.

Slade, Catharine. *Encyclopedia of Illustration Techniques.* Running Press, 1997.

Books About Books

Children's Book Council staff. *Children's Books: Awards and Prizes.* Children's Book Council, 1996.

Children's Books in Print/Subject Guide to Children's Books in Print. R. R. Bowker, annual.

Horning, Kathleen. *From Cover to Cover: Evaluating and Reviewing Children's Books.* HarperCollins, 1997.

Lewis, Valerie V., and Walter M. Mayes. *Valerie and Walter's Best Books for Children, Second Edition.* HarperResource, 2004.

Marcus, Leonard S., and Maurice Sendak, illust. *Dear Genius: The Letters of Ursula Nordstrom.* HarperCollins Juvenile Books, 2000.

Silvey, Anita, ed. *The Essential Guide to Children's Books and Their Creators.* Mariner Books, 2002.

Sutherland, Zena. *Children and Books, Ninth Edition.* Addison-Wesley, 1996.

Zipes, Jack, et al., eds. *The Norton Anthology of Children's Literature.* W.W. Norton, 2005.

Reference Books

Brogan, Katie. *Writer's Market.* Writer's Digest Books, annual.

Buzzeo, Toni, and Jane Kurtz. *Terrific Connections with Authors, Illustrators, and Storytellers: Real Space and Virtual Links.* Teacher Ideas Press, 1999.

Cox, Mary. *Artist's and Graphic Designer's Market.* Writer's Digest Books, annual.

Deval, Jacqueline. *Publicize Your Book: An Insider's Guide to Getting Your Book the Attention It Deserves.* Perigee, 2003.

Garner, Bryan A. *Dictionary of Modern American Usage.* Oxford University Press, 1998.

Gove, Philip Babcock, ed. *Webster's Third New International Dictionary.* Merriam Webster, 1993.

Kirsch, Jonathan. *Kirsch's Guide to the Book Contract: For Authors, Publishers, Editors and Agents.* Acrobat Books, 1998.

Literary Market Place. R. R. Bowker, annual.

Litowinsky, Olga. *It's a Bunny-Eat-Bunny World: A Writer's Guide to Surviving and Thriving in Today's Competitive Children's Book Market.* Walker and Co., 2001.

Pope, Alice, ed. *Children's Writer's and Illustrator's Market.* Writer's Digest Books, annual.

Poynter, Dan. *Dan Poynter's Self-Publishing Manual: How to Write, Print, and Sell Your Own Book, Sixteenth Edition.* Para Publishing, 2007.

Raab, Susan. *An Author's Guide to Children's Book Promotion.* Raab Associates, 2007.

University of Chicago Press staff. *The Chicago Manual of Style, Fifteenth Edition.* University of Chicago Press, 2003.

Magazines

Booklist
Published monthly
www.ala.org/booklist.

Children's Book Insider
Published monthly
www.write4kids.com/index.html

The Horn Book Magazine
Published bimonthly
www.hbook.com

The Lion and the Unicorn
Published three times a year
www.press.jhu.edu/journals/lion_and_the_unicorn

Once Upon a Time
Published quarterly
onceuponatimemag.com

Publisher's Weekly
Published weekly
www.publishersweekly.com

School Library Journal
Published monthly
www.slj.com

Organizations

Association of Author's Representatives
www.aar-online.org

The Author's Guild
www.authorsguild.org

Canadian Society of Children's Authors, Illustrators, and Performers
www.canscaip.org

The Children's Book Council
www.cbcbooks.org

Society of Children's Book Writers and Illustrators
www.scbwi.org

Society of Photographers and Artists Representatives
www.spar.org/index.html

Sample Materials

Welcome to this warehouse of samples! First come typical guidelines from a trade publisher, so you'll know what to expect. Actual guidelines vary a lot, so you should still write for guidelines from actual publishers you submit to. You'll also see samples of different kinds of cover and query letters and a sample manuscript format.

For more examples of cover and query letters, including one amusing look at what not to do, take a look at Jackie Ogburn's "Rites of Submission: Cover Letters and Queries," online at www.underdown.org/covlettr.htm.

In all the sample letters, where *Your Address* is called for, put your complete postal address, your telephone number, and your e-mail address.

Sample Guidelines from a Trade Publisher

Following these writer's guidelines are sample guidelines for illustrators.

SUBMISSION GUIDELINES

for Children's Book Writers

from a Pretty Good Publisher, Inc.

Pretty Good publishes children's books for the trade market for children of all ages. We publish both fiction and nonfiction but do not publish board books, reference books, or activity books.

Pretty Good reads all unsolicited manuscripts we receive, provided they are submitted to us on an exclusive basis through the mail. At present, we do not review or reply to submissions or queries made by e-mail or fax, in disk form, or consisting only of website addresses.

Manuscripts of fewer than 20 typed pages can be submitted in their entirety. For longer manuscripts, we prefer to receive a query letter, summary (not an outline), and three sample chapters. Please write Query on the envelope, and include a self-addressed stamped envelope (SASE) with your query.

Manuscripts should be typed double-spaced on white paper. We recommend that you make a copy of your manuscript before sending it, as we cannot be responsible for submissions lost in the mail or at our offices. Your name, address, and telephone number should appear on your manuscript as well as in your cover letter. Do not include illustrations.

Please submit your manuscript to the attention of the Trade Editorial Department at the address above.

Enclose a SASE with sufficient postage (not a check or cash) for our response and return of the manuscript, or for response only if the manuscript need not be returned. If you do not enclose a SASE, your manuscript will be discarded.

Please send only one or two manuscripts at a time. We make every effort to respond in three months but cannot guarantee that we will be able to do so, due to the volume of submissions. For confirmation that your project was received, include a self-addressed stamped postcard.

Before submitting a manuscript to us, we encourage you to review some of our published books in a library or bookstore or to take a look at our website (www.prettygoodpublishers.com). If you would like to request a catalog, please send a 9×12-inch self-addressed stamped envelope with $1.47 in postage.

Illustration samples should be sent to the attention of the Art Director. We prefer tear sheets or color photocopies. Slides and CD-ROM portfolios may not be reviewed. Samples are not returned; we will contact you if we are interested.

Questions about the status of a manuscript must by made by mail, in an envelope marked Manuscript Status, with a SASE enclosed. Please do not contact us until at least three months have elapsed, and do not contact us by phone.

SUBMISSION GUIDELINES

for Illustrators

from a Pretty Good Publisher, Inc.

Before you contact us, we suggest that you review our already published books through your local library, a well-stocked bookstore, or an online bookseller to get a sense of what kind of illustration styles we find appropriate for our young readers. You may also request one of our catalogs (if available), by sending an 8×10-inch self-addressed, stamped envelope with 4 ounces postage.

We have a portfolio drop-off day on _____. You may drop off a portfolio with the receptionist any time before 11 A.M. and pick it up again after 4 P.M. Please call ahead to make sure the Art Director will be in that day.

You are welcome to mail any samples you would like us to review or keep on file. We will circulate them and individual editors or designers may contact you if they wish to see more. One to four samples are sufficient. One black and white (if you work in black and white), and three in color are preferable. Good-quality photocopies are fine. You may send a book "dummy" if you wish to showcase your ability to create a picture book.

Do not send original art. Slides may be submitted but are not as convenient to view as printed samples. Do not submit samples on CD-ROM or other computer format; even if we have the necessary hardware and software to view them, we may not have the resources. For similar reasons, we are not reviewing online portfolios or websites.

If your work includes the ability to illustrate various types of people, landscapes, objects, or if you work in various mediums or styles, please include a mix of these capabilities. (However, please limit your style submissions to two or three.)

Identify each sample sent with your name, address, and phone number. Also include a self-addressed, stamped envelope (in the appropriate size) if you request returns.

Comment: *Most publishers post their guidelines somewhere on their websites, and all will send them to you on receipt of a SASE. Notice the item on illustration samples in the writer's guidelines, which I included because some publishers don't have separate illustrator's guidelines. That may be the only help an illustrator gets.*

Three Sample Cover Letters for Unpublished Authors

Please use these with caution. These are not presented as perfect examples of the craft of cover-letter writing, but as examples of approaches. You should adapt, improvise, and generally find your own way to best present your unique work. These are all addressed to editors, but you can take a similar approach when writing to agents. The biggest difference is that agents will want to hear more about you and other manuscripts; they're not interested if all you have is one.

Your Address

Date

Some Editor
Pretty Good Publishers Books for Young Readers
1 Main St.
Anymetropolis, HC 00000

Dear Editor,

When I remembered the time I gave my little sister a bloody nose in the backyard five minutes after Mom had praised her report card, I knew that I had the beginnings of a story. *Mom! She's Bothering Me Again!* is the story itself.

I hope you'll agree that the humor and drama of it—and the unsentimental ending—make this a worthy new rendition of a perennial theme.

In keeping with your company's policy, I have submitted this manuscript exclusively to you. I look forward to hearing from you soon.

Yours sincerely,

An Eager Author

Comment: *If you haven't been published, do like this author did and don't apologize (or even mention this fact). You still have relevant personal experience with which to hook an editor. Words like* humor *and* unsentimental *also suggest that you know what you're doing. Above all, keep these letters short and businesslike. A cover letter should make an editor want to read your story; now the story just has to live up to what you've promised! If you're writing nonfiction, personal experience is still a great approach, as the next letter demonstrates.*

Your Address

Date

A Learned Editor
Informative Books for Young Readers
99 High St.
Middleville, PB 00000

Dear Editor,

You and I know that sharks are far less dangerous to humans than the average SUV. But these primitive yet efficient creatures still excite fascination and fear in adults and children alike.

I drew on my years of experience studying sharks at the Jaws Research Institute and my unquenched enthusiasm for the subject to create *Shark!*—dramatic nonfiction for a middle-grade audience.

How can this compete with the dozens of books on the subject already on the market? By providing up-to-the-minute information on sharks, told from a first-person perspective by a scientist active in the field.

I've seen the books that Informative publishes and believe that my approach suits your list. I enclose a SASE for my manuscript's return if you do not agree.

With best wishes,

A Shark Scientist

Comment: *In this example, the author is a scientist. But you don't have to be an academic expert on a subject to write about it for children. You do have to know the latest research and be able to communicate it. First-person experiences are almost always a good way to catch an editor's eye; so is knowledge of what's out on the market. But be succinct, like this writer is. You don't have to describe the competing titles and compare yours to each of them. Knowledge of a company's publishing program is always a plus; it can even become the basis of a cover letter, as it is in the next example.*

Your Address

Date

Some Editor
Pretty Good Publishers Books for Young Readers
1 Main St.
Anymetropolis, HC 00000

Dear Editor,

My six-year-old son never gets tired of the goofy humor in *The Gerbil Looks Unhappy,* or the rambunctious antics of Eleanor in your easy-reader series. Thank you for publishing them!

Because PGP Books seems to welcome such wild and wacky stories, I'm hoping that you'll enjoy the enclosed, *Where's Davey?* an over-the-top adventure based on the (apparent) disappearance of one of my own children.

In the event that I'm wrong, I enclose a SASE for the return of the manuscript. I hope to hear from you soon.

With best wishes,

A Funny Author

Comment: *It impresses an editor if you display familiarity with a publisher's program, especially if you don't just mention such extremely well-known books as* Goodnight Moon *and* Where the Wild Things Are, *as you might if writing to HarperCollins. This isn't a form of name-dropping! It's also important to say something about the books and to compare them in approach to your book. Do not focus on the subject of the book; it's not too insightful to claim that a publisher who's done one book on dogs will obviously be a good home for another one.*

A Sample Cover Letter for Published Authors

The three approaches used previously will work well for you, too. All you need to do is add a brief paragraph about your writing experience for children. This example simply reworks one of the previous examples.

Your Address

Date

Some Editor
Pretty Good Publishers Books for Young Readers
1 Main St.
Anymetropolis, HC 00000

Dear Editor,

When I remembered the time I gave my little sister a bloody nose in the backyard five minutes after Mom had praised her report card, I knew that I had the beginnings of a story. *Mom! She's Bothering Me Again!* is the story itself.

I hope you'll agree that the humor and drama of it—and the unsentimental ending—make this a worthy new rendition of a perennial theme.

I'm the author of *Wombats and Dodoes* (Informative Books) and *The Thing in the Closet,* just released by Conglommo, Inc. I've also had several stories published in *Cricket.*

I have submitted this manuscript exclusively to you. I look forward to hearing from you soon.

Yours sincerely,

An Eager Published Author

Comment: *You can mention magazines as well as books, provided they're nationally distributed, mainstream publications. Books for adults are not relevant. Really!*

Letters for Illustrators

Life for illustrators is a little less complicated than it is for authors, at least when it comes to contacting publishers. When sending out a mailing of samples, you may not need a cover letter, although a short letter demonstrating your familiarity with the publisher's program and mentioning any relevant work you've done doesn't hurt. But the samples are what matter. However, if you're contacting an artist's representative in the hope that he or she will represent you, write a personal letter.

Your Address

Date

Ann Artrep
Ann Artrep Agency, Inc.
99 Hope St.
Midsize, PB 00000

Dear Ms. Artrep,

You may remember that we spoke briefly during the Children's Publishing Basics workshop in Bigtown recently, and you suggested that I send you some samples of my work.

I've been working in children's books for five years now, ever since I graduated from Cal Arts. I've been pretty busy recently, working for educational publishers, as you'll see from the samples.
I've also illustrated two trade books for Small Independent Co., *Look Ma, No Hands!* by Alison Charming, which just came out this year, and *Wash Day* by Alda Animals, a funny nonfiction book on how animals keep themselves clean. That's due out next year.

I'm ready to get a rep to help me take the next step up in my career and feel that you could be the one. I visited your website to get an idea of what you do and the kind of client you represent, and think I'd fit in well. I hope you agree. If you don't, I've enclosed a large SASE for the return of the samples.

Yours sincerely,

An Eager Illustrator

Comment: *Be sure to get the art rep's name right, and be personal, though professional. Mention how you heard about the rep, or who referred you to them, because so many reps are now looking only at people referred to them. And do give a short rundown of your career to date. The samples speak for themselves, but your letter helps put them in context.*

Two Sample Query Letters

Publishers often require query letters to reduce the volume of their submissions, particularly of longer manuscripts. Here you have to work harder to get their interest; with a shorter manuscript a reader will almost always glance at the manuscript, even if the cover letter is a downer. With a query letter, you have to make her want to request and then read the entire manuscript.

Your Address

Date

A Learned Editor
Informative Books for Young Readers
99 High St.
Middleville, PB 00000

Dear Editor,

You and I know that sharks are far less dangerous to humans than the average SUV. But these primitive yet efficient creatures still excite fascination and fear in adults and children alike.

I drew on my years of experience studying sharks at the Jaws Research Institute and my unquenched enthusiasm for the subject to create *Shark!*—dramatic nonfiction for a middle-grade audience. Eight compact chapters provide the latest information about the life cycle, special adaptations, and threats to the survival of the shark. I've also taken an in-depth look at human-shark incidents—and concluded that the shark often is the loser. A guide to shark species, book and web resources, and a diagram of shark anatomy round out the book.

Through personal contacts, I can also put together a complete set of full-color illustrations, and I enclose a sample of what's available, along with an outline and two chapters. The complete 76-page manuscript is available.

I've researched the market, and I believe that there's no book on this popular subject that not only provides up-to-the-minute information on sharks, but also is told from a first-person perspective by a scientist active in the field. I'm confident this approach will suit your list.
I enclose a SASE for your response.

With best wishes,

A Shark Scientist

Comment: *Compare this to the earlier cover letter about this hypothetical book. You need to include more information about the manuscript, because it's not in front of the editor. Because this is nonfiction for older readers, and potentially photo-illustrated, the author also lets the editor know that she can help gather those materials. Another plus is that the entire manuscript is available. Getting a contract offer for just a proposal is a possibility for nonfiction, if you're published, but if you aren't it's better to complete the manuscript before trying to place it.*

Your Address

Date

Some Editor
Pretty Good Publishers Books for Young Readers
1 Main St.
Anymetropolis, HC 00000

Dear Editor,

Do you remember the bully in eighth grade? Many middle-schoolers are confronting a contemporary version of that terrifying figure, as Josh does in this passage from my novel, *The Gauntlet:*

> "Hey, kid! Think you're cool, don'tcha, all dressed in black? How's that black gonna look with some red on it?"

> Josh stopped dead in the hall, looked quickly behind him. No one. He'd have to face Steven on his own.

You know these issues. Dealing with difference, and dealing with the reactions of those angered by it, are major challenges for our society. We can stand back and talk about them. But they are all-too-real, concrete problems for my protagonist, as he navigates the halls of a large public school.

The sample chapters I enclose will show you that *The Gauntlet* is no message-driven polemic, but a gripping story about Josh. Many YA novels have been published on this subject, especially recently, as we struggle to learn from Columbine. But there's little for the middle-schooler, and I believe there needs to be. I hope you agree, and I enclose a SASE for your response.

Yours sincerely,

A Determined Author

Comment: *An actual excerpt from your manuscript, provided it can stand the scrutiny, can be an effective lead-in to a query letter for a fiction manuscript. As with the nonfiction query letter, work hard to get across what's unique about your manuscript. Be creative, and strive to make your letter better than your samples. Make the editor want to read all 100+ pages of it.*

Sample Manuscript Format

Here's a sample manuscript, set up to both show and tell you what to do. I know it disturbs the nice clean look of the page, but be sure to include your name and address on the first page of the manuscript. If it gets separated from your cover letter and SASE, the editor will still be able to contact you.

Your name (optional—word or page count)
Street address
City, state/province, and post code
Telephone number
E-mail address

(leave a break of at least four lines)

Your Title

by Your Name
(leave a break of at least four lines)

Start your manuscript here. It should have margins of at least 1 inch on the sides, top, and bottom. Indent your paragraphs. Double-space between lines. Do not be tempted to save on paper by single-spacing a long manuscript. This will make it harder to read, and you want the editor's reading experience to be the best you can make it. For the same reason, use a common, easy-to-read typeface, no matter what your word processor offers.

You can number your pages, starting with the second page, in the upper-right corner, if your manuscript is longer than a picture book.

You can put "Copyright © (year) by (Your Name)" on the first page, but this is no longer necessary. Unpublished works are protected by current copyright law, even without this notation.

For presentation purposes, you can create a separate title page, starting the text on the second page, but this is not necessary for short manuscripts.

Index

Get proven techniques and expert advice for penning your tale.

"I can't imagine a thing Ron has left behind. Don't miss this!"
—Jerry B. Jenkins, co-author of *The Jesus Chronicles* and *Left Behind* series

THE COMPLETE IDIOT'S GUIDE TO

Writing Christian Fiction

Inside advice on crafting compelling, faith-based stories

Ron Benrey

ISBN: 978-1-59257-681-4

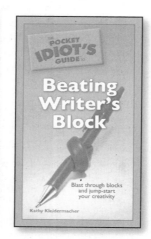

THE POCKET IDIOT'S GUIDE TO

Beating Writer's Block

Blast through blocks and jump-start your creativity

Kathy Kleidermacher

ISBN: 978-1-59257-640-1

THE COMPLETE IDIOT'S GUIDE TO

"This book will give you a much better chance ... of seeing print—and getting paid for it."
—Ellen Recknor, Spur Award winning novelist

Never-before-published interviews with bestselling authors!

Writing a Novel

Proven techniques for laying the foundation of a great novel

Tom Monteleone

ISBN: 978-1-59257-172-7

THE COMPLETE IDIOT'S GUIDE TO

CD-ROM
With dozens of document templates, lists of agents and writers' conferences, and more!

Getting Published
FOURTH EDITION

Get your book out of your head and into bookstores

Sheree Bykofsky and Jennifer Basye Sander

ISBN: 978-1-59257-518-3

THE COMPLETE IDIOT'S GUIDE TO

Expert tips on writing books teens love to read

Writing for Young Adults

Deborah Perlberg

ISBN: 978-1-59257-545-9

THE COMPLETE IDIOT'S GUIDE TO

"Dr. Rozakis has a knack for making even the most complex concepts simple, understandable, and memorable. ... She knows everything there is to know about grammar and style."
—Gaydon Sulahian, writing program coordinator, Institute for the Academic Advancement of Youth, Johns Hopkins University

Grammar and Style
SECOND EDITION

Rights and wrongs of sentence structure, word usage, spelling, and much, much more

Laurie E. Rozakis, Ph.D.

ISBN: 978-1-59257-115-4

Check out these and 20 other writer's reference books in *The Complete Idiot's Guide*® series!

ALPHA
idiotsguides.com